THE
ROYAL
WARDROBE

THE
ROYAL
WARDROBE

*A very fashionable
history of the monarchy*

ROSIE HARTE

HEADLINE

First published in 2023 by
HEADLINE PUBLISHING GROUP

1

Cataloguing in Publication Data is available from the British Library

Hardback ISBN: 978 1 4722 9746 4
Trade paperback ISBN: 978 1 0354 0428 5

Designed and typeset by EM&EN
Printed and bound in Great Britain by Clays Ltd, Elcograf S.p.A.

Headline's policy is to use papers that are natural, renewable and recyclable
products and made from wood grown in well-managed forests and other
controlled sources. The logging and manufacturing processes are expected
to conform to the environmental regulations of the country of origin.

HEADLINE PUBLISHING GROUP
An Hachette UK Company
Carmelite House
50 Victoria Embankment
London EC4Y 0DZ

www.headline.co.uk
www.hachette.co.uk

For Verity, Sarge, Jess, Grace and Sophie

Contents

Introduction

BUCKINGHAM PALACE. Sometime in the early 1900s. Christopher, a Prince of Greece and Denmark, has come to visit his aunt Alexandra, the wife of the newly crowned King of Great Britain, Ireland and the British Dominions. He has been summoned to her quarters, where the glamorous royal wife has pillaged the clothing storage at the Palace and laid out on her bed the dresses and accessories that once belonged to her mother-in-law, the late and legendary Queen Victoria.

'Now, Christo,' she says to her little nephew, her sharp blue eyes glinting with mischief, 'you've got to put this dress on.'

The dress, which more resembled a ball of frilled tartan taffeta, was once worn for the opening of the Great Exhibition in Paris back in 1855 and had been treasured by Victoria due to the significance of the event. For Victoria, preserving clothes was just as effective a tool for recording important life events as the mountain of diary entries she had made throughout her eighty-one years on earth.

Alexandra helped Christopher into the dress, stuck a bonnet on his head and handed him one of Victoria's old parasols.

'You must go down to Aunt Minnie's room and make her laugh,' she instructed, proud at her ability to transform the little Prince into the image of the iconic Queen. Christopher, in all his frills, followed his aunt down the long corridors of the Palace, past scandalized courtiers and servants. Alexandra then announced him at the entrance to Minnie's room as 'Her Majesty, Queen Victoria'.[1]

Though Alexandra may have found the whole episode very funny, those who saw Christopher on his procession to Aunt Minnie were divided in their feelings. It was unnerving to see someone wearing the clothes of the late Queen, interfering with the mystical aura that exists about the clothing of a person, especially the clothing of someone with such a powerful legacy.

This power, held in the stitches of Victoria's gowns, was not simply the product of one woman's sense of style, or even one woman's cultural impact, but rather the culmination of generations of careful strategy and showmanship handed down from her royal ancestors. The clothing culture that existed in the royal court was inexplicably linked to power and authority, with the difference between a successful and scandal-ridden ruler often coming down to their ability to dress for the job. The reigning monarch was encouraged to consider their public image from a very early age, with cautionary tales of the ruin that befell slovenly kings and extravagant queens fuelling their desire to get things right. The sentiment held by monarchs of the past was that visually impressing your fellow rulers was the key to earning their respect, and dazzling your public was the most effective tool for asserting your God-given authority over them; 'We be men and nay angels,' wrote Thomas Elyot in 1531, musing on the importance of royal splendour, 'we know nothing but by outward signification.'[2] Satisfying people's expectations of what a powerful ruler looked like was key to the survival of royal power.

The culture of dressing for power was so firmly established in court society that it meant all those in the monarch's circle could reap the illustrious benefits. When the royal wardrobe had been officially established in the medieval period, it was a department that concerned itself not only with the upkeep of the King and his clothes but also with managing his personal finances. It was a central pillar supporting the royal family, and as such it was a particularly special honour to be associated with the department. Chief Officers of the Wardrobe were often plucked from a high rank in society, laundresses were gifted emerald rings for their services to the Crown, and Ladies/Gentlemen of the Bedchamber, whose job involved assisting the monarch to get dressed, held such an intimate and valuable position at court that they could go on to form powerful relationships, wreck royal marriages and ignite political disruption.

Yet hidden behind all of this sparkle and spectacle there is the personal and the intimate, and this is the beauty of fashion history. It bridges a gap between ourselves and the people of the past in one of the oldest human rituals – getting dressed. Regardless of whether they were the Queen of England or a simple seventeenth-century farmhand, every person throughout history woke up each morning and decided what to wear. The clothes we choose for ourselves are shaped by everything from the jobs we do to the media we enjoy, and ultimately our wardrobes create a collage of our life story. This could not be more true than for those who lived in Britain centuries ago, for whom fashion was a tool with which you could present yourself to the world. It could display faith, class, or even political views, and this was particularly important for women, who had very little opportunity for independent self-expression. I have always found then that fashion is one of the best ways to introduce myself to a figure of the past, as it gives an incredibly intimate glimpse into their life and personality.

When looking at fashion history in general, there is rarely a moment where the royal family are not brought into the spotlight. From Queen Victoria's revolutionary white wedding gown to Princess Diana's revenge dress, their impact reaches into all aspects of society and has influenced what we have (and haven't!) worn throughout history. Their wardrobes continue to fascinate us, the 4-metre-wide hoop skirts of Elizabeth I and the codpieces of Henry VIII seem so foreign and bizarre that we can't help but wonder what the point of it all was? Despite the wealth of information that we have on monarchs of the past, it can sometimes feel hard to grasp the realities of their lives; yes, they fought wars and established laws, but what were they like as people? The further we look back in time, the more alien the people seem to us, but exploring some of the iconic pieces in their wardrobes can be a great place to start searching for the answers.

Fashion for the royal family has for generations been one of their most powerful tools, and often their most subtle weapon. Carefully, and with no expense spared in terms of time or funds, countless royals have crafted legendary wardrobes that spelt out their propaganda in golden embroidery, but if we read between the lines (or in this case, the stitches), we can tease out the more personal histories of the grand figures who wore them. Royal clothes are imbued with meaning, with history and with majesty, but at their core they tell a story, a story of complex individuals with fears, preferences, demands and insecurities just like us. In telling the stories of the royal family through their wardrobe, I hope to make these remarkable figures so much more tangible for you. I hope it will help you truly visualize and understand the men and women who have shaped our history and see them as more than just their titles.

Their clothes tell a story, you just need to know how to read them.

Part One

THE TUDORS

ON 28 JANUARY 1457, protected from the cold by the walls of Pembroke Castle, Margaret Beaufort went into labour. This was no normal birth in any sense; outside the castle the country was embroiled in a civil war that would see some of the most bloody and brutal battles to ever take place on English soil. Inside the castle walls Margaret was undertaking a battle of her own. Just shy of fourteen years old and notably petite for her age, the young girl was undergoing a labour that would leave lasting physical damage. This would be her first and only chance at motherhood, but her husband was nowhere to be seen. Twelve years her senior, Edmund Tudor, Earl of Richmond, had died just three months earlier, imprisoned for his role in the civil war and riddled with disease. When the ordeal was finally over, Margaret could hardly have imagined that the tiny baby in her arms would go on to father one of England's most famous dynasties.

This baby was Henry Tudor, and Henry Tudor was never meant to be King.

The Wars of the Roses, the brutal civil war that plagued Henry's childhood, was far from a clean-cut conflict. It manifested in various sputtering instalments over the course of the fifteenth century and involved a bitter power struggle between the Lancastrian King Henry VI and his rivals from the House of York. Henry VI's popularity had suffered many devastating blows, and his enemies had concluded that he was unfit for the role of King. As Henry Tudor grew up, he would have seen first-hand that kingship could be a remarkably frail concept. As a Lancastrian himself, Henry Tudor had two tentative links to the English throne. His father, Edmund Tudor, had been the King's half-brother, and though the Welsh Tudors enjoyed a good relationship with their royal relatives, it had been made very clear that Edmund and his children had no claim to the throne. Henry's strongest ties to royalty came from his mother, who was a direct descendant of King Edward III. Either way, it would have been fantasy to assume at his birth that Henry would ever ascend to the throne.

Henry Tudor's ties to royalty, regardless of how tentative they may have seemed, placed him in a volatile position. When King Henry VI had been overthrown in 1471, the young Tudor fled to Brittany. He had become the Lancastrian supporter's favourite candidate for the throne, which made him a prime target for the newly crowned Yorkist Kings, Edward IV and his successor, King Richard III. After fourteen years, Henry returned to England, bringing his Lancastrian army to face the forces of King Richard. After a gruelling battle at Bosworth Field on 22 August 1485, Henry Tudor and his ragtag army emerged victorious, and as the conflict came to a close, Richard III was cut down. The golden circlet that had once adorned his helmet was plucked from the thorn bush that it had rolled into and placed upon the head of the victorious Henry.

The Tudor age had begun.

HENRY VII

No sooner had that circlet been placed upon his head, Henry and his supporters began the journey to London to have him officially crowned as King. On this journey it would have become abundantly clear that the Battle of Bosworth Field was one win in a long fight to remain King. Henry had been quick to assert his right to the throne by emphasizing his mother's royal ancestry but there were plenty of others who had potentially stronger claims than his own. At any moment, foreign royalty from Portugal or Castille (who each sported stronger claims to the throne than Henry) could rise up and challenge him. The title of King could be lost just as quickly as it had been won.

Looking back at his half-uncle Henry VI, the new King would have understood that outward appearances could make or break a monarch. Henry VI had been repeatedly criticized for his appearance, often seen in public wearing the same simple blue gown that just did not satisfy the public's expectations of what a powerful ruler should look like. His consistently disappointing wardrobe 'lost many and won none'[1] of his people's hearts, and this dwindling public opinion played a key role in the calls for his replacement. Showmanship was an essential quality for the monarchy to have, as a man who was not seen as a king could never even dream of being respected as one. Henry needed to present himself as the true, rightful ruler of England and avoid the errors made by his half-uncle by crafting a flawlessly regal image. Dressing to emphasize power and status was not a new concept at the time, but the fragile situation that had birthed the dynasty meant that the Tudor monarchs would feel a constant pressure to utilize it to its fullest extent, and the three generations of Tudors would revolutionize the way clothes could be used to express an identity, setting a precedent for royal fashion that is still followed today.

When deciding how exactly he should dress himself, Henry looked to his precarious political situation. He was indebted to the nobles who had fought to put him on the throne and reliant on the subjugation of those he had defeated. In order to ensure his ascent to power was as seamless as possible and to enforce the point that he was the natural heir to the throne, Henry prioritized continuity in his wardrobe. He hired the Parisian tailor George Lovekyn to provide his clothing, the same tailor who had served both Edward IV and Richard III, and as a result Henry's clothes could hardly be differentiated from those monarchs before him. In Henry VII's reign, men's fashion was more medieval in style than what we today would consider 'Tudor', with heavy emphasis on highlighting the body's natural shape. The long gown (glaudekin) was the key part of the outfit, falling typically to the ankles and covering a doublet jacket and long hose. Men would wear square-toed shoes and a woollen cap on top of their typically shoulder-length hair.

The first and most important opportunity for Henry to present himself to the public came on 30 October 1485, the day of his coronation. No expenses were spared for this elaborate event, and great care was taken to make sure the proceedings of the coronation mirrored those of his predecessors, particularly of Edward IV. For the event itself, which took place at Westminster Abbey, Lovekyn created the traditional ceremonial robes for the King – a mantle of crimson velvet for his procession to the Abbey, cloth of gold for the ceremony itself, and one of purple velvet for afterwards. The importance of visual spectacle at coronations cannot be understated; the ritual has at its core a physical representation of the power that God has bestowed upon the monarch and, in turn, the monarch's acceptance of that duty. In order to set himself apart from his fellow man, Henry had to ensure that for this important occasion he dazzled his public, and so he did. 'With great pomp' he arrived at the Abbey, and as the golden Crown of St Edward was placed upon his head, his mother, Margaret Beaufort, 'wept marvellously'.[2] Many crucial events would take place in rapid succession after the coronation, including Henry's wedding to Elizabeth of York, a surprisingly low-key affair. Elizabeth was the daughter of Edward IV, and as an English princess she had a much stronger claim to the throne than her husband. Henry wanted there to be no confusion; he was King in his own right and certainly not because of his wife, and so the wedding ceremony was downplayed significantly. Elizabeth's coronation was even delayed until after the birth of their first child and heir, Prince Arthur. There would be no upstaging the new King, not even by his Queen.

Elizabeth had expensive tastes, her life as a princess had gifted her a keen eye for magnificence and her brief, previous engagement to the Dauphin of France had left her with an appreciation of popular French fashions. The process of dressing Elizabeth in the morning began with a linen smock and perhaps a quilted waistcoat if the weather was cold. Then she was laced into a kirtle, a close-fitting dress lined with canvas or buckram, with a stiffened bodice to help support the bust and hold the shape of the dress. For a working woman the kirtle would be enough, but wealthy women like Elizabeth would wear a gown on top. These gowns were made of wool or velvet with a long, often cumbersome train that would be looped over the arm to reveal the contrasting fabric of the kirtle beneath. At this time, women were expected to cover their hair for the sake of modesty, and wealthy women would use various elaborate headdresses to do so. The emerging English hood was the predominant style of the late 1400s (alternatively known as the 'gable hood', as it resembled the front of a gabled roof) and would have been the preference of Elizabeth; in fact, one of the only extant portraits of Elizabeth depicts her in a headdress of this style. The hood consisted of a structured and heavily decorated front, with decorated strips called 'lappets' dangling down the side of the face, and a black veil at the back of the head to conceal the hair. These hoods were worn over a linen coif (cap), onto which they could be pinned to hold them in place, and which ensured that the hood itself was protected from the oils of the hair.

What would it have felt like to wear all of these layers? Not nearly as stifling as you might think. The linen undershirts and coifs were essential; lightweight and breathable, they were the only part of the ensemble that touched bare skin, acting as a barrier between the body and the clothing and soaking up sweat. The silk and wool garments worn by wealthy ladies at court, as well as the expensive fur used to trim them, were delicate and often unwashable, so a protective barrier in the form of a shirt was a necessity. Linen shirts were cleaned regularly, and for women like Elizabeth often changed multiple times throughout the day in order to stay fresh and improve the longevity of outerwear. Though they may not have had a full understanding of the science, the Tudors understood that a bad smell, indicative of uncleanliness, could lead to possible health issues, and endeavoured wherever they could to keep clean and fresh. They were not sweating to an excessive degree, at least not as a result of their clothing, and would have been very comfortable in their layers. For much of the Tudor's reign, England was experiencing the Little Ice Age, a period of unusually cold weather that would have made heavy dressing a blessing rather than a curse. Even in the summer months, these outfits were not cumbersome, as the light, breathable nature of the natural fibres used kept the wearer well aerated.

Despite their rank, Henry and Elizabeth's clothes would have been relatively plain in comparison to their children and grandchildren's. With clothing being made from unpatterned fabrics and fur being reserved largely for ceremonial events, displays of wealth came from the cost of the colour of fabric instead. Most of Elizabeth's dresses were made of black velvet with contrasting borders and a scarlet underskirt, and Henry too had a fondness for black clothing.[3] As King, Henry would have had access to a wider range of colours and materials than the majority of his subjects, but the colour black, which required expensive quantities of madder red dye to achieve, was effective in communicating the wearer's wealth. As Henry and Elizabeth sat before their court in their moody-coloured clothing, they would have represented their vision for England as a whole – unified, modern and wealthy.

The royal couple shared much more than just a corresponding interest in fashion. Despite their marriage not originally being a love match, Henry and Elizabeth became utterly devoted to one another. With mistresses being a common occurrence for royals of the period, it's somewhat of a relief to know that Henry VII had no known affairs, and the duo enjoyed a happy married life that resulted in the birth of seven children. Henry was a provider for his family, with most of the clothes for his children being listed in his expenditure. Of their seven children, those who survived past infancy were Arthur, Margaret, Henry and Mary. As the Prince of Wales and eldest son, Arthur had preferential treatment when it came to his clothes and was always dressed appropriately for his station – Henry wanted to ensure that his son's royal reputation was fully established by the time he became King. Henry would often provide black clothes for his children, keeping in line with his own interests, yet the new generation of Tudors were particularly fond of brighter colours. The sisters Margaret and Mary would often be dressed in the same colourful clothes, such as the time in 1498 when they received matching gowns of green velvet with purple hems.[4] Interestingly, the first documented instance of the word 'orange' being used to describe a colour was in Elizabeth of York's wardrobe accounts after she purchased a dress of that colour for one of her daughters.[5]

Of course, as a doting husband, Henry would occasionally make royal wardrobe purchases for Elizabeth, but these were often only bedding, ceremonial clothes or the odd gift, sweetly documented in official records as for his 'dearest wife'.[6] The majority of Elizabeth's clothes were paid for out of her own pocket and her expensive tastes often landed her in debt, which Henry would pay off. In a sign of wifely devotion, Elizabeth would in return mend and embellish Henry's clothes by hand and was able to show off her particularly impressive embroidery skills. This may also have been an act of thrift; despite Henry's urge to project his kingly magnificence, he was also keen to ensure no unnecessary expenses were made. Henry's wardrobe moderation meant that following generations of Tudor royals would have ample funds to spend on their own clothing, but for now even his children would have to abide by his frugal ways. Often royal clothes would be repurposed, changing the sizes so that the growing children could continue wearing their clothes and adding or removing fur to make them seasonally appropriate.

English fashion remained largely unchanged in this period – at least until 2 October 1501, when a fashion revolution landed at Plymouth, Devon. This revolution came in the form of the fifteen-year-old Spanish Princess Katherine of Aragon, who had been brought to England to marry the future King, Prince Arthur. One of the first things Katherine would have noticed when she disembarked the boat from Spain was just how differently the women of this new country dressed. The English felt similarly, and eyewitnesses to her arrival looked on in bewilderment at the 'rich apparel of the Princess' and the 'strange fashions of the Spanish nation'.[7] A few days before her wedding, Katherine made her entry into London in a grand procession. Since her arrival, she had won the heart of her future husband and the approval of King Henry, who expressed his willingness to embrace her as his own child. This was her opportunity to showcase her Spanish finery to the English public. She rode into London in a loose-fitting gown with a pleated skirt draped over a Spanish farthingale (a series of wooden hoops connected by fabric creating a conical cage that a gown may be worn over). Her hair was kept away from her face by a wide, flat cap so that her piercing blue eyes could be seen by the large crowd that formed to greet her.

No expense was spared for her wedding ceremony, held two days later on 14 November. Henry and Elizabeth both spent a considerable amount of money on the wedding, despite the fact that Katherine's parents had urged them otherwise, claiming they did not want her to be a burden on the finances of England but rather to be the 'source of all kinds of happiness'.[8] This was just as important an event for Henry as it was for his son, as it was an opportunity for him to broadcast his carefully curated image of the Tudor dynasty on a global scale. Katherine's wedding dress was a Spanish gown, embellished with pearls and precious stones and made of white satin.[9] Her bridegroom, Arthur, wore white robes to match. Katherine's long, reddish-gold hair hung loose down her back – this would be one of the last times she could wear it down in public. Once she became a married woman, society dictated that she must hide it beneath a hood, except for on rare ceremonial occasions.

Katherine, perhaps begrudgingly, would have to change her wardrobe now that she was Princess of Wales to express her allegiance to her new country. She would have to part with the pleated skirts and elaborate headdresses of her homeland in favour of the English gown and gable hood. Eventually, the women of England would be influenced by their brief glimpse at continental fashion and slowly adopt the Spanish farthingale and sleeves, but for now Katherine would have to make do with her new English gowns and hoods. Leaving Spain had been a distressing experience for Katherine, and this did not escape King Henry's notice. To distract the young Princess from her sadness, he allowed Katherine to select a ring from the royal jewellery collection – just a taster of the finery she could expect in her time as Queen. Katherine would always be partial to jewellery, and this gesture from King Henry was very successful in calming her post-nuptial nerves. Soon after the wedding, Arthur and Katherine relocated to Ludlow, Wales, to hold their own court and practise governing before they ascended to the throne. Despite Arthur's poor health and Katherine's severe homesickness, the two took to holding a court with ease. They were popular in Wales, and their marriage was happy and harmonious. But in March 1502, both the Prince and Princess of Wales were struck down with a mysterious illness. The couple were kept separate, and

Katherine made a full recovery; her husband, however, would not be so lucky. On 2 April, the Prince of Wales succumbed to his illness after six months of marriage. He was just fifteen years old, and Katherine, herself no older, suddenly found herself a widow.

Henry was inconsolable after the death of his son, and likely concerned for the future of the Tudor family. He had lost an heir to the throne; what if he ran out of sons to continue the dynasty? A traditional mourning period was observed by all members of the royal court, during which it was compulsory for all those in attendance to dress in black mourning clothes. Unfortunately for the King, yet another tragedy would strike when, just one year later, his beloved wife, Elizabeth, died from childbirth complications at just thirty-seven years of age. Henry was crippled by this second death, and in his grief broke royal mourning protocols. Traditionally a mourning monarch would wear dark blue, so that they would still stand out from those in their court, but Henry, who now lived a solitary existence, could only bring himself to dress in black. On 21 April 1509, Henry himself would pass away, leaving the Crown to his fiery second son, Prince Henry.

HENRY VIII

In 1506 the Spanish Princess was struggling. As a widow, Katherine was no longer the Princess of Wales and found herself in a state of limbo. Both she, her ladies-in-waiting and the rest of her household had been moved to Durham House in London after a grieving King Henry VII had stopped providing financial support. Behind the scenes, her father was working hard to secure her another English royal marriage, but this was a complicated process and Katherine was running out of time. She had run low on money to feed and clothe herself and had been reduced to begging the King for money, which he was reluctant to give. Since the death of her husband, she had received only two new dresses and those she had brought with her from Spain no longer fit; in a letter to her father she confessed that she had had to sell some of the family jewels in order to purchase a new dress for herself. In a sign of her compassionate nature, Katherine admits that she is most concerned with seeing her 'servants and maidens so at a loss' as a result of her financial hardship.[10]

Eventually, a new marriage for Katherine was agreed upon and she was betrothed to Arthur's younger brother, Henry. Henry had always treated Katherine with respect and saw her sharp mind as an equal to his own, but there was, of course, the issue of the Bible. Canon law dictated it was unlawful for a man to marry his brother's widow, yet after careful investigation and a great deal of tact from Katherine, it was agreed that her first marriage had not been consummated, thus making it invalid and allowing her to marry Prince Henry. The marriage between the two young royals took place at a private ceremony on 11 June 1509, shortly after Prince Henry had ascended to the throne and become King Henry VIII, and Katherine, undoubtedly still shaken by her precarious situation over the previous years, was keen to put no foot wrong. She chose to wear a virginal white wedding dress with her hair loose and exposed.[11] Going without the hood that was expected of married and widowed women was a symbol of her purity, reinforcing her claim that her marriage to Arthur had never been consummated. At the time, it must have seemed a great relief to Katherine, who after so many years of turmoil could finally feel secure in her position. She could not have known at that point that she was to be the first of six wives fated to suffer at Henry's hand.

The seventeen-year-old King that Katherine married that day was nothing like the grotesque, corpulent figure we associate with an older Henry VIII. Like his father before him, Henry was never meant to be King but thankfully had been blessed with a boisterous and jovial temperament that won him the affection of many, including his new wife. He was unusually tall for his time, probably about 6 foot 2 inches, with a fine head of short, red hair. He had a fondness for sporting events that gave him a lean, athletic figure and a shapely set of calves of which he was exceptionally proud. Luckily for Henry, he would have ample opportunity to display his fine legs, as the length of male gowns shrank significantly in his early reign. The hemline of Henry's gowns would fall somewhere between mid-thigh and knee, and the gathering of the fabric made the ensemble seem boxy. This would have complimented Henry's tall figure, and with the increased interest in surface embellishment, he would have made an imposing and glittering regal figure. Henry was deeply inspired by the magnificent European courts of the time and wanted to be taken seriously for his fashionable endeavours. He made sure to have new clothes for every holy day, experimented with styles from far-off countries, covered himself in heavy jewellery and every square inch of his clothing was embroidered with gold or silver thread. His efforts were evidently successful, as he was once described as 'the best dressed sovereign in the world',[12] a title which he surely relished.

Unfortunately, all that glitter and finery could not conceal the King's more unsavoury characteristics; despite his typically amicable personality he could be incredibly short-tempered and prone to jealous outbursts. No one was allowed to upstage their King in any endeavour, especially not in fashion, and Henry was quick to make it quite literally impossible to do so. In 1510, just one year after his Coronation, Henry delivered his first Act of Parliament, which legally dictated what clothes could and couldn't be worn by members of the public. Legislation like this wasn't anything new: laws restricting fashionable dress had become particularly popular in fifteenth-century Europe as the emerging merchant class began to amass more money and were able to dress similarly to their aristocratic counterparts. To prevent confusion, 'acts of apparel' or 'sumptuary laws' were implemented, mostly to help enforce class boundaries by creating a visual distinction between ranks. Henry enacted four main sumptuary laws in his reign that used income, class and profession as the means to separate society.[13] Certain furs such as sable were to be worn only by those with the title of Earl (or higher), velvet and satin were off limits to those below the rank of government servant, and there were harsh restrictions on who could wear imported goods. Certain materials were reserved for royalty – purple silk, cloth of gold, and black-and-white ermine fur were to be worn by the King's family alone. Breaking these rules was punishable by heavy fines and they were followed closely by members of the royal court who did not want to anger their King. Interestingly, Henry's acts of apparel rarely applied to the clothing of women, and as such the ladies of his court easily outshone their male counterparts.

Katherine of Aragon took to the role of Queen like a duck to water. She had particularly traditional views of how a Queen should present herself, and these manifested through her clothing; where the King's wardrobe was filled with vibrant, bright colours, Katherine gravitated towards the deep and sumptuous shades favoured by the court of Henry VII. Despite these differences, in their early reign the King and Queen would occasionally be seen in matching ensembles, and they presented themselves as the model royal couple. Katherine was intelligent and resilient in nature, and over the course of her first few years as Queen she would become increasingly pious and turn to religion for comfort. Underneath her regal gowns she wore the habit of St Francis and dressed modestly in private as a sign of humility. Under the pressure of the royal court, she took a step back from pageants and entertainments and became a spectator rather than a participant in the events her husband so passionately enjoyed. Katherine and Henry were slowly drifting apart.

The first significant blow to their marriage came in 1511. Katherine had given birth to a son and heir on New Year's Day, but by the end of February the child had passed away. Katherine would experience multiple miscarriages and still-births over the course of her life, and her only surviving child was the young Princess Mary – not good enough for Henry, who had inherited the anxieties of his father and was desperate for a son to continue the Tudor dynasty. He was beginning to grow anxious; the possibility that he was trapped in a fruitless marriage was hauntingly apparent.

Katherine was five years older than Henry, and the stress of her royal duties caused her to age significantly faster. By 1525, Katherine was dressing to compensate for this, wearing the many jewels she had inherited as Queen, favouring ropes of pearls and large, religious brooches for her gowns – made of heavy velvet with a long court train. She overwhelmingly wore gowns of an English style but resorted back to Spanish fashions when it was prudent to do so – such as to secure favour from overseas allies with connections to her homeland. Surrounding her at all times were her ladies-in-waiting, a group of beautiful and stylish women from noble families who attended the Queen and kept her company. These glamorous young women did little to help the Queen's tumultuous marriage, as they were prone to distract from her. Henry's head was often turned by the sprightly characters and modern dresses of the ladies of Katherine's court, many of whom became his mistresses and bore him illegitimate children. That year, Henry's head was turned by a shiny new addition to his wife's entourage: Anne Boleyn.

By Tudor standards, Anne was no great beauty. She was short and slight, with a slender face, in a time where buxom figures were considered desirable. And while contemporary opinion praised the fairest of features, Anne's eyes and hair were the deepest brown, and her complexion sallow. Despite all of this, Anne electrified the Tudor court with the way she presented herself. In her youth she had spent a great deal of time in the French royal court, which had shaped her into the powerhouse of a woman that she was. Wit and humour came naturally to her, she was particularly fond of hunting and cards, and her skills in music and dancing were unmatched. The women of the French court had left an impact on Anne: from Queen Claude she had learnt to be dignified in all aspects of life, and Margaret of Alençon had encouraged her to pursue her own academic interests and remain well versed in contemporary issues. Above all, Anne had mastered the refined courtly art of flirtation, using both her physical and intangible assets to attract attention. Anne was praised in the French court for the ease with which she adopted their preferred style of dress, and it's not hard to imagine how alluring she must have looked in her revealing French gowns with her long hair laced with diamonds. In France, Anne had been considered stylish. In England? She was a fashion sensation. On her return in 1522, Anne brought with her the styles of the French court, popularizing the French gown, which was considerably less conservative than its English counterpart, and the French hood, a crescent-shaped headdress that sat far back on the skull to scandalously expose the hairline.

By the Christmas of 1525 the thirty-four-year-old King was infatuated with the twenty-four-year-old Anne and began his usual process of courting a mistress. Anne, however, was not easily swayed. Her sister, Mary Boleyn, had also been in the service of Queen Katherine and had become the King's mistress shortly before Anne returned to England. Anne had seen first-hand how quickly Henry's affections could wane and did not want to risk her chances of a proper marriage. Henry, who was used to his romantic pursuits being accepted readily was for the first time quite unsure how far his feelings were reciprocated. In February 1526, he made his first public display of affection towards Anne. He partook in a jousting tournament and had a new uniform embroidered with burning hearts and the motto 'Declare I Dare Not', a sign to all those in attendance that the King was pursuing a new mistress.[14] Unbeknownst to the public, Henry *had* declared his love to Anne, but she had refused to become his mistress. This did little to dissuade the King, rather it turned his affection for her into a rampant obsession. Henry was quick to bestow a great deal of gifts on Anne in an attempt to curry her favour; these included fabric for clothes, jewels and even the title of Marquess of Pembrokeshire, which Anne accepted heartily. Anne eventually returned Henry's affection but made it clear that she was saving herself for marriage.

A seed had now been planted in the King's head. In order to have the one thing he truly wanted, Katherine would have to go. As she approached forty, the chances of her producing an heir were diminishing and Henry used this as the driving force behind his argument for divorce. In May the following year, Anne and Henry made their first public appearance as a 'couple', and Anne's ensemble was notably impressive. She was draped in the many expensive jewels that she had received from the King and wearing a gown of the most luxurious fabrics. She was beginning to push the boundaries of what was acceptable for a woman of her status to wear, and the perceptive Queen Katherine would have realized by now that Henry was taking his relationship with Anne far more seriously than she had first thought. Anne was dressing for the rank she wanted, not the one she currently held.

On 22 June 1527, Henry came to visit Katherine in the Queen's apartments, bringing with him news that she had been dreading. He informed his wife that he believed their marriage to be invalid and was petitioning the Pope for a divorce. Katherine was inconsolable; after so many years of dedication, how could he so cruelly dismiss his wife like this? But the Spanish Princess had been raised for the role of Queen of England and was not prepared to abandon her marriage without a fight. Her royal upbringing had taught her the symbolic power that clothes held and she intended to utilize this to its fullest advantage. That year, Katherine began spending more money than ever before on her wardrobe, dressing with unusual luxury in an attempt to cement her position as Queen above Anne.[15] This may also have been a final attempt by Katherine to rekindle her marriage by appealing to Henry's love of finery, but this would unfortunately be a fruitless endeavour.

Despite all the chaos, Katherine was determined to carry on as if nothing had changed; she had done no wrong and saw no reason why the divorce should be granted. So she continued with her wifely duties. One such task was making Henry's shirts, a garment considered intimate and therefore a wife's job to create for their husband. Katherine had taken this role seriously throughout her marriage and took great pride in embroidering complex black patterns around the cuffs and collar – this 'blackwork' was a Spanish trend that she had introduced to England and it had become a fashion staple during her reign. All through this turbulent period she secretly continued to make Henry's shirts, a clear sign that she still viewed herself as his wife. Katherine's shirt-making continued until Christmas in 1530, when Anne Boleyn discovered a servant bringing her a delivery of linen to make the shirts. She flew into a terrible rage that Henry himself had to placate, as she could not stand that Katherine was still insisting on her place as the King's wife. From that point onwards, it became Anne's duty alone, although rather than make the shirts herself, Anne had them made by an expert tailor on her behalf.

By this point, Anne was Queen in all but name. Her clothing was now financed and organized by the royal wardrobe department, and she frequently wore gowns of sumptuous purple fabric or glittering cloth of gold, colours only to be worn by the immediate royal family. Henry made these exceptions for Anne and kept supplying her with finery to keep her keen whilst the complicated divorce proceedings played out. The process was long and not going in Henry's favour, largely because Katherine had taken to appealing for supporters and made some powerful allies in her fight to keep her title. In retaliation, Henry made a particularly low blow in an attempt to undermine Katherine's efforts: he sent the Duke of Norfolk to confiscate the Queen's jewels. Throughout her time in England, Katherine had amassed a fine collection of jewellery. Some she had brought over from Spain, some had been handed down from Queen to Queen, and others were gifts from Henry himself. When Katherine wore these jewels, it was a sign of her status, and they would have brought her comfort as a reminder that she had not yet lost this marital battle. When the Duke delivered the King's instructions, Katherine was angry, and rightfully so, for the King intended for the jewels to be brought to Anne Boleyn to keep her satisfied. 'It is against my conscience,' the Queen exclaimed, 'to give my jewels to adorn a person who is the scandal of Christendom!'[16] But Katherine quickly realized that this was not a request but a demand, and, ever the dedicated wife, she surrendered each and every piece.

The cold January air pierced its way into the King's Chapel at Whitehall Palace. Inside, the King was ecstatic: he had finally managed to secure the divorce from Katherine. It may have taken breaking England from the Catholic faith and establishing the Church of England to give Henry total control, but he had achieved his goal in the end. Outside the Chapel, Anne Boleyn, already in the early stages of pregnancy with the King's child, prepared to walk down the aisle. With Katherine sent away from the court forever and Princess Mary stripped of her title, the Crown was Anne's for the taking. Henry married his long-time mistress in private in the early hours of 25 January 1533. He had his ex-wife out of his life and a child – now legitimate – on the way. He had all he'd ever wanted.

Plans for Anne's coronation could now commence. Anne would have sensed the gravity of the event; this was to be England's first major ceremonial event since separating from papal authority and it needed to assert England's independent power. Anne herself may have been the one to plan the extravagant pageants and celebrations for the event, but she clashed with her father on how she should dress herself for the occasion. By June her pregnancy would be well underway, and she requested extra fabric to be added to her gown to disguise it, but her father thought she should be flaunting her condition. Anne had very few supporters as she came into power, but her one trump card was the chance she was carrying England's much-needed male heir. Her father tried to convince her to appear in an unlaced gown to draw attention to her belly and perhaps win extra support, but ultimately Anne won out.[17] On 1 June 1533, she appeared at Westminster Abbey for her coronation in a shimmering dress of white cloth of gold trimmed with regal ermine fur, her dark hair loose down her back and a gold circlet atop her head. Her gown was in the French style and Anne, independent and strong willed, would continue to dress like this throughout her reign. That is not to say she never wore English styles, for the next year a series of commemorative medallions were made in honour of Anne's coronation depicting the Queen in an English-style hood. Though Anne would always favour her French fashions, she knew it could be beneficial to adopt local garments to enforce her position as Queen of England.

When Anne arrived at the Cathedral, Henry embraced her and asked what she thought of the celebrations she had passed on her journey. 'I liked the city well enough,' she replied, then added with disappointment, 'I saw a great many caps on heads and heard but few tongues.'[18] The crowds that had gathered were there not to support Anne but rather jeer at her, even joking that the interlocking HA initials that were embroidered throughout the decorations could be read as 'ha ha!', like laughter. Removing one's cap was a basic sign of respect in Tudor England, and when her public refused to do so, Anne realized that she would have to work extra hard for her people's approval.

As Queen, Anne was a fierce presence in the royal court. She was outspoken, politically astute and encouraged her ladies-in-waiting to be well read and follow her lead. According to legend, Henry wrote the famous song 'Greensleeves' for his beloved Anne, and she certainly did enjoy dressing in that colour. In 1530, Henry purchased a gown of green damask for Anne, and in 1535, he gifted her an incredible amount of green satin and green cloth of gold. In the Queen's quarters, Anne decorated her bedding and furniture with the same colour and purchased green clothing for her daughter Elizabeth.[19] This may have been personal preference but it may also have been in homage to her new position as Tudor Queen, as green and white were the Tudor house colours.

Anne is also closely associated with the famous 'B' necklace that she is depicted wearing in her most famous portrait. Women in the sixteenth century were particularly fond of jewellery that incorporated their initials, either to display their family heritage or their titles, and Anne was no exception. Prior to her marriage she had a B, an A and an AB pendant, and once she married the King she may have adopted an interlocked HA (Henry and Anne) and AR (for Anne Regina, Regina meaning Queen).[20] As for the now-exiled Katherine of Aragon, who had been demoted to Dowager Princess of Wales, she refused to accept that she was no longer Queen and would continue to have her clothes embroidered with her and Henry's initials until her death in 1536.[21]

Anne's time as Queen was not without its challenges. She amassed a great number of enemies in the brief time she was on the throne, many of whom began plotting to remove her from power. She was a politically outspoken woman, had earned the wrath of passionate Catholics who saw her as the reason the King had broken from the Catholic Church, and many members of the public felt she was to blame for Katherine of Aragon's mistreatment. Furthermore, the child that Anne had been pregnant with at the time of her coronation was not the boy that Henry had been hoping for but rather another daughter – Princess Elizabeth. Like Katherine before her, Anne suffered many miscarriages and again Henry's patience ran thin. He had been convinced that his marriage to Anne would produce the male heir he desperately needed, but Anne was struggling, quite literally, to deliver.

In 1536, the Queen's enemies approached Henry claiming false charges of incest, adultery and treason against Anne (one such claim was that she laughed at the King's clothes behind his back) and an enraged Henry was ready to be rid of her. On 2 May that year, Anne was informed of the charges, and she immediately retreated to her chambers. Once in the safety of the Queen's apartments, Anne changed into an impressive gown of crimson velvet and cloth of gold.[22] She knew that now more than ever she needed to assert her position as Queen in order to make it through the upcoming trial unscathed. Anne had seen her clothes fill many roles in her life but now they would become her battle armour as she fought to retain her title and her life.

Despite Anne's best efforts, she was found guilty and sentenced to death. On Friday, 19 May, a scaffold was erected at the Tower of London ready for the Queen's execution, and as she was marched to her fate, the two-year-old Elizabeth would have been her main concern. For such an outspoken woman, Anne's final words were somewhat timid and made no attempt to defend herself, for if she defied the King now it would be little Elizabeth who would face the consequences. Instead, she made her final thoughts clear through her clothing, choosing to wear a grey damask gown over a scarlet petticoat, draped in a mantle of ermine fur and finished with an English hood.[23] The colour scarlet was closely associated with martyrdom, and ermine fur was restricted by law to members of the immediate royal family. This, combined with the English-style hood voiced Anne's belief that she was the rightful Queen of England and was being unjustly sent to her death. After her final speech to the crowd that had gathered, she removed her hood to reveal a netted coif, knelt before the block, and in one swing of the swordsman's blade, Anne Boleyn was dead.

That same day, one of Anne's ladies-in-waiting was busy making plans for her wedding dress. She had not yet been formally proposed to, but it had become common knowledge in society circles that the King had been courting her for a while now and would likely make her his next bride. This woman was Jane Seymour, and she was right to be making wedding plans. Just one day after the death of Anne Boleyn, Henry proposed, and within a few weeks' time the two would be married at York Place. For his third wedding, Henry chose to dress in white, the colour of purity. He wanted this marriage to be a clean slate; he had rid himself of his previous brides and wanted this to be seen as his first legitimate marriage.

Jane Seymour was twenty-seven when she married Henry, who was now forty-five. She came from a noble family and had first caught the King's eye when she was lady-in-waiting to Queen Anne, but it had not been her physical appearance that drew the King to her. Jane was not renowned for her beauty; she was of average height with exceptionally pale skin, a long face and small eyes and lips, but her demeanour was everything Henry was searching for. Perhaps growing tired of Anne's outspoken and fiery personality, the King was undoubtedly attracted to Jane's reserved demeanour; he now desired above all else a submissive wife who would fulfil her singular duty of providing an heir. Almost certainly Jane would have been anxious about marrying a man who had so mercilessly discarded two of his wives already, and so she strategically played into Henry's desires for a demure English bride to ensure her survival.

The clothes that made up Jane's royal wardrobe were significantly different to those found in Elizabeth of York's. Similar to how men's fashion had become more experimental, women's clothes were now significantly more detailed. Influenced heavily by the European styles of Katherine of Aragon and Anne Boleyn, the average woman at court would wear a low-cut gown of French inspiration with long, trumpeted sleeves that would be folded back up the arm to reveal the contrasting lining. On the forearms, interchangeable sleeves were pinned to the gown, and they would often be made with expensively decorated fabric. The bodice of the gown was laced up the front, and a panel of fabric called a placard was pinned over the laces to cover them; this placard would often be structured with whalebone to create a supportive yet flat silhouette. The skirt of the gown would typically open at the front to reveal the forepart – a panel of contrasting fabric worn underneath the gown. Beneath all of these layers a roll of stuffed fabric was worn around the waist to create volume in the skirts, and the ensemble would be finished with a considerable amount of jewellery and the still-fashionable French hood.

When Jane became Queen, she made the controversial choice to dictate to her ladies-in-waiting what they could and could not wear. Anne Bassett, for example, was a keen and fashionable young girl who upon being accepted into the Queen's service in 1537, was told in no uncertain terms by the Queen that she did not approve of her new French wardrobe. Frantically, Anne turned to her family friends at court to lend her the appropriate clothes, and a letter to her mother reveals: 'the Queen's pleasure is that Mrs. Anne shall wear no more her French apparel, so she must have a bonnet or two with frontlets [English-style hoods], an edge of pearl, a gown of black satin, and another of velvet' and that she should have extra fabric added to the low necklines of her gowns.[24] Anne and the other ladies of the court were not thrilled to have to dress in such an outdated style, but they had to please their Queen regardless. It's not known for certain why Jane enacted these rules, but it was most likely her attempt to stabilize a court still reeling from the loss of two queens, spurred by her desire to not become the third such loss. By enforcing a more formal and certainly more English code of dress for herself and her ladies, Jane would be able to present an image of a unified English court that was distinctly separate to the one presided over by Anne Boleyn. Jane's preference for an overtly patriotic style was strong, her wardrobe was vibrant and contained a much wider variety of colours than the Spanish Katherine of Aragon, preferring the rich, bright colours now popular in England. Her sleeves, of which she owned many pairs, were often embellished with embroidered strawberry leaves – a symbol traditionally associated with England.

The motto that Jane adopted as Queen was 'Bound to Obey and Serve', and that was exactly the way she lived her married life. Subservient in all ways, Jane managed to keep the increasingly temperamental King sweet on her, ultimately allowing her to gain favours for her family and even to restore Katherine of Aragon's daughter, Lady Mary, back into favour.

Jane was in all ways Henry's perfect bride and likely soothed his fiery temper, but for Jane things would quickly take a turn for the worse. In late May 1537, the court was overjoyed to see Queen Jane in an open-front gown, indicating that she was pregnant.[25] This open-front gown was favoured by expectant mothers, with the placard sitting behind the gown laces rather than being pinned in front, allowing them to be tied looser and the dress to expand as the pregnancy progressed. As Jane rose each day, her ladies would tie her gown looser and looser, exposing more of the placard; this acted as a visual countdown to the birth. On 9 October, Jane began a three-day labour, and it was not certain that she would survive. To Jane and Henry's great relief, she eventually delivered a healthy baby boy, Henry's heir to the throne, Prince Edward. A few days later, at Edward's christening, a still recovering Jane received guests whilst sitting in her bed of crimson and cloth of gold. She wore her fair hair loose about her shoulders and was draped in a crimson mantle trimmed with ermine fur. With Henry sitting proudly beside her, she would have looked every bit a powerful Tudor Queen.

But not all was well with Jane. The birth had been traumatic, and she had developed an infection from the resulting complications. A few days later, the infection brought about a severe fever that left the Queen bedbound, and on the night of Wednesday, 24 October, Jane Seymour passed away. Henry was left devastated by Jane's death and entered a period of intense mourning in which he wore exclusively black for three months; the royal court were required to observe mourning traditions until Easter the following year.[26] But despite Henry's grief, he now needed to be on the hunt for another bride, and since he had no current mistress to turn to, he had to actively search for his next Queen. This might seem bizarre, but Henry knew from his own father's experiences that just one son would not be enough. He had the heir, now he needed a spare. The King turned his gaze overseas, sending his court painter Hans Holbein to capture the image of the eligible women of European royalty in the hopes he might secure a marriage that was politically beneficial, as well as romantically.

One tiny, circular portrait that Holbein created stunned the King like no other. Encased in a frame carved as a Tudor rose, the woman that gazed out at the King was devastatingly beautiful; her soft, heavy-lidded eyes complimented the gentle roundness of her nose and the sweetness of her pink lips, and the heavily jewelled bodice of her Netherlandish gown gave her an air of regal brilliance. This woman was Anne of Cleves, a princess from the Duchy of Cleves in modern-day Germany. Though Cleves was not a particularly wealthy region, a marriage alliance would be politically beneficial for England, and so for Henry, she was an obvious choice. In December 1539, Henry's bride-to-be arrived in England but she didn't exactly overwhelm her new subjects. She came equipped with a wardrobe of her country's favoured styles and it seems the gowns were just slightly too foreign for English eyes. Described by onlookers as 'monstrous', her gowns featured a rounded skirt without the long train popular in England and draped in the masculine golden chains typical of Dutch bodices.[27] Whatever physical beauty she was said to have was entirely eclipsed by her foreign dresses, and no one dared to tell the King of this disappointment.

Henry himself was in high spirits as he awaited Anne's arrival; he anticipated a marriage that would bring him untold joy and rode quickly to greet his new bride. Despite now nearing fifty, the King still saw himself as the charming monarch of his youth, and he decided to surprise Anne in an act of typical English pageantry. On the journey to meet her, Henry switched his regal attire with the plain clothes of one of his gentlemen attendants. Inspired by tales of chivalric knights and handsome kings of times past, he believed that Anne would see through the ruse and easily identify her true love, triggering the start of a passionate marriage. Unfortunately, Henry's dream was not to be realized: Anne, understanding very little English language and even fewer English customs, saw the King's plain clothes and did not recognize him.[28] Henry was devastated, leaving the room to change into a regal coat of purple velvet and returning to a deeply embarrassed Anne. The king was enraged, and in his anger forgot to give Anne the furs he had bought for her. In a matter of moments Henry's opinion of his betrothed had changed dramatically; he no longer desired to be married to her. There was just too wide a cultural divide separating him from his foreign bride.

On 6 January 1540, Henry and Anne married in matching golden gowns. They were trimmed with black fur and heavily embroidered with flowers made of silver thread and pearls.[29] The splendour of their wedding day helped to mask Henry's displeasure, and indeed Anne herself would remain unaware that she did not please him until six months into their marriage, when he asked for an annulment. Unlike Katherine of Aragon, the significantly less confident Anne of Cleves did not put up much of a fight and stepped away from the Crown quickly. Henry rewarded her obedience, and she was given an honorary position in the royal family, as well as a great deal of land and money from the Crown. Anne retreated to her new home at Richmond Palace, where she lived happily as one of the wealthiest and most important women in the country. It was reported that each day she had a new gown to wear, most of which were in the styles popular in England.

The King knew exactly who he wanted as his next bride. While Henry's advisors worked hard to secure his annulment from Anne of Cleves, his heart had been stolen by one of her ladies-in-waiting. This lady was the charming Katheryn Howard, and the court looked on as the King bestowed upon her gifts of land and luxurious fabric, falling for her in a way he had not done for 'any other woman'.[30] It is not known exactly when Katheryn was born, but she may have been as young as fifteen when Henry began courting her. She was short and decently pretty, but like her cousin Anne Boleyn, she won Henry's heart with her witty personality, and by July 1540 she was married to her ageing King.

As Queen, Katheryn appointed the same tailor as all of Henry's previous wives, John Scut. Behind her vivacious exterior the new Queen hid an anxious heart; as a very young woman with little experience at the royal court, she would have found it comforting to be guided through her wardrobe choices by such a knowledgeable man. As her confidence as Queen began to grow, Katheryn would begin to take a more active role in the creation of her clothes. She was a stylish girl who gravitated towards French fashions and was known to have her motto 'No Other Will But His' embroidered on her sleeves, and on multiple occasions Katheryn provided specific instructions on how her jewellery and clothes should be made.

There are a few paintings that might depict Katheryn, but none have been officially identified as her. One of the most likely candidates is a small miniature of a woman in a tawny gown with silver sleeves and a heavily jewelled headdress. The woman's soft features and auburn hair match contemporary descriptions of the Queen, but it's her jewellery that gives her identity away. Around her neck she wears a stunning necklace laden with pearls that also appears in a Holbein portrait of Jane Seymour and, along with the pearled trim around the edge of her hood, matches the description of items given to Katheryn as a wedding gift from her new husband. It seems Henry was passing on the belongings of one wife to the next.

Henry's fifth wife has gained a reputation as a spoilt young Queen who had little in her head except vanity and a love for material things, but though it was rumoured she had a fresh new gown each day, she also had a charitable streak. She was moved by the suffering of prisoners in the Tower of London and often acted to improve their conditions. After hearing that the elderly Countess of Salisbury had gone two years in the Tower with no suitable clothing for cold weather, Katheryn instructed her own tailor to make the countess a wardrobe of winter clothes and nightgowns that she paid for out of her own purse. Katheryn's actions towards the incarcerated reveal to us a sensitive and astute young woman, a side of her personality that has since been overshadowed by the controversies of her later life.

Henry presented Katheryn with many jewels and a great deal of clothing throughout their marriage; he was utterly besotted by his young bride and hoped that her youth would increase his chances of having another child. Though it was claimed Katheryn's presence took years off the King's age, it was abundantly clear that – fast approaching fifty – he was not the man he once was. A suit of armour made for the King at this time measures 54 inches around the waist; a jousting accident a few years earlier had left him with an infected wound on his leg, preventing him from engaging in the sports that had kept his figure trim in his youth. The injury caused him constant pain, making him more unpleasant in temperament as the days went on, and the infection left a lingering smell of rotten flesh wherever he went.

On 1 November 1541, the Archbishop of Canterbury left a letter on the King's pew at the Chapel Royal, Hampton Court Palace. The contents of this letter would horrify the King. In it, the Archbishop explained how Katheryn Howard had slept with two men prior to her marriage to Henry and had recently begun an affair with one of his favourite young courtiers, Thomas Culpeper. Henry, reluctant to believe that his rose without a thorn was capable of such treachery, ordered an investigation into the affair. The exact nature of the young Queen's relationship with Culpeper is uncertain, but she explained in detail the way in which she had been groomed as a child by two men in the household she had been raised in, even making it clear that the choice to sleep with them had not been her own. Today we would view Katheryn's tragic childhood with sympathy, but to those in the Tudor court, she had committed a great crime against her husband by not disclosing her premarital status. Katheryn was arrested, banished from court and at Henry's request her beautiful clothes and jewels were seized. He gave exact orders on what clothes she should be permitted to wear – precisely six gowns and hoods, all in sombre colours, and none of the fine jewels she had become used to as Queen.[31] In February 1542, a terrified Katheryn was informed that she was accused of treason and manhandled by guards into the barge that would take her to the Tower of London. Here Katheryn was last seen by the public stepping off the boat in a gown of black velvet, one of the few she had been allowed to keep by her husband.[32] A few days later Katheryn, requiring the assistance of her ladies-in-waiting to walk, stepped onto the executioner's scaffold. A single swing of the axe was all it took to sever her little neck, and she was laid to rest in the nearby Chapel of St Peter ad Vincula near her cousin Anne Boleyn. She couldn't have been any older than twenty when she was killed.

Back at court, rumours were flying. Would the King take another wife? It was no secret that he was past his prime, yet he was still in need of another son. For a brief moment it was thought he might remarry Anne of Cleves, but instead the ailing King turned his attention towards the recently widowed courtier Katherine Parr, sending her sleeves and Italian dresses to declare his intentions.[33] Katherine's role as Queen and wife is often reduced to that of a humble nurse for an ageing King, yet in reality she was an extraordinarily glamorous woman. Most of her life had been spent in and around the royal court and so she would have confidently understood the role fashion could play in demonstrating one's place in the social hierarchy. In her first year as Queen, Katherine gravitated towards crimson and cloth of gold, but as she grew more assured in her position she turned to purple – the colour of royalty. Made using a mixture of expensive indigo and cochineal red dyes, the production process ensured that only the very wealthiest could afford to dress themselves in purple, and with the colour still firmly enshrined by sumptuary laws, its use by Katherine was a powerful statement of her position as a member of the royal family. Other colours, such as crimson, black, gold and silver, were similarly attributed to the elite, as they too were difficult and expensive to produce in textiles, and there was also white, whose elite status stemmed from its impracticality – indicating that the wearer did not need to engage in labour and could afford to replace their clothes regularly.

Symbols of royal strength were a key element in Katherine's wardrobe, and she played into her husband's desire for a united Tudor family by purchasing matching gowns for her immediate royal relatives. For the New Year's celebrations of 1544–5 she appeared alongside her stepchildren Mary, Elizabeth and Edward in matching gowns of glittering silver, going a step further by including Anne of Cleves in her display of royal unity, purchasing a silver gown for her to wear too.[34] At no point in his reign did Henry's anxieties about the future of the Tudor dynasty wane; he feared that he might undo all that his father had done to bring their family to the throne, but Katherine's strategic wardrobe choices helped to soothe him.

This was a smart move, and her focus on a united royal family led to Katherine restoring Princess Elizabeth to her father's favour; as a result, Katherine became an important maternal figure in the young girl's life. She was worldly, a keen writer and in fact the first woman to publish a book in English. Her wardrobe reflects this, as she kept her finger firmly on the beating pulse of European fashion, adopting items such as the ostrich feather fan or Spanish farthingale as soon as they became popular. Her writing revolved around her personal opinions on religion, which some of her enemies at court branded heretical. In 1546, a warrant was issued for her arrest on the grounds that she was a dangerous religious reformist but, exercising great tact and flattery, the sharp-witted Queen Katherine managed to sway her husband into dismissing it. To apologize for the trauma he had undoubtedly caused his wife, Henry ordered five jewellers from across Europe to bring to court jewels, gowns and furs 'as they shall think best for the pleasure of . . . our dearest wife'.[35]

By 1547 King Henry was a sickly man. It became abundantly clear to him that his time with the living was running out and he began preparations for his death. He asked to be buried beside Jane Seymour, his 'one true and loving wife', yet he did not forget his devoted Katherine Parr.[36] She had diligently been dispelling any rumours of the King's ill health from court, but on the night of 27 January, Henry called her to his bedside. He informed Katherine that after his death she would be cared for as if she were still Queen, with a generous yearly salary and her pick of his clothes, which she could sell for a fine sum of money. Henry was evidently thankful that in his final years of life he had such a devoted wife and calm marriage.

Henry VIII died in the early hours of 28 January, as a result of complications from his leg injury.

EDWARD VI

THE NEW KING was inconsolable. The news had finally been broken to Edward that he had ascended to the throne. This outburst is entirely understandable when you consider that Edward was only nine years old and far more concerned with the fact his dear father had passed away than the gravity of having become King. He had known that this day would one day come; all his life he had been raised with all the ceremony and pomp befitting a future King of England and it would have been impossible to ignore just how important this child was. The day of his birth, back in 1537, had seen the country enter a frenzy of celebration at the arrival of the long-awaited heir: church bells rang and banners were raised, as was customary, but the public too were quick to join the festivities. Street parties were held, bonfires lit, and there was a strong feeling of relief and thanksgiving in the air. None, however, were quite as grateful as Edward's own parents. In birthing a healthy baby boy, his mother, Jane, had done what none of Henry's other wives could achieve, giving Henry the male heir he had become so obsessed with attaining. Henry's paranoia would affect Edward's early life. He was almost immediately separated from his mother and brought to his own quarters, where he could be tended to by nursemaids and servants. The plague was rife in the country, and Henry wanted his son in a controlled environment where every toy, shirt and shoe that was handed to the Prince could be thoroughly cleaned. He could not risk losing so precious a child. As an infant, Edward's clothes were organized and selected for him by Lady Bryan, his governess, who took her duties very seriously.

She ensured that the young Prince would always appear his best whenever guests came to visit him and was responsible for organizing the jewels and fine fabrics he wore from a very young age. A Holbein portrait made of Edward when he was barely fourteen months old shows the type of finery Bryan felt was necessary: a fine coat of scarlet wool with long hanging sleeves falling from the back of the shoulders.[37] These sleeves could be used by Lady Bryan to steady the young boy as he learnt to walk.

Throughout his childhood years, Edward had a close relationship with his father. Henry spent many days at his son's residences, playing with the young boy and holding him proudly at the windows so that his adoring public could see their future King. The Prince's clothes were financed and ordered by Henry, so his wardrobe often reflected the preferences of his father. By his sixth birthday, Edward had been breeched, meaning he now dressed in the clothes expected of adults (as opposed to the skirts worn by children of both genders), and in a portrait from 1546 we can truly see how deep Henry's influence ran in his son's clothing.[38] Edward's powerful stance is identical to the pose adopted by Henry in most of his portraits, which was an attempt to make the young Prince seem much more imposing than he would have been at eight years old. He wears a velvet gown lined with lynx fur and a white satin doublet embroidered with gold thread.

Every aspect of the ensemble could easily have been worn by Henry VIII, even down to the codpiece.

Codpieces were an important part of early Tudor fashion. They had originated in the medieval period as a simple triangular piece of fabric used to provide modesty for men as their doublets and gowns began to shrink in length, but by the sixteenth century they were used to emphasize rather than conceal. By the 1540s the codpiece was often padded with fabric to increase its size and embellished with ribbons or embroidery to draw attention to it, and it was even occasionally used to hold money or other small items. The codpiece appealed to monarchs like Henry VIII as a very visual means to highlight their virility, especially if they were under pressure to produce an heir. Despite his young age, Edward would already have begun to experience the same pressure to continue the Tudor dynasty once he became King. As he was still so young at the time of his coronation, the possibility he might die before providing an heir was very real, meaning the dynasty was still weak. To compensate for this, his clothes seem to have been padded in an attempt to make him seem stronger and more manly than he was.

Where his father had a great many marriages, Edward had none. He was briefly engaged to Mary of Scotland, but that had fallen through when she was sent to France to marry their future king. Various English noblewomen were suggested, but Edward, who seemed to have adopted his father's love of finery, specifically requested a foreign bride, who would be dressed more sumptuously and stylishly than his country-women.[39] In the end, Edward did not get the chance to marry. In January 1553, the young King became incredibly ill and over the following months his condition worsened to an agonizing state. He had contracted some form of respiratory illness, perhaps tuberculosis, and he himself was aware that he would not survive the year. As he lay in bed, the fifteen-year-old King declared: 'I am glad to die,' and on 6 July 1553, he finally succumbed to his illness.

MARY I

IN 1553, MARY TUDOR was preparing for a monumental occasion. Her brother, King Edward, had passed away, and in accordance with her father's wishes she was next in line for the throne. This suited Mary just fine, for she had a great deal of support from the English people, and with the blood of her mother, Katherine of Aragon, running through her veins she was confident she would be a powerful ruler despite the prejudice surrounding her gender. It's not hard to imagine, then, the shock that Mary must have felt when she discovered she had been written out of the line of succession and replaced by another: Lady Jane Grey.

Jane Grey was a grandniece of Henry VIII and a devout Protestant, which is exactly what had placed her in this precarious situation. Edward VI and his advisors had worked hard to establish England as a Protestant nation, and with Mary known to be a passionate and confident Catholic they did not want her on the throne to undo all they had achieved. They decided instead that Jane Grey was the next most acceptable choice.

To say that Jane was suited to a life of royalty would be false. She was an introverted young girl who had little interest in the glitter and finery of court life, dressing instead in plain gowns and renouncing the notion that costly apparel could prove one's power.[40] She had even been rejected as a choice of bride for Edward VI on account of her plain appearance. At only sixteen years old, a terrified Jane collapsed to the floor when she was informed of her new lot in life. Bursting into tears, she lamented how underprepared she was for such a monumental role but vowed regardless to do her very best. For a girl that much preferred Plato to pageantry, Jane was about to be thrust suddenly into the spotlight.

The first time Jane made a public appearance in her new title was on 10 July 1553, passing through the gates of the Tower of London to be proclaimed Queen of England. Her gown for this occasion was made of green velvet and her white headdress was laden with precious jewels, befitting her new status but likely not her own choice.[41] As she arrived at the Tower, her handsome face was sour, for she often struggled to hide her disgust when she was forced to wear clothes of such elaborate finery. Her devoted husband travelled with her in an ensemble of white and gold – side by side they made up the Tudor family colours, a visual representation of their right to rule. Hidden beneath the skirts of her gown, Jane struggled to walk in a pair of Italian high-heeled chopine shoes, as where her Tudor relatives had all been impressively tall, Jane was extremely petite. The shoes allowed her to seem more regal and imposing, but also more similar to the core members of the royal family, creating a sense that she was the natural successor to the Tudor legacy.

Nine days later, Jane's life would take another dramatic turn. Her first appearance as Queen had not quite done the trick, as the public still believed that Mary, as a Princess of the blood, had a stronger claim to the throne and deserved to be in her place. They rallied behind Mary thick and fast, and realizing the odds were no longer in their favour, Jane's council (the very men who had schemed to have her made Queen in the first place) jumped ship to save their skins. On 19 July, Jane was stripped of her title and imprisoned in the Tower of London, where she was executed early the following year. She was a young girl caught in the unstable tides of power changing hands, and her life was cut short through no fault of her own. The public consciousness moved on quickly, for Mary Tudor was now finally Queen of England.

Jane Grey's brief stint as Queen was hardly the first obstacle to the throne that Mary had overcome. Up until the age of seventeen, Mary had been the sole heir of Henry VIII, and she had flaunted the wardrobe to prove it. Soon after her birth, a wide variety of expensive fabrics had been purchased: white satin, damask and tinsel, all to be made into small gowns trimmed with regal ermine fur. Ermine fur was a non-negotiable for royal fashion and continues to feature in ceremonial robes worn by the aristocracy today. A small brown stoat, an ermine's fur changes to pure white during the winter months, save for a dark tip on the end of the tail, and it was fur in this 'pure' state that was so prized amongst the elite. They also enjoyed the 'powdered ermine' variety – wherein the black tails were arranged in a linear pattern across the fur. By the age of four, Mary's wardrobe had been bolstered by her parents with a steady flow of new dresses, now in much more vibrant colours.[42] As she tottered around the royal nursery in her gowns of blue, silver, crimson, violet and green, there was no doubt at all as to who was currently first in line for the throne.

Things had changed suddenly for Mary when her parents' marriage had been dissolved. She had been stripped of her title as Princess, removed from the line of succession, made to serve her new half-sister Elizabeth, and, most painfully for Mary, she had been refused permission to visit her mother ever again. When Katherine of Aragon passed away in 1536 she left for her daughter the expensive furs from her gowns and a golden cross from her homeland of Spain, comparatively cheap yet concealed within was a fragment of the true cross – evidently a prized possession of Katherine's.[43] The furs were delivered to Mary; the cross, however, was withheld from her. That same year, Mary's new stepmother, Jane Seymour, extended a hand and welcomed her back into her father's favour. Now with the knowledge of how suddenly and drastically her position in life could change, Mary was keen to keep a low profile, reining in her expectations for clothing and assuring others that she was 'satisfied to wear whatever the King shall appoint'.[44]

This is not to say that Mary was impassive about her clothes; on the contrary, her love of fashion was very well documented at court, and she was noted as 'one of those ladies who takes the greatest pleasure in clothes'.[45] Throughout her reign, ambassadors would report back to their masters and mistresses that if they wished to please Mary, then they should send her gifts of dresses and accessories, and after receiving a selection of clothes from the Queen of Portugal in 1554, Mary spent days admiring their beauty and a week later had 'not yet finished looking at them and rejoicing over them'.[46] For Mary, the clothes she wore during her first few years as Queen likely held a very special significance; for the first time in her life, she had total freedom in the clothes she wore, and they represented the new power she had come into. Not just as a ruler, but the power to decide her own religion, husband and wardrobe.

With the path to the Crown now clear, a triumphant Mary and her supporters made their grand entry to the nation's capital, with the new Queen dazzling the crowd in a French gown of purple velvet scattered all over with pearls and gold embroidery.[47] By autumn the time had arrived for Mary's coronation, and on 1 October she was brought through the streets of London to Westminster Abbey, where she would be crowned the first ruling Queen of England. For this important occasion she wore an impressive robe of cloth of gold embroidered with Tudor roses, and atop her head she wore a finely jewelled crown. She must have been quite the sight, for the crown was so heavy she had to use her hands to hold it in place for the entire journey.[48]

Mary had a lot more weighing on her mind than simply that crown. She was very aware that despite being the more popular choice of monarch (because unlike Jane Grey, her reign followed the natural line of succession), she was still quite obviously a woman. Today, Britain's queens are amongst our most beloved monarchs, but by Tudor standards the prospect of a female monarch was repugnant – a perverted twist on the natural order of society that deemed women subservient to their husbands, to their fathers, to men as a whole. Laws were introduced by parliament clarifying that any power held by kings would be bestowed equally upon queens, but the court of public opinion would require a great deal more convincing before warming to the idea of having a woman in charge.[49] Mary would have difficult waters to navigate and a tough crowd to please.

Mary was a headstrong queen, with a clear vision of how she saw her reign playing out. She may not have been raised for the job of ruling like her brother had been, but she was committed to the task that now lay before her, dedicating time and effort to understanding the issues and politics surrounding her. In her quest to get things right, Mary adopted a system of dressing that consisted of two separate styles for private and public occasions.[50] For her day-to-day wear, the Queen wore a loose gown that fastened at the front but was left open below the waist to display the decorated underskirt. The sleeves were tight-fitting and fell to the wrist, with the shoulders gently padded to create volume, and were scarcely decorated; instead, the sleeves were slashed to create patterns for the lining of the gown to be pulled through. For important occasions, Mary wore a more traditional gown of French inspiration, similar to the styles worn in the court of Henry VIII. Mary seems not to have enjoyed the low, square neckline of this style and wore them with a partlet – a panel of fabric used to cover the decolletage that featured a high, turned-out collar. Eventually, Mary would begin to have the partlet sewn into her gowns, and it is almost certainly this style that she wore for her wedding to the Spanish Prince Philip on 25 July 1554; the dress appears in records as made of richly brocaded violet velvet and white satin.[51]

Mary had always known that she would have to marry. Being a female monarch did not mean she was exempt from the succession anxieties that had plagued her father, in fact they were more prevalent than ever. If Mary bore no children, it would be her half-sister, the Protestant Elizabeth Tudor, who would next come to the throne, a possibility that spelt the crushing defeat of Mary's personal mission to return England to the Catholic faith. She had set her sights on the young Prince Philip of Spain, a pleasingly attractive option both for his handsome face and his connections to Mary's ancestral homeland through her mother, for which she felt great affection. Her advisors, on the other hand, were worried that a foreign match might see the Prince try to assert his superiority over the Queen by right of being her husband, thereby rendering England a Spanish puppet, and begged Mary to consider instead an English groom. Mary was unrelenting, and her Spanish Prince was shipped to England, dressed in white and placed at the altar.

It seemed at first that the marriage was a success, as not long after the wedding the Queen announced her pregnancy to the court. She did so through visual means: 'richly apparelled, and her belly laid out, so that all men might see she was with child'.[52] It was a prominent bragging point for Mary, her swelling stomach proof to the world that she was capable of continuing her bloodline, and capable of sustaining the Catholic dynasty she aspired to – certainly something worth emphasizing through dress. It would be a short-lived happiness however, as with each month that passed, and as the due date came and went with no sign of labour, Mary was forced to admit with great embarrassment that there may have been no baby at all. She had instead been experiencing a phantom pregnancy. To rub salt into the wound, not long after the ordeal, Prince Philip, who had been an attentive husband despite reciprocating little of the affection that his much older wife bestowed upon him, left to busy himself with military and political matters overseas. The desertion left Mary crippled with sadness and once again she turned to her trusty wardrobe to remedy the situation.

When Philip and his Spanish entourage had arrived in England, they had not been pleased by what they saw. One Spanish courtier, a member of Philip's cohorts, reported with disgust on the appearance of English women's dress: 'All the women here wear petticoats of coloured cloth without admixture of silk . . . satin or velvet, very badly cut. Their shoes are sometimes of velvet, but more often of leather, and they wear black stockings and show their legs up to the knee when walking. As their skirts are not long they are passably immodest when walking, and even when seated.'[53] He goes on to detail all the ways that English ladies failed to live up to Spanish standards and the Queen, 'small, and rather flabby', was by no means exempt.

Now separated from her husband, Mary began to transform her wardrobe: the dark, conservative styles so favoured in Spain began to multiply in their numbers as she worked to tempt Philip back into her embrace. She seems to have delighted in wearing one particularly impressive pearl that Philip had given to her. Known as 'La Peregrina', this striking teardrop pearl was the largest that had ever been discovered when it was found in Panama in 1513. It was quickly claimed by the Spanish and presented to Philip and the royal family. It was a poignant gesture of matrimonial power when Mary received the jewel from her husband, and bore even more emotional significance when Mary wore it proudly suspended from a brooch on her bodice. After Mary's death, it returned to the Spanish royal family and was granted the status of crown jewel, passing through the hands of many Spanish queens. Eventually, by the nineteenth century, it had lost its crown jewel status and found a home instead at the auction houses, where in 1969 it was bought by the actor Richard Burton as a Valentine's Day gift for his uber-glamorous wife, Elizabeth Taylor. Mary's transformation in appearance during the breakdown of her marriage is reminiscent of the wardrobe changes undertaken by Katherine of Aragon as she tried to stave off her impending divorce all those years ago, and while that wasn't to be the fate suffered by her daughter's marriage, Philip would scarcely make any further effort to return to see his wife for the rest of their union.

As the 1550s drew to a close, Mary's reputation was in shambles. It was under her rule that England had suffered the disastrous loss of Calais, the final piece of French territory that had been under English control, for which Mary grieved solemnly. Her quest for a Catholic England had also descended into ruins, for it was Mary who had overseen the burning of Protestant leaders at the stake, a mass prosecution that earnt her the moniker 'Bloody Mary' by subsequent generations. She was also, as she entered her forties, still without that much coveted heir.

After a brief return to England by Philip in 1557, Mary was once again exhibiting signs of pregnancy. Her due date was early the next year, and whilst Mary believed with passion that this was finally a fruitful labour, the rest of the country were hardly convinced. Mary begged her husband to return to her side, but Philip was far too busy with his own political issues to bend to the wishes of the wife he thought very little of, and on 17 November 1558, Mary passed away with no child to deliver. She had suffered yet another phantom pregnancy, likely the result of the very same tumour that caused her death. Mary was buried in a nun's habit, unloved by much of her country and, most painfully for Mary, unloved by her husband.[54]

ELIZABETH I

AGAINST ALL ODDS, Elizabeth Tudor was crowned Queen of England and Ireland (the latter having come under English rule during the reign of Henry VIII) on 17 November 1558. At just twenty-five, she had already experienced a great many adversities on her journey to the Crown. From losing her mother to being written out of the line of succession on multiple occasions, the fact that she had made it to the throne at all was a miracle.

That day in Westminster Abbey, Elizabeth sat resplendent in a shimmering robe of cloth of gold, and eagle-eyed Tudor viewers would have noticed it was the exact same gown worn by her sister, Queen Mary, for her coronation.[55] This was not out of familial love, but rather thrift, for the royal purse strings would be tight in the new Queen's reign as a result of her family's lavish spending habits. Elizabeth was not particularly keen to establish similarities between herself and her late sister, for Mary's poor reputation had ensured that the country Elizabeth inherited was still quite seriously opposed to being ruled over by a Queen. She needed to present as many differences as possible to sever herself from the negative associations now linked with her sister and promise the nation that through her they would emerge into a better, more refined age. It was to be a complicated task, but one that the new Queen was no stranger to; her tumultuous childhood had ensured Elizabeth front-row seats to the world of court politics and made her painfully aware of the deadly consequences of being a woman in power.

First and foremost, she had seen her mother, the ambitious and intelligent Anne Boleyn, struck down in her prime by political opponents. Before this first childhood tragedy, Elizabeth had been catered for finely; she had been raised away from her mother (a common choice for wealthy families of the time), but distance had not affected Anne's desire to ensure her daughter was given the best start in life. The little red-headed Princess would be seen in gowns of velvet and satin, orange to match her hair as well as green, white or yellow. Anne Boleyn was particular about the clothes that her daughter wore and did not hesitate to send back items of clothing that did not meet her high standards.[56] After Anne's execution, Henry VIII declared his youngest daughter to be illegitimate, stripping her of her title of Princess and almost entirely forgetting about her. This sudden change for Elizabeth would have been obvious to her even at such a young age, and her wardrobe gives us insight into the conditions of her living in this period. As a quickly growing toddler, Elizabeth had outgrown the clothes purchased by her mother within a few months, but there would be no replacements.[57] Her father, Henry, was now far too concerned with the family he was to have with his new bride to care about his young daughter, and Elizabeth's governess often had to beg for clothes in order to dress her.

Elizabeth made a gradual return to court life at the welcoming invitation of her stepmother Katheryn Howard, who gifted her with jewels and attention, and held her in high regard thanks to their blood relationship through Anne

Boleyn. After only a year of this comfort, Elizabeth became a spectator to Queen Katheryn's dramatic fall from grace as her scandalous affairs were revealed to the world. It would, however, be the relationship with Queen Katherine Parr that was most influential in shaping the young Elizabeth. Katherine took the motherless young girl under her wing, fashioning her into a mirror image of herself – highly educated, staunchly Protestant and extremely stylish. Elizabeth formed a close bond with her stepmother and after the death of Henry VIII, she moved permanently into Katherine's household.

Their close relationship should have meant that this move was comforting for Elizabeth, but the clothes adopted by her in her teenage years reveal a great deal of trauma that would impact the rest of her life. Katherine Parr remarried soon after the death of the King, to a courtier called Thomas Seymour, and it was during those first few years of living under their roof that reports of Seymour's inappropriate behaviour towards Elizabeth emerged. He was unusually fond of her and began making secret visits to her bedchamber early each morning, slipping beneath the covers to kiss or tickle Elizabeth whilst she fought to retain her modesty. Her protective maids rallied around her and began to devise ways in which Elizabeth could hide from Seymour's uncomfortable intrusions, though by making her bedchamber inaccessible, his advances only became dangerously more public. One terrible autumn day, whilst Elizabeth strolled in the gardens of Hanworth, she was set upon by Seymour, who, under the guise of mere humour, used a dagger to slice her gown into ribbons of fabric.[58]

When Katherine Parr died in 1548 from childbirth complications, Seymour considered marrying Elizabeth to gain control over her brother, the young King Edward VI. His plot and his behaviour towards Elizabeth were quickly uncovered, and they were both interrogated at the Tower of London.

Thomas Seymour was executed on charges of treason and while Elizabeth may have been spared, she was left shaken by the ordeal. At just fifteen years old, she had learnt first-hand how important sexual purity was for an unmarried Tudor woman and to avoid any further scrutiny on the matter, Elizabeth adopted an extremely modest style of dress.[59] She did away with vibrant fabrics and embellished laces, putting her piety and Protestant morals at the front of her public image to dispel any rumours of misguided virtue.

How then was Elizabeth to avoid the many pitfalls that were laid before her, simply for daring to be born a woman? It seems that the only choice for her was to rise above her gender and stress that she was on a path different from all other women of her age by abandoning the life cycle of events typically expected of wealthy Tudor women. Though marriage had seemed like a legitimate possibility early in her reign, it would soon become one of those many aspects of mundane life that Elizabeth forswore; she had seen from her sister Mary's experience that the authority of a Queen could be diluted once she took a husband, and she was keen to avoid this. Her sister's purple wedding gown, which like her coronation robes, had been retained by Elizabeth possibly for use at her own hypothetical wedding, was left to gather dust and the 'Virgin Queen' would continue to flaunt fashion reserved for unmarried women well into her old age to hammer home the point of her independence.[60] Symbols of purity were strong features in Elizabeth's wardrobe. Pearls were sewn all over her dresses and her hair was frequently left free around her shoulders. As one observer put it 'her bosom was uncovered, as all the English ladies have it, till they marry' right the way up until her death.[61]

Elizabeth was ambitious about England's position on the world's stage, and it was under her patronage that more

English trade routes were established across the globe and frequent voyages across the Atlantic were undertaken to try to establish colonies in the Americas. These ventures not only allowed England to become a key player in trade industries that had thus far been dominated by the Spanish and Portuguese, but they also brought back a wide variety of dyes, fabrics and other materials that could be used to enrich the wardrobes of the wealthy. Fashion in the Elizabethan period underwent many dramatic transformations that morphed the human figure into some pretty bizarre shapes. Whalebone, with its malleable and durable qualities, which was now brought back to England in abundance, formed the basis for many new items in women's wardrobes. Chief amongst these were 'pairs of bodies', a precursor to the corset and structured with whalebone that gave the wearer a fashionable straight posture and conical torso. It also had a practical function, as it was used to hold in place the farthingale, which with the support of whalebone had grown from the understated triangular Spanish style to a drum-shaped French equivalent, over which vast quantities of expensively embroidered skirts were arranged into intricate pleats. These contraptions, which extended from the waist at a 90-degree angle and essentially created a protective barrier around the wearer, were hardly practical and required special training with a practised dance master in order to successfully manoeuvre. Even then, there were times that these skirts simply could not be tamed, and it was once recorded that Elizabeth's ladies had to eat their meal on the floor beside her, as there was no room left at the table for their gigantic farthingales.[62]

Clearly, then, the underpinnings of women's clothing had transformed to reflect the prospering of trade, but similar changes also occurred with outerwear. Sleeves were padded to give them epic proportions, and women now had a variety of very different gown styles that they could pick from, each from different regions of Europe. Outside the walls of the royal court, xenophobic moralists criticized the people of England for their extreme interest in foreign fashion, but the Queen would take little notice.[63] From Flanders Elizabeth wore puffed, gigot sleeves, and from Poland she adopted extremely long and pointed bodices that dipped far below the natural waist. The gowns were typically high-necked and trimmed with an impressive ruff, and with the introduction of the starching process in the 1560s these ruffs could become larger and more dramatic than ever before. As mentioned earlier, Elizabeth enjoyed the liberty of exposing her décolletage with swooping, low necklines for much longer than her married contemporaries did, but she would also occasionally wear gowns inspired by men's doublets, which featured high neck-lines and buttons down the front. Doublets would have played nicely into Elizabeth's developing mythos that she defied contemporary notions of gender, and it's worth noting that surviving examples of women's doublets often do not differ in construction from those worn by men. With no bust darts added to them, the garment would effectively compress the wearer's chest, giving them a masculine appearance.[64]

Menswear was, in this era, becoming slightly more man-ageable as they bid farewell to the bulky layers of earlier years. Inspired by the Spanish, doublets were tight-fitting with a low, padded waistline that resulted in a protruding (peascod) belly and short yet very voluminous hose, which were emphasized by wearing a girdle belt to cinch the waist. This focus on a slim figure with curved hips was particularly feminine to contem-porary eyes and contrasted the increasingly more masculine style of dress occasionally adopted by the Queen and the ladies of her entourage.[65] Walking through one of Elizabeth's great palaces would have been a feast for the eyes: men and women alike would glisten with golden embellishment and vibrant fabric as they sought to gain the approval of their fashion-savvy Queen.

Elizabeth presided over her court with an iron fist, upholding a high standard of dress not only for herself but for her courtiers too. In an era where imagery was an integral part of visual culture, to have a mastery of its meaning could make or break an individual. Her personal preferences were governed by these complex rules of symbolism and were carefully selected to promote her image of the powerful virgin Queen. She wore her clothes like armour, perhaps compensating for the underlying anxiety she felt being both a woman and a woman without an heir. It's worth noting too that while the image of the Virgin Queen in armour is a popular trope in her modern media depictions, not a single suit was made for the real Queen Elizabeth I.

Colour at the Tudor court had always been linked with various meanings and messages, and the late Tudor court would have been a remarkably colourful place to be. Over the century, new colours and dyes had been introduced to England that would not have been as easily accessible to previous rulers. Elizabeth was then faced by a great many choices of colour with which to utilize their meanings; perhaps green for youth or red for power? What about orange for courage? Or yellow for hope? Eventually, she settled upon a very distinctive set of colours. In July 1564, the Queen announced, in reference to black and white, that 'these are my colours', and the statement is certainly reflected in the contents of her wardrobe.[66] Black was a popular choice from a fashionable perspective as it would contrast nicely with the heavy gold embellishment favoured at the time, and would have complimented Elizabeth's fashionably pale complexion, but it also held great symbolic meaning. With black representing constancy and white representing purity, Elizabeth was enforcing an image of both capable ruler and respectable woman.

One of the earliest examples of the Queen selecting her own iconography actually comes from her time as Princess, when she gifted a French psalter to a friend containing a drawing of an armillary sphere.[67] Armillary spheres (celestial globes made of interlocking rings) appear frequently in the jewellery and embroidery found in Elizabeth's gowns and would have represented her position as God's voice on earth, a remnant of Katherine Parr's religious education and a reminder of the monarch's role as God's chosen leader. The armillary sphere was then taken up by members of Elizabeth's court, along with her black-and-white motif, incorporating it into their dress as a way of expressing their loyalty – a sort of unofficial uniform for the court of Elizabeth I. Devotion to the monarch could also be exhibited through presenting costly jewellery pieces, particularly at New Year celebrations, that would often contain symbolic messages of their own. Elizabeth valued wit very highly, and as such the gifts presented to her contained extremely complex references. Thankfully for us, the Tudors created many guides to symbolism, such as Cesare Ripa's *Iconologia*, that allow us to translate the meanings behind the icons in Elizabeth's wardrobe.

One of the most richly symbolic ensembles worn by Elizabeth I appears in a painting known as the 'Rainbow Portrait', created towards the very end of her life. Here, the still virginal Queen stands with one hand holding a rainbow, her hair curling around her neck and her gown laced with pearls. Her bright-orange mantle is embroidered with hyper-realistic eyes and ears, a sign that as monarch she has total control of her realm with the ability to see and hear all that takes place within it. A richly jewelled snake, representative of wisdom, weaves its way up the sleeve of her gown, clasping in its mouth a glistening heart – together the two symbols represent the Queen's ability to reign with both strength and compassion, and the armillary sphere on its head reminds us that she will always rule with God in mind. These symbols are typical of Elizabeth and helped to shape her into the mystical deity she needed to present herself as. Icons of wisdom, governance and strength were used to remind her public of the many military victories she had overseen throughout her reign and helped to dispel the contemporary feeling that a woman was not capable of wielding such power.

The Rainbow Portrait was made in the final years of the Queen's life, when she was in her late sixties, but the woman who gazes out of the frame looks barely a day over thirty. There are no wrinkles, no imperfections, not even a single grey hair running through her fiery locks. In Tudor society, a woman's youth and beauty were her most important features, as they were directly linked to her societal duty of bearing children for her husband. As Elizabeth grew older and her already meagre looks were weathered away by smallpox scars and exhaustion, she would feel increasing pressure to yet again rise above the expectations placed upon her gender by defying time itself. As part of her intense control over her image, Elizabeth approved of very few portraits that were painted of her, and those that caused her 'great offence' were burned before they could be seen by the public.[68] Those portraits from early in her reign that she approved of were then used as templates for artists throughout the rest of her life, resulting in the image of an eternally young Queen. These portraits often focus very little on Elizabeth's face, and she instead becomes a companion to her clothing. She is not a woman, but rather just another aspect of the symbolism of the monarchy.

In these paintings, the immortal Queen's skin is pale, though the veins she would have had painted onto her face and neck to flaunt her skin's transparency have faded from the canvas over time. Her dark eyes are left unframed, as she has plucked away her eyebrows to extend her forehead. Women for many generations now had found that high, graceful foreheads were the pinnacle of beauty and would often pluck their hairlines back or remove their eyebrows and eyelashes to draw attention to it. Hair was piled up on top of the head, usually uncovered or draped with a sheer veil to again extend the forehead. Elizabeth's position as Queen meant she was the model for beauty standards at the time, and many women used harsh dye to copy their Queen's vibrant red hair. Eventually, Elizabeth herself would struggle to meet those very beauty standards that she herself had set; as a result of the toxic lead-based foundation she had used to lighten her complexion, she was rapidly losing hair, and she turned to wearing elaborate wigs to disguise her balding.[69] The toxic foundation left her face leathery in texture and to combat this Elizabeth would glaze her face with a concoction of egg whites.[70]

Elizabeth, like so many of her Tudor relatives, had only come to the throne by a miracle, and though she was the last Tudor monarch, she had, through carefully orchestrating her image and wardrobe, transformed the monarchy into something powerful. They were untouchable, mythical beings that rose above age and gender – more gods than mere mortals. She had succeeded in masking the inner turmoil of the monarchy and ensured that whoever came after her would inherit a powerful legacy. This shrouding of personality has made the royals of years past seem inaccessible to us, but at the same time they intrigue us and no amount of symbolism can deter our urge to uncover who Elizabeth truly was.

One of the questions that is repeated time and time again is what did Elizabeth think of her mother, Anne Boleyn? The two women shared a great deal in common, but being so young when her mother was executed, it's questionable whether Elizabeth would have any concrete memory of her. There are few records of the Queen speaking of Anne, but it's possible she may have carried a part of her mother with her throughout her reign. On one of her famously graceful fingers, Elizabeth wore a remarkable little ring made of mother of pearl and rubies, which carried a mystery still unsolved today. The bezel of this ring, which has come to be known as the Chequers Ring, is decorated with Elizabeth's initials and opens up to reveal the miniature portraits of two women. One woman is easily identifiable as Elizabeth herself, but the other woman has sparked some debate: her French hood informs us that she was likely from a time before Elizabeth's reign, and many have suggested that this could be either Anne Boleyn or Katherine Parr. Whichever woman you choose to see in the painting, it's undeniable that the powerful Queen Elizabeth I was shaped by the mother figures in her life. Both were strong-willed, intelligent and strategic, and it's not hard to imagine Elizabeth opening that little locket to catch a glimpse of the woman within for comfort and guidance.

On 24 March 1603, the Tudor dynasty would finally come to an end. In the months that preceded, the elderly Elizabeth had slipped into a depression triggered by the deaths of many close friends, and in the early hours of that morning she too would pass away. The cause of her death is contested, but it has been suggested that the inch-thick base of lead make-up she wore each day was a contributing factor. Or perhaps, as has often been theorized, it was her coronation ring that was to blame, as it had not been removed for over forty-five years and had literally grown into her skin. As her body lay in Richmond Palace, Elizabeth's cousin, Robert Carey, slipped the Chequers Ring from her finger and set out on a journey to announce her death to the new King. He rode north, travelling beyond the border into Scotland, to the home of England's long-time conflicting neighbours – the Scottish royal family. Here, Robert presented the tiny ring to King James of Scotland, and as the gem passed from subject to King, so too did the fate of the Crown. A new age was about to begin.

Part Two

THE STUARTS

WHEN ELIZABETH I DIED without an heir, the line of succession had to be traced back through the Tudor family tree until it reached the sister of Henry VIII, Margaret Tudor, and her descendants. The Crown now landed on the head of James Stuart, Margaret's great-grandson and the current King of Scotland – a controversial choice seeing as Scotland and England had a long-lasting animosity.

Remarkably, the typical xenophobic tendencies of the English were subdued at the prospect of a new Scottish King, largely due to the fact that for the first time in forty-four years there would once again be a royal family. The English court had grown accustomed to revolving around one singular monarch, who had vowed to never marry and consequently never have children. In Elizabeth's final, reclusive years, the court had likely been a very boring place for the young nobles who had congregated there in search of excitement and romance. James, however, came to England with a ready-made, perfectly prepared, cookie-cutter royal family. He had a beautiful and lively foreign bride, as well as three healthy children – an heir, a spare, and a pretty young princess to marry off to some far-away noble. This handsome young family brought with them the promise of excitement but also stability for the future of the country. James had become King of Scotland at only a few months old, and coming to the English throne at the age of thirty-six meant that he already had a wealth of experience under his belt. He had been very successful in maintaining peace and dispelling feuds in his native country, and this combined with the foundation established by Elizabeth I meant that the reign of the Stuart dynasty should have been an uneventful one.

It most certainly was not.

JAMES I

THERE WAS NO GREAT transformation in fashion at the start of the seventeenth century, but the unique personal tastes of King James and his family make them a fascinating cast of characters who were, for better or worse, not afraid to go against the grain of what was considered fashionable, or even acceptable. James was an intelligent man, scholarly in interests, and would likely in another life have been a man of academia rather than King. He once penned a manual for his son to teach him how to rule, and frequently reflected on the topic of kingship in his prose, revealing his very strong opinion that it should be the monarch who has the utmost authority over his country. This blunt, intellectual approach to the right to rule perhaps explains the underwhelming state of his clothes, as James cared very little for the intricacies of visual propaganda that had entirely dictated the wardrobe of his predecessor. It seems as though James felt that the frills and laces of fashion were redundant tools in comparison to his lengthy theories, and that his written word was sufficient to justify his authority.

The new King had a particular way of living that he refused to change, preferring to eat the same meals and dress in the same clothes each day until they were totally worn out from use.[1] The elongated doublet and lengthy hose that made up the male wardrobe was cut into an unfashionably baggy style at the King's request, making an otherwise slender man seem strangely corpulent. Overall, he was a rather uninspiring figure, who would have easily gone undetected in his own court had it not been for the sizable gems that adorned his figure. Along with the Chequers Ring, James had inherited the many pieces of jewellery owned by Elizabeth I, a collection that was as vast as it was valuable. Where Elizabeth and her Tudor relatives had worn these jewels typically as pendants or brooches, James began wearing them as hat pins, making even the plainest of caps seem as star-studded as any crown. In 1604, not long after his accession to the English throne, James had a very special piece of jewellery created to hold pride of place within the royal collection. Jewellery pieces belonging to both Elizabeth I and James's mother Mary, Queen of Scots, were deconstructed and reset into the Mirror of Great Britain, a very large and dramatic brooch of diamonds.[2] Just like the Tudors, the Stuarts were keen on upcycling clothes to make them fashionable again rather than discarding them for entirely new pieces, and jewellery was no exception to this. Over the following centuries, the royal family would deconstruct and reconstruct their jewellery in order to fit changing trends, switching their diamonds from settings of gold to silver and finally platinum, from brooches to necklaces and tiaras, until the pieces are virtually unrecognizable. The Mirror is a clear example, and as a combination of both English and Scottish royal jewels, it also functioned as a metaphor for James's monumental achievement in uniting both those Kingdoms under one monarch.

It was said that the King chose to pad his doublets to protect himself from assassination attempts, further distorting his appearance. It wasn't uncommon for men to do this, but the nature of the King's padding in particular received special criticism, indicating that James could very well have been motivated by paranoia rather than fashion. His frumpy clothes may have protected him from daggers and blades but they did give him a soft underbelly that his political enemies could strike at. The court of King James was described by moralist critics as 'a nursery of lust', and that its sins manifested themselves in the lavish clothes worn by the courtiers.[3] Elizabeth I had kept her court under strict guidance, and her elaborate wardrobe had helped to enshrine her in a veil of magic. She utilized clothing in her pursuit to become an untouchable goddess in the eyes of her people, which had provided her with a level of protection from moralist criticism. At the end of the Tudor reign. the court circle was criticized, but the monarch in particular, in all her benevolent glory, was exempt from these onslaughts. In the reign of James I, however, the monarch was seen as the *instigator* of court debauchery and entirely deserving of moralist attacks. In dressing no differently from the common folk surrounding him, James had knocked himself down from the pedestal of monarchy – he was just a man. A man with faults, and the critics began to pick at these with vigour.

James was certainly an easy target for mockery. He was an odd-looking man of average height, with uncoordinated limbs and a head that seemed almost too big for his body. He had a nasty habit of openly fiddling with the crotch of his breeches in public and unfortunately the most striking thing about him was his smell. James was known to severely neglect his personal hygiene, opting to simply wash the tips of his fingers with a napkin after eating rather than bathing in full. Elizabeth I had enjoyed a very luxurious bathing ritual in a bathroom that was fittingly regal. In the now destroyed Palace of Whitehall, Elizabeth's opulent bathroom was covered with beautiful green tiles. The bath was filled by an elaborate fountain of carved oysters, and there was a small music room off to the side so that the Queen could be serenaded whilst she bathed.[4] James inherited this bathroom, but evidently it went unused.

A principal criticism of James and his court was the King's overwhelming fondness for the young noblemen that surrounded him. While James cared very little for the clothes on his own body, he was entertained to no end by the handsomely dressed men that filled his palaces. He was quick to compliment a finely cut cape or an elegant lace ruff, and soon power-hungry families were dressing their sons and brothers in the most expensive clothes to parade under the King's nose. In 1604, James had repealed the sumptuary laws established by monarchs before him, giving these young men the opportunity to wear the most extravagant clothes in their fight for his attention.[5] What exactly were they fighting for? The royal court, which comprised the royal family, nobles and their attendants, was the prime opportunity for social climbing. For centuries now, loyalty and obedience from courtiers had been rewarded by the monarch, and whether this came in the form of clothing, promotions or a new title, being close to the King certainly paid off. There was no better position to hold at court than the 'royal favourite', an unofficial title for the individual who captured the monarch's favour on a personal level. This closeness to the Crown gave the favourite more influence than perhaps anyone else at court, making it the most desirable position.

Let's not forget that James had a wife. In the beginning, the marriage between James and Anne of Denmark had been a happy and passionate one, but they began to drift apart after disagreements on how their children should be raised and Anne's sudden conversion to Catholicism. By the time of their arrival in England their relationship was frosty, and the King often found himself out on hunts to avoid his wife and her ladies. It was on one of these hunts in 1614 that King James first met George Villiers, the second son of some lesser noble, and immediately became quite desperately attracted to him. A new wardrobe was prepared for George, and he was given the position of cup-bearer to the King, allowing him free access to converse and bond with James. The King's fondness for the twenty-one-year-old grew and eventually George was appointed Gentleman of the Bedchamber, where each morning he would dress the King and provide him with companionship throughout the day. George was lifted up the social ladder by the man who sat at the very top, and in the space of just ten years James had given his companion so many gifts of land and titles that he was now the most influential man in the country (outside of the royal family, of course). George had gone from the son of some little-known nobleman to the Duke of Buckingham, all because he had captured the fancy of the King, and while the exact nature of their relationship is unknown, they did refer to each other privately as husband and wife.

George's newfound wealth and power meant that he had many enemies, but one thing they could not deny was that George Villiers was perhaps the most attractive and handsomely dressed man they had ever met. He was said to have the face of an angel, and simply looking at his clothes was a biblical experience; on a diplomatic mission to France in 1625, a Parisian wrote of George: 'It must be confessed that the Duke of Buckingham had the finest outfit one could see in a lifetime. I am moved to describe it.'⁶ He goes on to detail the lace ruff, diamond jewellery and six strands of pearls wrapped around George's torso with such reverence you would think he is describing a King. George gives us insight into just how

King James might have chosen to dress himself had he appreciated the power of clothes just a little bit more, and just how deeply the people of the seventeenth century could be moved by fashion.

So what about the Queen? We've established that Anne and her husband did not particularly get along, and this is largely because James had refused to allow Anne to be a hands-on parent to their children Henry, Charles and Elizabeth. The royal couple also had quite polarized interests; while James preferred hunting and scholarly pursuits, Anne moved in more cultured circles. She took an interest in art, architecture, music and performance and made sure that her court was filled with vibrant entertainment and equally vibrant people. It comes as no surprise, then, that there was an air of theatricality in her wardrobe. Upon her arrival in England, Anne had received the clothes once worn by Elizabeth I and she had them altered for use in her own wardrobe and for costumes at court masques.[7] Masques were the primary form of entertainment in the Stuart court, events filled with acting, music, dance and elaborate sets. Anne typically commissioned the playwright Ben Jonson and the designer Inigo Jones to organize her masques, and they worked together to create performances that Her Majesty and her ladies could take part in. Typically, a masque would be themed around ancient legends or mythology and framed in a way that made the participating royals seem like the heroes of the story, upholding peace and virtue on the stage just as they were expected to do in real life. Despite the positive intentions, these masques could often be controversial. The 'Masque of Blackness' saw the Queen and her ladies play daughters of an African god in full blackface, which even then was shocking to audiences, and the 'Masque of Beauty' saw 3 per cent of the court's yearly budget spent on just one night of performance.[8] The Queen's frivolity was yet another aspect for critics to attack.

Some of the designs for Inigo Jones's costumes still survive today – vibrantly coloured and whimsically constructed, and they are also extremely revealing. With our twenty-first-century standards, we might imagine it scandalous to see a Queen or her ladies-in-waiting dancing publicly in a state of undress, but this may very well have been at the request of Anne herself. The Queen was vocally proud of her full and pale bosom and frequently wore dresses with outrageously low necklines. In 1617, a Venetian ambassador noted with amazement that one of her dresses exposed her breasts 'bare down to the pit of her stomach'.[9] Anne's preference for revealing outfits was followed by the other ladies of her court, who used red cochineal dye to redden their nipples and painted veins onto their chest to make their skin seem paler. Other radically revealing changes to women's dress (which definitely wouldn't seem as radical to us!) included the folding back of the sleeves to reveal the wrist and the shortening of skirts to show off fashionable shoes decorated with ribbons or oversized rosettes. Unlike the cleavage, these were parts of the female body which it had never been fashionable to show off. For the Jacobean court, ankles and wrists were like newly revealed forbidden fruit.

These novel styles were eclipsed, however, by one of Anne's more dated preferences – the farthingale. Outside of the court, it had become popular for women to go without the barrel-shaped hoops left over from the reign of Elizabeth I, but Anne refused to let them go. Her contemporaries were astounded by the sheer size of her farthingales, and she struck a truly impressive figure, with one ambassador reporting that there was no exaggeration necessary when he said her skirts reached a circumference of 4 feet wide![10] Farthingales were now tilted upwards at the back, all part of the early Stuart interest in elongating the female figure. This was complemented by vertically standing ruffs and tall, gravity-defying hairstyles made by arranging the hair over stuffed fabric pouches. Anne and her ladies would have made quite a scene walking through the Palace hallways, resting their hands on the shelf of their farthingales to stop them from swinging wildly. A remnant of Elizabeth I's power-dressing agenda, the farthingale forced the wearer to take up space, demand attention, and created almost a halo of distance between the female body and those around her. Anne's reluctance to move on from the garment signalled a continuity of female superiority, causing significant friction in what was now a King-led court. At the 1613 wedding of Princess Elizabeth, so many women arrived dressed in farthingales that male attendees began to complain that there was no room left for them to stand.[11] This debacle prompted the father of the bride, King James, to demand that farthingales be banned from court functions from then on, but his requests were ignored and Queen Anne continued to wear them until her death in 1619.

There were many other instances when James attempted to intervene on popular fashion. Scandal was rife in his court, and he would not have wanted to give any ammunition to his critics. In 1620, James instructed clergymen to preach against 'the insolence of our women' and their preference for wearing masculine clothes.[12] Women had now turned to large-brimmed hats, relaxed-fitting doublets and the shoulder-length hair typically worn by their male counterparts, which had aroused many moralist complaints. The preaching was unsuccessful and this style would go on to become the foundation for women's fashion in the following years. In 1615, James had tried to ban another fashion he deemed offensive: the increasingly popular yellow ruff. It was a matter of urgency, as his court had become the scene of a crime when a young woman, Lady Frances Howard, had poisoned one of the King's favourite courtiers, Sir Thomas Overbury. Frances was incensed at Overbury, who had been working to prevent her from orchestrating a marriage for herself, and had employed the assistance of a woman called Anne Turner to help sneak poison into the meals of her victim, eventually killing him. Anne Turner was well known at court, an independent businesswoman who ran several houses of ill-repute in London, where illicit affairs could be carried out between secretive couples. She also had monopoly over the saffron-based starch industry, which she used to create bright-yellow ruffs. Both the nature of the murder and the fame of the individuals involved made it a popular story for the public to follow and soon, inspired by the trade of Anne Turner, the yellow starched ruff became the latest craze in Jacobean London. The trend persisted even after Anne Turner's execution and King James, who perhaps viewed the ruffs as a reminder of his court's biggest scandal, wanted them and their negative associations dead and buried.[13] Despite his best efforts, these attempts at regulation were ultimately unsuccessful and the Turner murder case was one of the biggest blows to the monarchy during his reign. Anne Turner's yellow ruffs were seized upon by critics and for nearly fifty years they were used as an example of King James's inability to control the morals of his court circle.

James's one saving grace was his eldest son, Prince Henry. He had from a young age been at the receiving end of his father's philosophizing on the nature of kingship and took on board many of the points that James himself struggled to abide by. Henry's personal interests rendered him an athletic boy, excelling at riding, tennis and particularly golf, which had been brought to England by King James and his Scottish court. He leant more towards culture than academia and was a keen participant in masques, particularly in those themed around military history or legendary heroes. James wrote a poignant letter to his son upon his ascension to the English throne, explaining to him the fine balance that must be achieved by a king – how he must always present himself with grandeur but not let this hinder his dignity. In the same letter, James instils in his son the need to be humble about his place in the world and that his new position as heir apparent should not 'make [him] proud or insolent, for a King's son and heir was [he] before, and no more [is he] now'.[14] Henry clearly took this guidance to heart, as the young Prince's wardrobe would be markedly less showy than his mother's but far more refined than his father's.

In his teenage years, Henry and his circle of friends stood out from the court of his father, both for their cultured, grounded behaviour and their distinct sense of style. Henry had adopted for himself the clean-cut, more practical fashions of Spain and Italy for which he was praised, in contrast to the frilly French-inspired garments worn by the rest of the court circle. There was a very clear divide in taste between father and son, for James had come to take a diplomatic stance against foreign clothes. On one occasion, the King was presented with a hat made of Spanish block, which he 'cast from him, swearing he neither loved them nor their fashions'.[15] The chasm that had formed between King and heir would likely have distressed the courtiers, as they would have to make a conscious decision about whom they should display allegiance for. Should they continue to dress in their typical style to show favour for the King? Or would it be more strategic to switch to Prince Henry's polished preferences to secure their future at court? Thankfully for these ambitious lords and ladies, the conflict came to an end when, on 17 March 1625, the King passed away and his son took to the throne.

The only thing is it wasn't Henry who became the second Stuart King of England. It was his younger brother, Prince Charles.

CHARLES I

Short, even for his age, Charles had always lived in the shadow of his confident older brother. When Charles was nine, Henry stole the cap of a nearby bishop and placed it on his little brother's head. This, Henry decided, was Charles's destiny in life and he declared that when he was King, he would make Charles Archbishop of Canterbury so that the long robes that came with the role would forever conceal his frail little legs. Charles was justifiably upset and tore the cap from his head, stamping it into the ground and insisting he would do no such thing.[16] Henry's words, though unkind, do reveal to us how Charles looked as a boy. When his family moved to London from Scotland in 1603, the three-year-old Charles had stayed behind on account of his weakened physical state. He had a stammer that took great effort to mask and a hereditary case of rickets left his legs weakened and incapable of supporting his body. A special set of boots reinforced with metal were created for the young Charles to help strengthen his bones and these clearly worked wonders, as he would soon grow into a fine horse rider and tournament competitor. Fortunately, he would never have to become Archbishop – in 1612, Prince Henry succumbed to a terrible case of typhoid fever, leaving little Prince Charles as heir to the throne.

Upon the death of his father in 1625, Charles's first action as King was to find himself a Queen. He settled upon Henrietta Maria, the fifteen-year-old sister of the King of France, and wasted no time in sending George Villiers (still a prominent figure in the royal court) to escort his new bride to England. When she first arrived at court, Henrietta Maria wore the wide farthingales and stiff ruffs that had filled the court of King James I, but being both short and slender the little Queen was overpowered by these dresses. Eventually growing fed up with these unflattering gowns, she set about devising a new dress style that would, within a year, become the standard for fashion at court. With a separate bodice and skirt, this new style had a high waistline, typically emphasized by a contrasting ribbon belt, and was made of plain, watery satins. Sleeves were wide, softly billowing out and finishing just below the elbow in a flounce of spiked lace. And with farthingales now a thing of the past, the skirts (which were often so long that they would need to be carried in the wearer's arms as they walked) were supported by layers of richly decorated petticoats instead. Henrietta Maria preferred her dresses in soft, earthy tones with ropes of pearls to make up for the lack of embellishment. The necklines were low, almost falling off the shoulder, but courtly modesty was protected with a delicate lace collar draped across the shoulders.

Henrietta Maria's new wardrobe raised quite a few eyebrows, including those of her new husband. In 1625, King Charles was forced to dismiss his wife's French attendants on account of their wild spending habits; the ladies who had accompanied the new Queen from her homeland had racked up substantial bills with local tailors and tradespeople, which now needed to be settled out of English pocket.[17] The Queen also began wearing her hair cropped fashionably short, arranged in tight ringlets around the face with the rest of the hair pulled into a bun at the back of the head. This, along with the overall relaxation of clothing, inspired more grumbling from puritanical moralists. It seems, however, that the Queen couldn't care less; the new styles made her seem taller and more regal, and, most importantly, they made her comfortable. Both King and Queen were visibly awkward in more formal, ceremonial clothing and the styles that they personally chose suited them and their personalities much better.

Charles, as one of the most passionate patrons of art in royal history, had his wardrobe well documented in portraits. Not unlike his wife, the King adopted a visibly simpler tone for his clothing. His long, pointed doublet and breeches were of plain fabrics and paired with soft leather boots and gauntlet gloves. A wide-brimmed hat was worn slanted on the head, balancing out hair that was cut shorter on one side than it was on the other. This was a popular hairstyle for both men and women, known as a lovelock, but despite being a prominent feature of fashion in this period, the exact origins of the style are difficult to trace. Puritans, who saw the lock as a tool that the devil may use to drag the wearer to the depths of hell, credited the style to the Native Americans of Virginia. Other evidence, however, suggests it was a nod to tales of chivalric knights from the Middle Ages, seeing as the lovelock always fell on the left side of the body, over the heart. Though lovelocks could often be plaited, Charles allowed his to fall loosely over his shoulder and embellished it with a ribbon or large pearl pendant.

The resulting style that emerged for both men and women was one of intentional disarray, a calculated messiness and informality that needed to be carefully monitored in order to prevent the wearer from seeming legitimately slovenly. Charles and Henrietta Maria, who had a shared desire for order and structure in society, took up the task of regulating their court. This was no small feat, as the court now boasted no fewer than 2,000 members within its ranks. The couple chose to divide and conquer, sectioning their palaces based on social hierarchy, with certain rooms only permissible to those with the most prestigious titles. Those who did make it into the presence of the royal family were expected to follow strict clothing rules. For example, though they were a popular fixture in men's fashionable dress, boots and spurs were not to make an appearance in the royal presence at any formal occasion.[18] Courtiers were expected to dress as befitted someone of their rank, which in the absence of sumptuary legislation was a lot harder to ascertain, making it not uncommon for courtiers to find themselves up to their ears in fashion-related debts.

Don't let appearances fool you – though the clothes of the King were visibly plainer than those of his predecessors, they were still extraordinarily expensive. Between March and September 1627, Charles spent an astronomical £9,884 on fashion alone, significantly overstepping his yearly clothing budget. The sheer extravagance of Charles's spending can only be truly gauged by comparing it to the expenditure of the average working man, who could entirely dress himself for under a pound – less than what members of the royal court would spend on a single hat.[19] Finances were a tricky problem for Charles during his reign: his multiple expensive military campaigns saw him unfairly raising taxes, incurring the wrath of the people and Parliament, which he refused to cooperate with. Conflicts began to emerge in Ireland and Scotland as Charles's public lost faith in him, and Parliament too became unconvinced of his capability to rule. In 1642 this chaos came to a head when Charles, threatened by his lack of control, declared war against his Parliament, triggering the official start of the English Civil War.

Henrietta Maria played an active role in the war effort. Throughout the 1640s, the mounting tensions displaced the Queen's interest in fashion, and with the country's leading source of style inspiration now otherwise occupied, women's fashion stagnated. Waistlines dropped to a more natural level, and the ridiculously long skirts returned to floor length. What the Queen was now concerned with was money. Without the assistance of Parliament, Charles needed to fund his Royalist army in whatever way he could, and so a careful plan was set in motion. One that hinged entirely on the tact of the Queen.

On 23 February 1642, Henrietta Maria set sail for the Netherlands with her daughter Mary, under the guise of escorting the Princess to meet her new husband there. In truth, she was smuggling some of Britain's crown jewels to sell on the famed Dutch diamond market, hoping to raise funds for her husband's struggling army. What the Queen hadn't expected, however, was the Dutch sympathy for the Parliamentarian cause and their awareness of the fact that the jewels technically weren't hers to sell. The Dutch, like the disgruntled British Parliament, thought that the crown jewels were not the personal property of the monarch, but rather belonged to the state. They demanded that Henrietta Maria provide written proof of ownership, and as a result she only managed to pawn pieces from her personal collection, fetching a fraction of the sum that the crown jewels had been valued at.[20] The money raised was used to provide ships, troops and ammunition for the King's army, but the Royalist efforts would eventually be fruitless. Charles retreated from London to Windsor, letting the capital fall to the Parliamentarian soldiers.

On 20 January 1649, King Charles became the first English king to stand trial. It was an unprecedented occasion, resulting from both his defeat on the battlefield and a continued undermining of the mysticism of the monarchy over the previous few years. In 1643, after taking control of London, the Parliamentarians had made it a point to force their way into the Treasury at Westminster Abbey to take inventory of the royal regalia contained within. The regalia were the robes, crowns, orb and sceptres that had been used by the monarchy at their coronations since the rule of Edward the Confessor exactly 600 years previously, and they were the most important items in representing the power that the King of England was meant to have. Henry Marten, the Member of Parliament sent to oversee the task, looked down at these powerful symbols and declared 'there would be no further use for these Toys and Trifles', and promptly turned to dress one of his companions in the coronation robes and crown.[21] As the Parliamentarians laughed and pranced around the Treasury in the royal robes, they were effectively destroying all mysticism attached to these once sacred items. The very concept of the monarchy itself was beginning to be dismantled.

When Charles arrived for his trial, he fixed the gathered court with a steely gaze. A few men in the crowd bristled as the King took his seat and made no move to take off his large black hat, a sign of clear disrespect towards those that had dared to challenge the crown. His clothes were severe – swathes of dark silk only punctuated by the glorious star of the Order of the Garter that was embroidered on his cloak, its diamond encrusted surface reflecting the dim light of the room brilliantly. The King was aged in appearance, now forty-eight years old, with wild hair and a thick, unkempt beard from months of being held in captivity. He stood accused of tyranny and treason against his people and after four appearances before the judges he was found guilty and sentenced to death. There was to be no new King – the monarchy was abolished.

Charles was rushed quickly to his room at Whitehall Palace to await his execution. Once inside, he slipped an emerald and diamond ring from his finger and had it sent to his laundress, who in turn sent back a little wooden box. When Charles opened the chest, all he found inside were fragments of diamonds and precious stones, mainly pieces that had once been sewn into his clothes. 'You see all the wealth now in my power,' he said to his Gentleman of the Bedchamber, for with all his most valuable pieces having been sold abroad to fund the war effort, this was all he had left to give to loved ones as gifts of remembrance.[22] On the morning of 30 January, Charles dressed with special care. He placed a white silk cap on his head, slipped on a pair of leather gloves, fixed the badge of the Order of Saint George on his person and slung a cape over his shoulders.

The King was then marched through the Banqueting Hall and brought outside to the scaffold in front of the Palace, where a gathering crowd of his subjects stood fighting the cold. Despite the temperature (it was so cold that the river Thames had frozen over), Charles did not shiver. He had carefully chosen to wear two shirts under his doublet, one of linen and another of blue silk, so that he wouldn't catch a chill on the scaffold and have it mistaken for fear. With one swing of the axe, the King was dead.

In the wake of Charles's death, the royal family scattered. His children, including his eldest son and should-have-been heir Charles, fled to mainland Europe, seeking shelter in the courts of their relatives. Parliament moved quickly to liquidize the assets of the Crown for use in governing the country and bolstering its armed forces. They had their work cut out for them, as the emphasis that royals of the past had placed on their everyday and ceremonial clothing meant that there was a wealth of material for Parliament to exploit. In the year of Charles I's death, the decision was made to sell the clothes belonging to the late King, his Queen and his eldest son in order to pay off debts and fund the government. The contents of the royal wardrobes at the Tower of London, Somerset House, Hampton Court and Windsor were inventoried and sold off, with clothes belonging to many of the previous Stuart and Tudor royals being among the pieces lost to buyers both local and abroad. In the most important act of all, the crown jewels were broken up, the valuable stones sold and the gold melted down into coins. With the position of King now abolished, Parliament could see no further use for these symbolic pieces and likely felt their cause would benefit from further symbolic destruction of the power of the monarchy.

Unfortunately, the plan didn't quite work out how it was meant to. Those few personal pieces of the King's wardrobe that had been auctioned off now resided in the homes of those sympathetic to the royalist cause, who harboured a tiny flame that kept the spirit of the monarchy alive. These pieces of royal history were treasured like holy relics by the families who owned them, with some even claiming that items once belonging to the martyred King carried mystical healing powers. Though the Parliamentarians thought they had destroyed the most important aspects of the monarchy, the King lived on in the minds of the people and was preserved in the stitches of his clothes.

CHARLES II

ON 29 MAY 1660, the eldest son of Charles I arrived in London to a rapturous celebration. After eleven years as a republic, the decision had been made to restore the English monarchy and the new King, thirty-year-old Charles II, and his Stuart relatives were invited back to reign after many years of exile.

Charles had spent the period after his father's death in the courts of his relatives in France and Holland, watching from afar as the country he had thought he would one day rule was reinvented and reorganized. The period between the reigns of the two King Charleses, known as the Interregnum, saw Parliament try with great difficulty to form an effective method of governing that did not centre around a monarch. It appeared, however, that the gap left by the absent monarchy was too vast and too historic to fill with ease, and the role of Lord Protector was created to function in its place – a role that had more similarities than differences to its royal predecessor than it first seemed. The court of the Lord Protector was established at former royal palaces, where Oliver Cromwell, the Parliamentarian general selected to fill the role, was referred to by various titles linked to royalty, and despite the position not being a hereditary one, his daughters were often addressed as princesses. Royal tradition was far too ingrained in society for it to be shaken off so quickly, even by those who had fought to have it abolished.

Parliament was at this point overwhelmingly Puritan, and as such their personal views permeated their government of the country. The contemporary puritanical belief that outward displays of vanity were inherently sinful saw England become a lesser player in the grand scheme of European fashion; only conservative, demure styles were encouraged in society. This enforced moral regulation bled into the rest of everyday life, with various popular practices and forms of entertainment being abolished, such as Christmas celebrations and horse racing. After Cromwell's death in 1658, the new regime became increasingly fragile, culminating in near-unanimous cries for the Stuart dynasty to be reinstated. Charles's arrival in London not only signalled the restoration of the monarchy but the return of life and culture as it had once been.

That is not to say that Charles was prepared to make all the same mistakes as his father. His team of advisors carefully considered how he should present himself upon his arrival, and the initial decision was to offer him to his subjects as a man of conservative tastes to avoid any unsavoury associations between the monarchy and lavish overindulgence.[23] But on the contrary, the people of England were excited for the change that the monarchy would bring and were anticipating all the spectacle associated with traditionally popular monarchs. Though Charles may not have personally been inclined to pomp and ceremony, his mother and siblings with whom he returned to England were keen to see him reintroduce the court order they had known before their exile. Experiencing pressure from both within and without the royal family, Charles and his advisors devised a new approach, one that saw Charles borrowing from the practices of the most glamorous royal court of the time, that of his cousin Louis XIV of France.

King Louis, also known as the Sun King, set the standard for royal splendour in the seventeenth century. With his keen eye, Louis had tightened his grip over an unruly court by establishing an absurdly high standard of dress that was dictated by complex and specific rules for each occasion.[24] Charles was inspired by his stylish cousin and decided that his retinue for his return to England should contain a Parisian tailor, Claude Sourceau, so that his new royal wardrobe would reflect some of the glamour of the French court. But though Charles was inspired by the *styles* of France, he understood that the specific rules of dress established by Louis would have no place in the English court. Having to source appropriately luxurious outfits for each unique occasion in the court calendar had bankrupted many of the French nobility, and with his position as King hinged entirely on his acceptance by royalist sympathizers, Charles could not afford to alienate his allies by taking a dictatorial stance towards fashion. Instead, Charles was far more concerned with the entertainment that court life could provide him, and in the face of wild theatrical performances and pretty court ladies, fashion would not be one of his primary concerns. Charles's personal approach to fashion was one of apathy, a trait that was to the detriment of his grandfather James I but, in the wake of Oliver Cromwell's puritanical seriousness, served Charles quite well, as he seemed to pose no threat of excessive moral regulation.

One notable tradition from the French court that was implemented by Charles was the levee, the ritual dressing of the King each morning. Members of the court were granted access to Charles's bedchamber in the mornings and evenings to discuss with him their concerns and queries on various important matters whilst he dressed. Giving courtiers regular opportunities to make their opinions known was a successful tool in rebranding the monarchy; in contrast to the court of Charles I and Henrietta Maria, with their highly exclusive court geography, the new King was presenting himself as an accessible figure.[25] The levee would come to exist in a more formal context in the reign of James II, but later monarchs would find the practice cumbersome. Though it would continue until the 1930s, the levee was pushed later into the day and transformed into a reception wherein the gentlemen of high society could be presented to the King in his throne room.

There was over a year's wait between Charles's arrival in England and his coronation, and though it was traditional to leave a gap between the accession of a monarch and their coronation, this was an unusually long period of time. The delay was necessary, however, as those in charge of organizing the coronation needed every minute they could to plan the events of the ceremony and accompanying celebrations. Charles took a hands-on approach, instructing that the proceedings should follow the exact rubric established by medieval kings of years past, and no corners should be cut when it came to providing the public with the spectacle they were anticipating. His clothes for the ceremony, which consisted of a purple velvet robe lined with powdered ermine fur and worn over a doublet and breeches of scarlet satin, mirrored those worn by the previous Stuart kings to create a sense of continuity. But there was one glaring problem: no coronation of medieval inspiration could be completed without the crown jewels, and these were now no longer in existence. The majority of the coronation planning was spent preparing replacements for the lost regalia, and for a total of £13,000 two new crowns, an orb, sceptres, ceremonial sword, spurs, rings and bracelets were created.[26] These pieces would go on to be used for the coronation of every monarch thereafter.

At the start of his reign, Charles dressed in the styles popular in France: a short doublet that cut off just above the hips, exposing a flounce of linen shirt and from which vast quantities of ribbons would spill. Petticoat-breeches were the preferred choice for trousers: they fell to the knee and were so wide that it was not unheard of for a man to put both legs into one trunk and go about his entire day before noticing his mistake. The legs were concealed by stockings and finished with slightly heeled shoes, and around the knee large flounces of coloured lace were worn. Known as 'cannons', these cartwheels of fabric could reach truly epic proportions and were distinctively French in origin. Charles would often wear a wide-brimmed hat, from under which his long, dark hair fell in thick, fashionable curls past his shoulders.

Though Charles's relaxed personality ensured his wardrobe would never reach the same levels of excess as his French counterparts, his clothes still caused some grief for the usually merry monarch. Finances were a particular issue, as with no personal family fortune from which he could fund his lifestyle, Charles was totally dependent on the yearly allowance that Parliament decided for him. Though this salary was over a million pounds, by 1667 Charles was struggling to pay the bills of the various craftsmen employed to create his wardrobe and had established unpopular new taxes in a futile attempt to pay off these debts.[27] Furthermore, the French fashions that filled the royal court were coming under fire for their rejection of regional identity. The English, the critics were saying, should be ashamed that unlike the rest of Europe they had no costume that they could proudly claim as their own. Their argument also concerned fabric, as imported textiles made up the majority of English fashionable dress, leaving the local production industries in a fragile state.[28]

Charles announced his solution to these problems to his council on 7 October 1666. He was introducing a newer, simpler style of dress for men at court that he vowed never to alter, one that was specifically designed to teach the nobility thrift.[29] This new ensemble consisted of a knee-length coat left open at the front to expose a vest, which we would today identify as a very long waistcoat. The vest, worn over a linen shirt, was long enough that it covered the breeches, causing them to reduce in size and embellishment; they were now slim and finished just below the knee. Sleek construction was prioritized over excessive surface embellishment and the King wore them almost exclusively in fabrics of English manufacture. This new style was not only effective at reducing the cost of fashionable clothing but also formed the basis of a primitive version of the three-piece suit that would dominate male dress for the foreseeable future.

Though the suit may have assisted Charles with his finances going forward, he still needed a more permanent source of income to help clear his existing debts. In 1672, after noticing just how profitable the transatlantic slave trade was becoming, Charles established the Royal African Company. For most of the century, British colonizers living in the American colonies had been purchasing enslaved Africans from Dutch privateers to provide labour for their intensive tobacco farming. The Royal African Company was Charles's answer to this foreign competition, and with his younger brother James at the helm of operations, the company was responsible for transporting more enslaved Africans to the Americas than any other organization of its kind. The profits generated by the Royal African Company would inspire future generations of royals to keep a hand in the slave trade until its abolition in the early nineteenth century in order to fund their lifestyles. As England continued its colonial expansion, it became impossible to ignore the overlap between the royal wardrobe and the violent method of its funding. We shall see in later chapters just how intrinsically the clothes of the monarchy came to represent the suffering caused by British colonialism.

In 1662, Charles had agreed to marry the Portuguese Princess Catherine of Braganza, in exchange for lucrative trading privileges in Brazil and the ownership of Portuguese-governed territories in Africa and India. Catherine was young and woefully unprepared to fill the boots of her fashionable predecessor, Henrietta Maria; she had been raised in a convent and her style was described as more befitting a widow than a young princess. Her skin was tanned, her eyes and hair 'angelic' and dark, yet none of these features seemed to win over her hedonistic new husband.[30] Catherine and her Portuguese entourage were the talk of the court for all the wrong reasons: they arrived wearing a specific type of farthingale that was typical in Portugal but monstrously oversized in comparison to the slim skirts of English ladies, prompting the King to joke that his new wife resembled a bat more than a Queen.

Though the royal marriage would gradually become more amicable, with Charles frequently praising Catherine's good character, the Queen would always have to fight for her husband's attention. It was common knowledge amongst court circles that Charles had a wandering eye, taking many mistresses throughout his reign who would often exert more influence upon court life and fashion than Catherine ever could. The most notorious of these mistresses was Barbara Villiers, who had begun her affair with Charles when he was still in exile and accompanied him upon his return to England. Tall and slender, Barbara quickly established herself as the fashionable epicentre of the royal court, a fact that did not change after Charles's marriage. Soon after the new Queen's arrival, Charles insisted on Barbara receiving the prestigious position of Lady of the Bedchamber, where she would assist Catherine to dress, an embarrassingly public promotion of a mistress which caused the Queen to faint with distress upon realizing the King's intention.[31] Despite her initial concerns, Catherine's image was only improved by Barbara's fashionable hand in her dressing, and within a few years she was following all of the most stylish trends established by Charles's mistresses.

Barbara's task of dressing the Queen began with a chemise undershirt, followed by petticoats and a heavily brocaded skirt laced with metallic threads. A slender, bonded bodice was next, finishing far below the waist in a sharp point and with a wide, oval-shaped neckline that sat off the shoulders. The sleeves of this bodice would have been short, revealing flounces of the chemise sleeves that cut off at the elbow. A single strand of pearls was placed around Catherine's neck, two on each ear, and her hair was arranged into tight ringlets and piled against the side of her face in a style known as 'hurluberlu'. The diarist and avid observer of royal fashion Samuel Pepys noted that the Queen looked 'mighty pretty' in her new style but he asserted that the true arbiter of fashion would always be the king's mistress, no matter who that happened to be at the time.[32]

By 1663 Charles's lifestyle of partying and pleasure had begun to take its toll, and he noticed that his once lustrous and dark hair was turning grey.[33] The solution was a periwig, a long and finely curled wig made to match his natural hair colour, under which the hair was cut short against the scalp.

Periwigs were available in cheaper versions made of goat and horsehair, but for wealthy men like Charles, human hair was preferred. Typically from the head, but also from some more unconventional locations . . .

No periwigs belonging to Charles survive today, but in 1775 a small group of Scottish nobles came together to create a club centred around a century-old wig that had once belonged to the merry monarch. The club, creatively titled the 'Wig Club', was an offshoot of the sex-focused drinking clubs popular in high society and above all prided itself on the ownership of a 'renowned wig worn by the sovereign composed of the privy-hairs of royal courtesans'.[34] You've read that correctly: a periwig, once owned by Charles II, made using the pubic hair of his mistresses. The club members treated the wig with reverence, devising rituals to pay their respects to both the item and the sexual prowess of its original owner, including having new members of the club kiss it and vow to add to its volume with clippings from their own bedroom escapades. The early years of the wig's existence are murky, but according to club legend, Charles II gifted it to his friend the Earl of Moray, who then passed it down through his family as a revered heirloom until one of his descendants founded the Wig Club. The later history of the wig provides little more clarity to the story: after the club was disbanded in the early nineteenth century, it continued to pass from owner to owner until it disappeared entirely – its last known location being a lawyer's office in Scotland in the 1930s.

A lack of primary evidence supporting the early years of the wig's history has led to some debate as to the reliability of the claim that it was made of the pubic hair of Barbara Villiers and her fellow royal mistresses. Though it may be that the wig truly *was* the fruit of Charles's romantic labours, it is equally plausible that the story of the wig's origin was embellished to bolster the reputation of the sex clubs of the eighteenth century, with its members seeking to fabricate a piece of royal fashion that spoke to their unique interests. Charles II, with his wealth of mistresses, of course seemed the obvious choice for a raunchy royal figurehead.

Though Charles II fathered fourteen confirmed children throughout the course of his life, none of them were with his legal wife. In 1685, after expressing his sadness at having mistreated Catherine with his wandering affections and begging for his mistresses to be well cared for in his absence, Charles passed away leaving no legitimate heir to the throne. The mantle of King was taken up instead by his brother James.

JAMES II

JAMES'S CORONATION was one of immense luxury. Having taken inspiration from the glamorous court of Louis XIV of France, no expense was spared for such a magnificent occasion. Continuing with tradition, James wore a crimson velvet robe with a matching mantle over his shoulders, both trimmed with ermine fur and gold embroidery. Crowned beside him was his wife, Mary of Modena, in a gown of purple velvet fastened down the front of her bodice by a line of diamond brooches. The scalloped edge of her skirt was pinned open to reveal a magnificent silver petticoat embroidered with golden foliage, and a matching mantle over 5 metres long was tied to her shoulders by ropes of pearls.[35] As the excited crowd gazed at their new King and Queen, the crown on top of James's head slipped and nearly fell, a haunting omen of the chaos that would fill his brief reign.[36]

At fifty-one years of age, James was the oldest monarch to come to the English throne, and so it makes sense for us to first explore his time as Duke of York. Growing up, it became abundantly clear that James was as visually different as was possible from his older brother; while Charles was dark, James was fair, with blond hair and blue eyes. Yet though James had a far more serious temperament than his predecessor, both brothers were united in their love for women, and though it was the tall, Italian Mary of Modena that was crowned beside James in 1685, she was not his first bride. During the Interregnum, when James had followed his scorned family into exile, he had met Anne Hyde, a lady-in-waiting to his sister, and the two began an illicit romance. By 1660 Anne was pregnant, and though James had previously pledged to marry her, now that his family was restored to the English throne nobody *really* expected the brother of the King to go through with his promise of marrying a commoner. James was determined to prove them wrong, however, and married Anne in a secret ceremony on 3 September 1660.

Portraits of Anne reveal a full-figured woman with mousy hair and soft, dark eyes, dressed in swathes of satin that seem almost dangerously revealing. This style of gown fastened up the front with little golden hooks, and was shapeless, often without boning to structure them, and revealed the chemise and much of the wearer's physique beneath. The style emerged earlier in the seventeenth century as night wear, but in the wake of the Restoration, when both men and women's dress was becoming increasingly more structured, the liberating *déshabillé* nightgown became a far more prominent feature in people's daytime wardrobes. Dressing in such a way was an indicator of status, as only those of the highest social standing were given permission to appear *déshabillé* in public. This was a poignant choice for Anne, for her upbringing as a commoner would affect not only her own social perception but also that of her children – establishing her elevated position in society through dress was key.

On the days that King Charles did not host his court, James and Anne Hyde took up the responsibility instead, providing an appealing alternative for those who found the court of Charles II not to their liking. In his manner of dressing, James was very matter of fact, reflecting his brother's apathy for fashion. James and Charles tended to act as a unit when it came to changes in their style, with James adopting the vest and suit at the same time as his brother, and when James adopted a periwig for himself, Charles quickly followed suit.[37]

In the late 1660s, James and Anne became drawn to the Catholic faith, privately converting before being publicly outed in 1673. The response was divided: on the one hand, a Catholic royal so close to the throne was a dangerous prospect, but on the other, James *did* have a stellar reputation with the public. After all, he had been at the forefront of the firefighting operations during the 1666 Great Fire of London, which had destroyed a significant portion of the city. As James was heir apparent, the religion of his children, Princess Mary and Princess Anne, was of paramount importance to King Charles II. While he could not dictate to James and Anne what religion they should follow, he could ensure their daughters were separated from any Catholic influence and raised strictly Anglican. For now, the threat of a Catholic royal family was slim.

Yet James would further push the public's willingness to accept his Catholicism when after the death of Anne Hyde in 1671 he chose to marry Mary of Modena, a Catholic Princess from Northern Italy, meaning that upon their accession in 1685 there would be both a Catholic King and Queen on the throne. As Queen, Mary enjoyed the benefits the role afforded her, having multiple new shoes to wear every week and a fresh pair of gloves for each day. She took part in a developing passion for adopting men's dress, which appealed to women but perplexed their husbands. 'It was an odd sight,' wrote Samuel Pepys, after observing a group of noblewomen dressed in vests, cravats and periwigs, just like him, 'and a sight that did not please me.'[38]

Disruption would permeate the reign of James II; rebellions and the distrust of his Parliament were fostered by his Catholic allegiance, only worsened by his pushes for religious tolerance and belief in the absolute power of the monarch. At first, nerves were quelled by James's two daughters, both of whom were staunchly Protestant and his only living children, but this security fizzled out when Mary of Modena gave birth in 1688 to a son who, on account of his gender, overtook his older half-sisters in the line of succession. This new baby, surrounded by unfiltered Catholic influence, was physical proof that a Catholic dynasty was emerging in England, and with such a grave threat hanging over their heads, a group of Protestant nobles made the decision to invite James's eldest daughter, Mary, and her husband, Prince William of Orange Nassau, to come to England with an army. Their intervention was well received by the British public and culminated in a quick defeat of James and his forces. The King, Queen and their new son fled to France, seeking shelter at the court of Louis XIV and watching with remorse as the Crown was offered to James's daughter Mary. James II was King no more.

WILLIAM III AND MARY II

'WHEN I LOOK BACK on what I was last year and what I now am,' wrote Queen Mary II at the turn of 1689, 'it amazes me to see how well I ended the last and how ill I begin this year.'[39] The last few months had been particularly difficult; after hearing that her father had fled to France, she lost a great deal of sleep over the inevitability of being called to return to England. It seemed obvious to many that the twenty-six-year-old Princess was the rightful successor to her father's empty throne, yet Mary was well aware that she lacked the skills necessary for the job. Her education had been pitiful, an unfortunate reality for many women of her generation, for whom the quality of their studies had declined in the wake of the Restoration. She also could not stand the thought of leaving her cosy little court in the Netherlands, where she had moved after her wedding and mastered the manners and ways of living, something she feared she would struggle to replicate in the country to which she had now grown a 'perfect stranger'.[40] The silver lining in this situation was that travelling to England would reunite her with her beloved husband, William, who had left her at the end of the previous year to assist in the 'Glorious Revolution' that had deposed James II. His arrival in England had been a welcome one, with the crowds that gathered to greet him dressing in Dutch orange to show their support.[41]

Mary arrived in London in mid-February, and was taken straight to Whitehall Palace to meet William; once in private the couple wept a great deal. They mourned the loss of the life they had led back in the Netherlands, one of reserved dignity and minimal extravagance. With the Crown now being offered to Mary, this was all about to change.

Such touching displays of marital devotion were common between William and Mary, but their marriage had not begun with such a happy tone. When a teenaged Mary had been told that she was to marry her first cousin, she reportedly wept for days; there was nothing the tall, glamorous young Princess loathed more than the thought of marrying the short, asthmatic and downright *boring* Dutch Prince. William himself was hardly pleased with the proposal, for he felt that he was marrying beneath his status. Being the daughter of a King and a commoner, Mary had only half the royal pedigree that he boasted. The experience of moving to her husband's court in Holland was as much of a shock to Mary as it was to return to England over a decade later, but her charming personality quickly won people over. She took her duties seriously and fell into a comfortable rhythm of devotion and modest court performance, spending most of her time embroidering with her ladies-in-waiting, creating complex patterns despite her poor eyesight. As a foreign Princess in the Dutch court, Mary paid careful attention to the clothes she promoted; the lavish and often risqué dresses of the English court would not have gone down well and so she made a conscious effort to limit the native influences in her wardrobe.[42]

In a royal marriage there are two roles to fill. First, there is the individual who inherits the throne through blood, and ergo exercises sovereign power in the relationship – the King or Queen Regnant. As the eldest eligible child of James II (his son by Mary of Modena having been declared unfit for the throne by Parliament on account of his Catholicism), Mary was poised to inherit the title of Queen Regnant, leaving her husband to fulfil the second role, that of consort. The consort became entitled to the style of King, Queen or Prince only through their marriage, and therefore deferred in authority to their spouse. William did not find this an appealing prospect; it seemed a slight on his masculinity to expect him to become submissive to his wife, and after all, he was a grandchild of Charles I, giving him a claim to the throne in his own right. Taking into account William's complaints and Mary's uncertainty, Parliament made the unprecedented decision to offer the throne to both of them. William and Mary were to rule their Kingdom equally, and together.

A situation as unique as this posed its own unique problems, notably with the coronation. If William and Mary were to be crowned together, they were going to need more than one set of regalia. The new set that had been made for Charles II was to be used by William, leaving Mary with the brunt of the problem. She could use the crown and sceptres that had been prepared for her stepmother's coronation back in 1685, but as these pieces had been made for a consort, they were significantly less impressive than what was typically used for a reigning monarch. This would not do for Mary – she needed to assert that she had the same claim to power as her husband – and so a brand-new set of regalia was made for her from the pieces that had been used for Mary of Modena.[43] Mary and William would have crowns of equal brilliance.

Despite initially feeling wary of the vanity that seemed to preoccupy the English court, Mary soon found her footing in this new fashion environment. The predominant style of dress that filled Mary's wardrobe was the mantua, a new type of formalwear that had risen to astronomic popularity in European society and would remain the central pillar of court dress throughout the next century. Having evolved from *déshabillé* nightgowns, the mantua was a coat-like gown pinned to the front of the bodice, usually leaving a gap open to reveal a stomacher, an inverted triangle of fabric that sat pinned to the structured undergarments beneath, often richly embroidered or decorated with jewellery. The bodice was tight-fitting with sleeves clinging to the upper arms before bursting into cartwheels of fine lace at the elbow. The skirt of the mantua opened at the front, pulled apart and pinned at the wearer's lower back to reveal a slender underskirt of matching fabric. This pinned-back skirt fell into a waterfall of neatly arranged folds trailing behind like a long, slender train. Mary, like many women of her time, paired the mantua with a frelange cap – multiple tiers of intricate bobbin lace that sat high above the wearer's head, supported by wire to maintain its upright position. The slender cut of the mantua, the popularity of striped fabrics and the epic size of the frelange caps of the time gave women the illusion of height, even if they were not naturally blessed with tallness like their Queen was. The rigidity of the ensemble instilled in its wearer a natural appearance of elegance; it truly was a perfect uniform to wear to court at a time when graceful movement was so highly prized.

Mary certainly had an eye for all that glittered. Her mantuas were made of heavy fabrics threaded with shimmering gold and silver and she would often be seen clasping a glistening fan painted with scenes from the Far East. Mary was particularly fascinated by the imports that arrived from Asia, popularizing the use of Indian calico and silks in England, purchasing intricate Persian rugs and commissioning rooms in her palaces to be decorated with textiles and furnishings of South Asian manufacture.[44] She certainly had an appreciation for high-quality craftsmanship and had a sure sense of individual taste when it came to the arts. She was also very keen on jewellery and would never be seen without handfuls of brilliant diamonds all over her body. The pins that held her mantua skirt in place were bouquets of precious gems, her stomacher was lined with impressively large brooches, and her hair was roped with strings of diamonds and pearls. Mary dazzled her court; young, charming and perceptive, she was its glistening apex of style and culture, but as the 1690s progressed, disaster was looming on the horizon.

In comparison to other members of the royal family, Mary's health had always been steady, thanks to her rigorous dedication to physical exercise. Other than a miscarriage at the start of her marriage that had left her unable to conceive, Mary had experienced no major medical issues in her thirty-two years, making her sudden contraction of smallpox in late 1694 a shock for the country. In the early hours of 28 December, Mary succumbed to her illness, plunging both England and Holland into a period of intense mourning for the Queen they had come to view as not only impressively glamorous but confident and capable at ruling in her own right. Despite her initial worries about her suitability for the throne, Mary had proved herself to be a quick learner and left behind a respected legacy and a husband deep in mourning. William, who had spent the nights leading up to his wife's death sleeping restlessly beside her on a temporary camp bed, was inconsolable – an unusual sight for a man who was so famously stoic, prompting one observer to declare: 'The marble weeps!'[45]

To make matters worse, William was infuriated to discover that the French court had refused to enter a period of mourning for his late wife. James II, who had taken refuge there, had never truly forgiven his daughter for her hand in his usurpation and instructed the French King to forgo the typical period of mourning that was carried out in honour of foreign monarchs. William would hold this grudge until James himself passed away in 1701, ordering the English court to only dress in purple half-mourning as opposed to the formal black that James's status should have afforded him.[46] This may have brought the King peace, but it incensed his sister-in-law, Princess Anne, who despite having sided with William and Mary back in 1689, harboured fond memories of her father and still wished to mourn him. Anne herself would receive satisfaction for this slight by mourning her father after the death of King William, only acknowledging her brother-in-law's passing with the occasional petty purple tassel of half-mourning on her dresses. William and Anne's rivalry was fierce, and it now needed to be swiftly remedied; the King, plain at the best of times but now practically lifeless in his depressive state, needed assistance in upholding the standard of splendour that Queen Mary had established at court. As a peace offering, William presented Anne with the jewellery collection of her late sister and Anne, pacified for the time being, stepped up to the task of overseeing court life.[47]

Though William's intervention in the deposition of James II had been a welcome one, as an individual he had never been quite as warmly received by the English as his wife had been. It became obvious very early into his reign that he far preferred his homeland and showed an obvious bias towards the Dutch nobles that he had brought with him, incensing his new subjects. It didn't help that he spent most of his time holed up in his favourite royal residence, Hampton Court Palace, far outside of the nation's capital, distancing himself from his public. Eventually, William came out of his shell, participating in public appearances and assisting his wife in rejuvenating the court culture, though by and large he relied upon Mary to handle the majority of sartorial splendour in the royal marriage, particularly during the long periods he spent away from England on military campaigns.

Though William may not have been the most stylish individual, and he certainly didn't care much for fashion personally, it would be incorrect to assume that he was slovenly or even simple in appearance. He was a pragmatic man and understood that his clothing could be used as a tool to disguise the waning authority of the monarchy – throughout his reign the power of the Crown had become eclipsed by that of the government. William's suits were finely cut, typically made of scarlet silk embroidered with silver thread, a trend mirrored in the furnishings of his royal apartments at Hampton Court.[48] He finished his outfits with an impressive amount of gold or white lace, which during his reign had become the ultimate display of wealth and style, to the point that it had become an unofficial expectation for court dress – the King being no exception, using it to trim his cravats, his shirt cuffs, his nightcaps and even to embellish his furniture.

On 21 February 1702, the fifty-one-year-old King went for a brisk ride through the grounds of his retreat at Hampton Court and fell from his horse after it stumbled on a molehill. William stepped away with only minor injuries but during his recovery period the King, who had always suffered with his respiratory health, fell gravely ill with pneumonia. He passed away at Kensington Palace on 8 March and was buried at Westminster Abbey beside his beloved wife and Queen.

ANNE

ON 11 MARCH 1702, a hush fell over the House of Lords. Any minute now, Queen Anne, sister-in-law to the late King William, would enter the Houses of Parliament to give her first address. Anne had gone to great pains to ensure that she made the best first impression at her debut engagement with her new title. Having spent years dutifully assisting her family throughout their reigns, Anne had been able to assess what made a successful ruler, or an unsuccessful one, and she realized that what the *English* people wanted was a truly *English* monarch. William III's foreign birth and lifelong preference for his homeland had never sat well with his subjects, and it was clear to Anne that what the public coveted now was an unapologetically patriotic ruler. The Queen and her advisors were quick to draw parallels between her current situation and that of Elizabeth I over a hundred years previously. Both Anne and Elizabeth were the children of non-royal mothers, were never intended to rule and had to navigate the treacherous waters of being a woman in power – Elizabeth's epic legacy was testament that her method of ruling would be a successful framework to emulate, and Anne immediately set in motion a visual campaign to emphasize her ties to that legendary English Queen.

It was at her first appearance in the House of Lords that the country got their first glimpse of Anne-turned-Elizabeth in action; she was dressed in a red robe trimmed with ermine fur and shimmering gold silk braid, and observers immediately noted its similarity to the dresses seen in paintings of Elizabeth I.[49] Around her neck Anne wore a heavy gold chain from which the badge of Saint George hung, and around her left arm the ribbon of the garter was tied. These last two pieces were part of the uniform of the Order of the Garter, England's most prestigious order of chivalry.

Having first been established in the 1340s by King Edward III, the order is composed of the monarch and twenty-four 'Knights Companion' of their choosing, with Ladies Companion not being introduced until the twentieth century. The Stuart kings had taken particular interest in orders of chivalry, with both King Charles' refining the uniform for the Order of the Garter and James II introducing its Scottish equivalent, the Order of the Thistle. When the Order of the Garter took part in ceremonial events, they wore a uniform of a deep blue velvet mantle lined with white silk, a matching cap with a white ostrich feather, and a white and red Tudor-style doublet and hose that had been created by Charles II. The titular garter was deep blue and covered in precious jewels, worn on the left calf of the Knights Companion. With the patriotic ties that the Order upheld, Anne was not keen to let this opportunity pass her by, choosing to wear the garter on her left arm so that it would be visible to the public, rather than concealed beneath her skirts. This uniform change would go on to be followed by all subsequent female monarchs and Ladies Companion.

'I know my heart to be entirely English,' declared Anne in her address to the Lords, and stressed the importance of uniting the Kingdoms of England and Scotland.[50] Though both regions were ruled by the same Stuart monarch, they had independent governing bodies that Anne wished to merge. In 1707, the Acts of Union were passed, joining the two Kingdoms into one, under the name of Great Britain. As a result, Anne was the first monarch to be styled Queen of Great Britain and Ireland.

Having come to the throne at thirty-seven years old, Anne already had plenty of experience of life at court, where she and her husband, Prince George of Denmark, had been central figures for many years now. When Anne became Queen, she insisted upon the same dedication to etiquette that she had followed all throughout her life thus far, almost to an excessive degree. In 1689, when a celebratory court assembly had been hosted for the arrival of the new King and Queen, she had refused to sit at her seat as it had been placed slightly too close to her sister's throne, and insisted it be moved to the distance appropriate for a woman of her status.[51] As Queen, she closely scrutinized the appearance of her courtiers and was always swift to identify a fashion faux pas, such as when one unfortunate nobleman's son appeared for the first time at court dressed in a wig too short to be considered appropriately formal. Anne questioned him and quipped that should she continue to allow small blunders such as this, she supposed she 'must soon expect to see all officers come to court in boots and spurs'[52] – both of which were considered egregiously casual. The young man returned home at once, changed his wig and returned to a much warmer reception from his Queen.

Anne's response to this wiggy misunderstanding gives us some insight into her reasoning for enforcing such high standards upon her courtiers. Rebelling against a monarch by pushing the boundaries of formal clothing was a slippery slope to defying their authority in other, more important political matters. By closely monitoring the wardrobes of her courtiers, she established a level of control over the conduct of those around her. Anne was astute in this way, taking her political duties very seriously and attending more cabinet meetings than any monarch had previously. The monarchy now had comparatively less political authority than generations before, but Anne's control over her courtiers and her awareness of current issues meant that she would retain *influence* in Parliament, if not total power. Anne also mastered the art of discretion, refusing to discuss important political topics casually whilst hosting at her palaces, a skill that continues to hold paramount importance amongst royalty today. Gossip at court was a powerful tool, and one that the Queen was not willing to dispense freely. Unfortunately for Anne, her courtiers often read her professionalism as banality, complaining frequently that she was uninspiring or boring in both appearance and character. In 1711, the Queen invited Dean Swift and about twenty other courtiers to keep her company in her private quarters, and he later reported miserably that all they were permitted to do was to stand around the Queen as she held her fan to her lips, occasionally breaking the silence with one or two words directed to those closest to her, before she finally departed for dinner.[53]

The truth of the matter was that Anne's discretion was infinitely helped by her naturally shy personality. She far preferred the company of a select few friends that she knew she could trust, and with them she formed vibrant and passionate relationships. Most prominent of these companions was Sarah Churchill, the Duchess of Marlborough, whose assertive and outspoken nature provided a crutch for Anne to cling to in the most difficult periods of her reign. The duo had been inseparable since the 1670s, when Sarah had first appeared at court as a Maid of Honour to Mary of Modena, and her presence in royal life had only grown since Anne became Queen.

Sarah's companionship was rewarded with some of the most prestigious roles available, such as Keeper of the Privy purse, responsible for managing Anne's personal finances, a position that had never before been filled by a woman. The Duchess was evidently proud of her job and flaunted it freely by wearing the golden key of the Keeper of the Privy Purse tied to her waist by a ribbon.[54] She was also made Mistress of the Robes, putting her in control of organizing and deciding the clothes that Anne would wear each day and helping her dress each morning. The physical and emotional closeness that these roles fostered between the two women allowed Sarah to tease out continual rewards for both herself and her family, including social and military promotions for her husband and a sizable lifelong pension from the Queen's own purse. Sarah also had first pick of any of Anne's cast-offs; each January, before making her annual order of clothes, the Queen would lay out the dresses she no longer wanted and allow her ladies to take home their favourites.[55] Sarah decorated her estate, Blenheim Palace, with the clothes and furnishings that Anne had given her and prized them for both their sentimental value and their luxury, as the Queen had a preference for heavy gold brocades, making her gowns extraordinarily expensive. The Duchess of Marlborough was the prime example for her time of what a relationship with the monarch could do and illustrated the inexplicable link that had formed between the royal wardrobe and power.

Anne's dependence upon her close friendships only deepened with each of her pregnancies. In 1683, she had married Prince George of Denmark, an arranged match that blossomed into a supportive and caring relationship, and one that saw Anne fall pregnant seventeen times over the span of seventeen years. Tragically, twelve of those pregnancies resulted in miscarriage or stillbirth, and the surviving five children would not survive into adulthood. As well as being emotionally wounded by the ordeals, Anne's physical health rapidly deteriorated, and by the time she had come to the throne she was unable to walk for long periods without support. As time went on her ailments worsened, and Anne had to be transported around her court in a wheelchair or a sedan chair.[56]

Keen not to let her disability prevent her from projecting her majesty, Anne persisted in wearing mantuas made of heavy metallic threads and laden with clusters of jewels when attending formal functions. Ahead of one thanksgiving service at St Paul's Cathedral in 1708, Anne lamented to the Duchess of Marlborough that 'heavy clothes are so uneasy to me', yet being aware of the hundreds of eyes that would undoubtedly be upon her, she went on to say that she 'had a mind to be fine' for the event and intended to cover her gown with a liberal smattering of diamonds despite the strain it would place upon her.[57] When recounting her time with the Queen, Sarah confirmed in her own words that her companion's ailments made it so that 'she could not endure heavy clothes'.[58] In private and when enshrined behind the walls of the court, Anne did not subject herself to this level of discomfort, dressing instead in loose-fitting gowns for her own pleasure. Later in life, the Queen attracted a mixture of both pity and horror, with one courtier noting that her gout-riddled frame was made only more 'frightful by her negligent dress'.[59]

Of all the personal tragedies that befell Queen Anne throughout her life, it would be the death of her longest-lived child and sole heir to the throne, Prince William, that would wound her deepest. Born not even a year after the deposition of James II, Anne and many of the British public viewed the delivery of a seemingly healthy baby boy as a reward from God for defending the Protestant faith, and William would grow up hailed as a hero of his religion. Unfortunately, he would also become an increasingly sickly child, and on the night of his eleventh birthday party, the young Prince developed a severe case of smallpox, succumbing to the disease less than a week later. Anne was devastated, and a mourning period was immediately enforced at court. Carefully regulated periods of mourning were yet another aspect of court life that Anne strictly monitored, with a very specific dress code for those in attendance: for men, suits of 'black cloth, with plain linen, black swords, and white gloves' were acceptable, and ladies' mantuas should be of black silk and paired with white gloves.[60] Mourning periods were a frequent occurrence during Anne's reign, much to the chagrin of court dressmakers. These businesses, which made their money by regularly supplying fashion-conscious courtiers with expensive dresses and suits, could be financially crippled by the dry spell that court mourning caused. With multiple consecutive months (in some cases as much as half a year) spent in the same regulation black clothes, courtiers felt little need to replenish their wardrobes, and textiles tradesmen suffered financially as a result.

It was tragedies such as these that brought Anne ever closer to her husband and consort, George of Denmark. Tall, fair and not unkind on the eyes, the Prince Consort was not known as a fashion revolutionary and rather followed along with the standards set by his more style-conscious courtiers. Periwigs were still as prevalent as ever, often arranged in two peaks at the top of the head in a manner that was frequently replicated in women's hairstyling. Men's suits became increasingly more tailored, with coats cut close to the torso before flaring out at the hip like a skirt, prompting some moralists to complain of the newfound effeminacy of men's dress. The sobriety that Charles II had hoped for when introducing this style had by this time been fully abandoned, with every inch of the suit being embroidered with shimmering metallic threads. This was a heavy and uncomfortable fashion, but one that had been known to save lives: on 8 March 1711, an assassin attempted to murder the Earl of Oxford but his knife was deflected by the thick gold brocade that covered the Earl's waistcoat, one he had chosen especially to honour the anniversary of Queen Anne's accession.[61]

George was known to take fashion cues from his wife and kept in line with her patriotic ideals by adopting and flaunting styles of local manufacture, rather than attempting to cling to the clothes of his native Denmark. This was the role that George adopted throughout his marriage – unlike William III, he showed no real interest in maintaining authority over his wife. George was happy to play the role of a supportive husband whilst his wife dealt with important political matters, declaring upon her accession that he 'shall do naught but what she commands me'.[62]

Prince George's death in 1708 would see Anne turn to her close female friendships for support, but her childhood companion, the Duchess of Marlborough, would offer little comfort. Over the course of that year, the two women's relationship had become increasingly strained, as Sarah attempted with her usual extrovert force to sway the Queen's political beliefs to win favour for her family. Becoming weary of this constant berating, Anne began to distance herself from the Duchess and instead drew closer to her other ladies-in-waiting, who offered her a more sensitive and sympathetic environment. Earlier in the year, Anne had decided not to wear a collection of jewels that Sarah had selected for a thanksgiving service, something that the Duchess viewed as evidence of her waning influence in her mistress's life. During the ensuing carriage ride to St Paul's Cathedral, the duo bickered fiercely over the jewellery, concluding with Sarah's harsh command that the Queen 'Be silent!'[63] Anne was now fully disenchanted with her companion, and when Sarah stubbornly refused to wear mourning dress after the death of Prince George to protest her diminishing authority, Anne became well and truly incensed. By 1710 there had been no improvement, and the Queen decided to formally dismiss Sarah and her husband, demanding that she return the golden key she had taken such pride in displaying and leave the royal court for good.

When Anne passed away on 1 August 1714, she was a sorry sight to behold. Having suffered two consecutive strokes, she had been left struggling to speak or move, comforted by her ladies-in-waiting whilst her head was shaved as part of a futile treatment to preserve her life. Now finally free from a lifetime of painful health conditions, Anne was laid to rest beside Prince George and nine of their children.

Above. Two generations of Tudor style. On the top step we see Henry VII in his long gown and Elizabeth of York holding her dramatic skirts. Below stands Henry VIII in his doublet and hose and Jane Seymour in an English style hood.

Right. Anne Boleyn, Henry VIII's ill-fated second bride. Here she wears her famous 'B' necklace, and a French hood trimmed with pearls.

Left. Edward VI just prior to his accession. His white doublet is embroidered with gold and padded to make him seem more imposing.

Below, left. The rainbow portrait of Elizabeth I, a painting rich with symbolism.

Below. The Chequers ring, worn by Elizabeth I until her death. The bottom portrait shows the Queen, the top depicts one of her mother figures – either Anne Boleyn or Katherine Parr.

James I & VI and his wife Anne. The Queen wears a French farthingale skirt, a relic from the reign of Elizabeth I that King James attempted to ban.

After Anne's death, women's fashion took a simpler approach. Henrietta Maria's wardrobe featured no French farthingales and instead used a softer and more natural silhouette.

A not-so-happy royal couple. Charles II wears a short French doublet and petticoat-breeches with cannons around his knees. Beside him, Catherine of Braganza wears a fashionable English dress with a 'hurluberlu' hairstyle.

In 1666, King Charles II introduced a new style of menswear to his court – an early version of the three-piece suit. For his wedding to Mary of Modena in 1673, the future King James II wore this gold and silver suit.

A mantua from the late Stuart period. The over gown has been pulled back and pinned into a waterfall of fabric behind the skirt. For much of the eighteenth century this was the most popular style for women at court.

Mary II and William III surrounded by their courtiers. The ladies wear mantuas and lace caps, the gentlemen wear suits and periwigs.

The genius Queen – Caroline of Ansbach. Her love of science and
the natural world is reflected in the metallic floral skirt she wears over
a bell-shaped hoop.

A British *robe à la française*, this popular style of court dress was very similar to its parent garment – the mantua. This one dates from 1750 and is arranged over a set of wide panniers.

The King's birthday ball – the most luxurious date in the court calendar when everybody dressed their best. To the left, George III and Queen Charlotte sit watching the Prince of Wales and Princess Royal dance in their lavish court finery.

Caroline of Brunswick in court dress. Queen Charlotte's stance on hoop skirts meant that court fashion could look frumpy and ridiculous, especially as women's waistlines began to rise.

In 1822, King George IV made his historic visit to Scotland. The fashion-obsessed King relished in playing dress-up for the trip and had his Highland dress memorialised in this very flattering painting by Sir David Wilkie.

Part Three

THE FOUR GEORGES

ANNE HAD KNOWN ever since the death of Prince William that she was destined to conclude the Stuart line just as her model, Elizabeth I, had done for the Tudors. In light of this, the decision was made in 1701 to elect an heir presumptive, no mean feat seeing as over fifty members of the extended royal family with strong claims to the throne had to be skipped over on account of their Catholicism. In the quest to declare an heir the Stuarts traced their family tree right back up to King James I and his daughter, Elizabeth, Queen of Bohemia, settling on *her* daughter Electress Sophia of Hanover.

Born in 1630 and married to the Elector of a dinky little principality in present-day Germany, the Electress was sharp, witty and very beautiful – traits that had not waned at the age of seventy, when she was declared heir presumptive. She was passionate about the role she was to inherit, taking a keen interest in British customs and political affairs so that she might effortlessly pass for a native when she ventured to her ancestral homeland. Despite her zeal, Sophia would never become Queen of Great Britain and Ireland – she passed away just two months before Queen Anne. Instead, it was her son, the fifty-four-year-old George Ludwig, who would begin the British dynasty of Hanoverian royals. This new generation of monarchs would begin in much the same way as their Stuart relatives, arriving with a preprepared royal family to both irk and entertain their new public, and just like the Stuarts, the reigns of the four consecutive King Georges would be filled with chaos and disputes.

GEORGE I

On Saturday, 18 September 1714, a crowd, composed of nobles and commoners alike, gathered at Greenwich. The streets were lined with people clamouring to catch a first glimpse of their new King as he arrived from Germany by barge. Some courtiers already knew what was in store, for ever since the nomination of Sophia of Hanover as heir presumptive, her court had received a continuous trickle of British visitors keen to make an early first impression on their soon-to-be royal family. These courtiers might have managed to meet George Ludwig whilst at Herrenhausen Palace, but only if their visit coincided with one of the brief periods that the Prince spent at home in between his frequent military campaigns. The reviews were mixed: while the Electress Sophia had been labelled 'the most knowing and entertaining woman of the age' and praised for the vivacity with which she had effortlessly animated what was otherwise considered a rather dull set of electoral palaces, her son was said to be so cold he drew all life from the court around him.[1] The Earl of Chesterfield, in an oft-cited assessment, labelled George 'an honest, dull, German gentleman'.[2]

The man who stepped out in front of the crowds at Greenwich Palace was short but athletically built, with skin so weathered and tanned from years spent fighting in foreign wars that his own mother once declared he could pass for a Spaniard. His eyes were blue, his periwig dark brown, and his choice of clothing wasn't anything to write home about. The new King's arrival couldn't have been further from the carefully orchestrated Tudor-inspired splendour that Queen Anne had employed for her first monarchical appearance. Amongst those that George brought with him were his two Turkish servants Mehemet and Mustapha (who were soon to become the envy of all ambitious British courtiers), his two 'mistresses', and the glamorous Prince and Princess of Wales, George Augustus and Caroline of Ansbach. All in all, they were a truly curious group of individuals. The King's arrival at Greenwich, which culminated in anti-climax when he made a rapid and unceremonious beeline for his bedchamber, was followed two days later by a triumphant entry to London ahead of his coronation. The reign of King George had well and truly begun.

The public disappointment that had surrounded George's arrival would continue to underscore his reign. As a practical military man, his approach to fashion was one of efficiency, resulting in a comely appearance that was smart but hardly reaching the level of splendour typically expected of royalty. Horace Walpole, the son of Britain's first Prime Minister, gave a detailed description of the time he was introduced to the King as a young boy, recounting his 'plain coat, waistcoat and breeches of snuff-coloured [brown] cloth, with stockings of the same colour, and a blue ribbon [sash] over all' – a stark contrast to the brightly coloured silks and expensive metallic brocades that his courtiers flaunted.[3]

There was also the issue of the King's unwavering preference for his homeland. Unlike his mother, George had never been enthusiastic about the prospect of inheriting the British

Crown and had scarcely even attempted to learn English in preparation for the job, choosing instead to communicate with his new advisors in French, their only common tongue. He was reclusive and rarely made an effort to appear before his public, and made frequent visits back to his native Hanover, which only further endangered his public opinion. In neglecting his British subjects, George inadvertently sparked a conflict between the scorned British courtiers and the German nobility he had brought with him, who scoffed at every cultural difference in their contest for the King's favour. At one court assembly in April 1716, the German Countess of Buckenburgh snarkily noted aloud that 'English women do not look like ladies of quality but make themselves look as pitifully and sneakingly as they could . . . whereas those that are foreigners hold up their heads and hold out their breasts and make themselves look as great and stately as they can'. Lady Deloraine, a British aristocrat who took particular offence to the Countess's remark, replied frostily, 'We show our quality by our birth and titles, Madam, not by sticking out our bosoms.'[4]

George's favouritism was something that the British had foreseen, as their last foreign ruler, William III, had liberally awarded his Dutch friends prestigious titles and positions at court. To prevent a repeat of this, a condition had been included in the Act of Settlement inviting the Hanoverians to rule that forbade them from appointing foreign individuals to public offices. George, who had come from a small court that he could easily micromanage, was uneasy at the prospect of having to select total strangers for the more intimate roles at court. Chief amongst these was the Groom of the Stole, the head of the royal bedchamber who was responsible for overseeing the organization of the King's clothing and assisting with both his dressing and his personal hygiene. The intimacy of such a task meant that the Groom and his master would often be inseparable, and the post was typically held by a royal favourite whom the monarch felt most at ease around. If they were not already a favourite, they likely soon would be, as the Groom enjoyed unfiltered and private access to the King which they could use to bolster their influence at court. When the role had first been explained to King George, he made the controversial decision not to appoint anyone to the task, at least not formally, which put a damper on the mood of eager British courtiers who were desperate to sink their claws of influence into the new King. George stated that he was aware that whoever he chose would, by the nature of the job, 'be always near [my] person and therefore [I am] resolved to know the man very well';[5] in fact, George would wait until 1719 before appointing an Englishman whom he felt he could trust.

In the meantime, George entrusted the duties of this coveted role to his two *valets de chambre*, Mustapha and Mehemet, who had been in his service for the last twenty-five years. They had first come to work for George after they had been captured in one of his military campaigns but had quickly risen through the ranks of service and by the time of their arrival at the English court they were both extremely wealthy men with unparalleled influence on their master. Both men and their families were treated to fine apartments conveniently close to those of the King and were the envy of all British courtiers who had hoped to fill their positions. It was Mehemet who was responsible for ordering the King's clothes, and he did so by purchasing from the same Hanoverian tradesmen that George had relied on previously, with no attempt made to promote local British trade. Mehemet's task of ordering the King's clothes awarded him the position of de facto Keeper of the Privy Purse, yet another highly desirable job that earned him many a jealous glare from the English.[6]

Between Queen Anne's obsession with dress codes and George I's unfashionable sobriety, the British court of the early eighteenth century had become entirely isolated from the trends of regular society. Anne had made it very clear exactly what sort of clothes were acceptable in her presence, and her courtiers had refined the art of appealing to her taste across the course of her reign. Under George, who offered no guidance to set the standard, fashion at the early Georgian court gradually fossilized, becoming a relic of the past century with styles that differed greatly to the clothes worn by aristocrats in the rest of their daily lives. It was now only within the walls of the royal palaces that you could expect to see long sweeping trains, frock coats covered entirely in metallic embroidery, and decorative swords; these were now part of an unofficial court uniform that the most ambitious members of high society studied with expert precision. Cesar de Saussure, a Swiss visitor to court, summarized this style divide best when he observed that 'Englishmen are usually very plainly dressed, they scarcely ever wear gold on their clothes' but that they were, however, 'very lavish in other ways . . . persons of rank are richly dressed when they go to court'.[7]

One of the most iconic items of eighteenth-century court dress was red heels, a trend brought into existence by Louis XIV of France in the 1670s which quickly spread to all major European courts. The striking scarlet heels were a social marker, indicating that the wearer did not need to muddy their shoes with manual labour, and were often flaunted in royal portraiture with a strategically forward-thrust leg. These too were confined within the Palace walls – no fashion-conscious citizen would be seen dead wearing them to pay calls or visit the assembly rooms.

Though the court was beginning to lose its relevance as an arbiter of fashion, it held its appeal for the political and social benefits it afforded those in attendance. Visiting a royal palace could present you with the chance to network with socialites, politicians and members of the royal family alike, and access was a coveted opportunity. No invitations were issued for court gatherings, nor were any clear instructions given to clarify what sort of person was allowed to attend; instead it was fashion that was used to judge who could gain access to the royal palaces. Ushers who stood guard on the stairs that lead to the King's drawing room would take note of each passing guest and, based on the quality of their dress, would decide who to admit and who to send away. The reasoning behind this system was that any individual who had reason to be in the presence of the royal family would also have the wealth and status to afford the best and most stylish clothes, and if you couldn't afford to dress the part, you probably weren't important enough to meet the King. This was, of course, not particularly efficient, and in 1714, Dudley Ryder, a young law student desperate to make contacts to advance his career, cracked the code for sneaking into court. By wearing a combination of his own smartest clothes and those borrowed from his better-off friends, Dudley managed to gain entry to many gatherings hosted at the royal court. He did, however, run into problems at important celebratory events such as the King's birthday, which required an even higher standard of dress, and was far too expensive for Dudley to mimic. On these occasions he would resort to bribing the guards, which usually did the trick.[8]

George brought with him no Queen when he arrived in England, though the mother of his children was still very much alive. In 1685, he had married Sophia Dorothea of Celle, a vibrant young aristocrat who captivated the Hanoverian court with her thickly curled hair, dark eyes and blush-pinched cheeks. She was without a doubt the most stylish woman within the electoral palaces, flaunting her plump white shoulders in French dresses with provocatively low necklines. They had been designed for that very reason, implemented by France's King Louis XIV so that he might freely ogle the décolletages of his female courtiers, and Sophia Dorothea's French mother had filled her daughter's wardrobes with them. It seems, however, that the only person immune to the charms of Sophia Dorothea was her own dull husband, who took little interest in his wife and left her to her own devices at court. Abandoned and lonely, the young bride's affections roamed freely, and she fell madly in love with the visiting Count Philip Christoph von Königsmarck, beginning a secret affair that ended in disaster when Sophia Dorothea's in-laws discovered the romantic rendezvous and reported back to her husband. George had his wife imprisoned and a divorce was swiftly arranged, with the handsome Count disappearing from society altogether. Königsmarck, rumour has it, had been discovered tangled in the bedsheets of his royal mistress and was murdered at the request of George I's father, who was keen to protect the reputation of his son, and his body was hidden beneath the floorboards of Sophia Dorothea's bedchamber.[9]

In the absence of a Queen, it was the King's two 'mistresses' who attempted to fill her role in the English court. First there was Melusine von der Schulenburg, Duchess of Kendal, who exhibited the most control over the King and was rumoured to be his second wife. She was no great style icon and in character was almost as dull as the King; Horace Walpole could scarcely recall her appearance when he had made his first trip to court, noting only that looming behind the King 'stood a very tall, lean, ill-favoured old lady; but I did not retain the least idea of her features, nor know of what colour her dress was'.[10] It wasn't only Walpole who focused on the Duchess of Kendal's strikingly tall and slender physique, but the country at large. Jealous courtiers created snide nicknames for the King's favourites, and Melusine was cruelly branded 'the Maypole', for her unfashionably gaunt appearance. Her counterpart received the equally wicked moniker of 'the Elephant'; she was the buxom Sophia Charlotte von Kielmansegg, Countess of Darlington. As a young woman in the Hanoverian court she had been a key figure, her good humour and lively character had kept her a frequent topic of gossip, and her style was up to date and sufficiently glitzy for a woman of her status. As she grew older and gained more weight, the Countess traded the tight court mantuas for sack gowns, coat-like dresses that hung loose over the body in wide pleats. She also did away with stays, a precursor to the corset that was used to support the bust and carry the weight of heavy court gowns.[11] By the time of her arrival to the English court she had gained enough weight for the English to use it as a weapon in their attacks against her; they were deeply envious of her close relationship to the King and came to the conclusion that she *must* be sleeping with him, just as Melusine was, in order to gain social power. In reality, these rumours could not have been further from the truth; unbeknownst to the court, Sophia Charlotte was George's half-sister, the illegitimate daughter of his father, Elector Ernst Augustus. There is no proof to suggest that George engaged in an incestuous relationship with Sophia Charlotte, but rather her influence stemmed from George's respect for her position as his sister, regardless of her illegitimacy.

These faux queens were hotly despised by courtiers, and their reputations would continue to plummet in an impressively epic manner over the coming years. In the 1720s, the two women, Melusine in particular, found themselves at the centre of one of the worst financial scandals in British history – the South Sea Bubble. The South Sea company had been established in 1711 in an attempt to alleviate the mounting national debt but had quickly become one of the most glamorous investments available. That may seem like an interesting choice of words to describe a financial bubble, especially considering that the company made its money by transporting enslaved Africans to the Americas, but the immense wealth that the company directors predicted it would produce enchanted high society. The company's reputation was bolstered when the King himself invested, and by 1720 there was nothing that people wanted to discuss more than the South Sea Company, with one British Countess deeming it 'very unfashionable not to be [investing] in the south sea'.[12] That year, the court circle was eclipsed by that of the South Sea Company, with aristocrats and royals clamouring to pay court instead to the directors of this illustrious organization. Sophia Charlotte and Melusine had both invested and profited greatly, particularly the latter, who flaunted her increased wealth at the birthday of King George that year, parading around the crowded court in a gown laced head to toe with jewels.

Disaster was soon to strike – in September the value of South Sea stocks dropped by a staggering 80 per cent, leaving hundreds of families up and down the country destitute. It was revealed that the Spanish Empire, which the company had promised to trade with, had enforced high taxes on all imports and limited the number of British trade ships to a fraction of what the company needed to sustain itself. Panicking, the company directors had resorted to insider trading and bribery to create the illusion of a successful business. Robert Knight, the company treasurer, had viewed an investment from the King as necessary to distract from their true financial situation, and identified Melusine and Sophia Charlotte as essential figures in winning his support. He bribed the two women to soften the King's ear to the company, a task which the Maypole managed successfully, situating her firmly at the beating heart of this scandal. An angry mob formed, hunting for someone to blame for the hardships they now suffered, and Melusine, whose position as the King's mistress protected her from total financial ruin, was their priority target. She was criticized harshly in the press, with prints depicting her in the overtly lavish dresses she had bought with her bribe money, accepting her secret payments from Robert Knight.

In 1727, George and Melusine packed their bags in preparation for another one of their regular summer holidays back to Hanover. On 20 June, as the King's carriage was making its journey between Delden and Nordhorn, George began to complain of stomach pains but urged the carriage to continue. Not long after, his courtiers noticed with alarm that his face was beginning to droop and that he had lost control of his right arm, and within moments the King had slipped from consciousness. He had suffered a stroke, and passed away just a few days later, his body laid to rest in Hanover, the place he adored more than any other.

GEORGE II

WHEN THE HANOVERIAN royals had come to England, the new Prince and Princess of Wales had shone out magnificently from behind the shadow of the dour George I. In the sartorial sense, the duo stole the King's crown with little effort at all. Prince George Augustus was unfortunately the spitting image of his father – short, with a strikingly prominent nose and bulging blue eyes – but was rendered infinitely more attractive by his regal deportment and dedication to proper dressing, always making it his business to be as richly dressed as possible. He could, when the occasion called, upstage the competition effortlessly. Velvet suits with rows of diamond buttons filled his wardrobe, and at the drop of a hat he could procure a coat of gold brocade so thick and detailed that the designs seemed to grow from the fabric.

Falling in stride with her husband, Wilhelmina Charlotte Caroline (known best as Caroline of Ansbach) was equally as radiant. Tall, full-figured, with a large bosom and a head of shimmering blonde hair, she enchanted her new subjects. Her successes were elevated infinitely by her commitment to learning English and, by the time of her arrival in Britain, she was the best English speaker out of the entire imported royal family. Caroline was considered the darling of the lot.

King George I was certainly not threatened by the young couple's glitz and glamour and was happy to surrender the responsibility of hosting court events, a task that Caroline in particular snapped up and performed with vigour.

The Prince and Princess adored one another, and the country in turn adored them. The early years of their marriage would be amongst the best of their lives, and they would both express an interest in preserving the memory of their youth and beauty during this period through portraiture. In their forties, when commissioning a series of miniature paintings, the Queen commanded the artist Frederick Zincke to 'make the King's picture young, not above twenty-five' while George suggested that his wife should be depicted as she was at age twenty-eight.[13]

Their happiness was soured, however, by the bitter feud that had begun to fester between King George I and his son. Only a year after their arrival in England, it was widely reported that the King and Prince would spend their time together either bickering fiercely or simply ignoring one another, much to the concern of the country at large, who began to fret that 'their own private ends will destroy us all'.[14] Courtiers split their loyalties – those who concerned themselves with the power of the present 'devoting themselves to the wearer of the crown' and those who flirted with the excitement of the future courting instead 'the expectant' Prince of Wales.[15] The growing rift was cataclysmic and was as personal as it was political. Things came to a head when, at the 1717 christening of George and Caroline's second son, the Prince of Wales found himself embroiled in a vicious argument with the Duke of Newcastle, whom King George I had selected as the baby's godfather. The Duke, having difficulty understanding the Prince of Wales's strong German accent, believed that in the midst of the confrontation he had been challenged to a fight, and when the Prince refused to apologize for the confusion, the King banished his son and daughter-in-law from court and they retreated bitterly to Leicester House.

King George II's 1727 coronation was, as might be expected, a particularly glamorous occasion, though not without its faults. Queen Caroline was the star of the show, at least as far as royal performance was concerned. She moved gracefully through Westminster Abbey despite the fact that her 'extravagantly fine' dress was weighed down by nearly a quarter of a million pounds' worth of jewels, with only some of the weight eased by those carrying her train – her ladies in pink silk dresses and her three daughters in shimmering silver.[16] Then there was George himself, struggling beneath his velvet and ermine robes in the heat of what was already an unusually warm and stifling October day. His procession cap, a crimson velvet mess of ill-fitting fabric, kept slumping unceremoniously over the eyes of an already grouchy King, incensing him further still, and it's not hard to imagine how pinched his usually stately face would have looked.[17] George was quick-tempered at the best of times, but the pressure of ruling would only exacerbate his nerves. The smallest things could set him off, and his daughter Anne once explained that 'when he is in his worst humours, and the devil to everybody that comes near him, it is always because one of his pages has powdered his periwig ill, or a housemaid set a chair where it does not used to stand'.[18] It was not uncommon to see the King brandishing his cane like a sword in the face of a courtier who had asked him a pointless question or kicking his hat or wig across the room as means to vent his frustration.[19]

George found the best outlet for his temper on the battlefield. He shared with his father an affinity for military pursuits and would go down in history as the last British monarch to lead soldiers into battle. When not on a military progress, the army continued to fill the mind of King George, and he dedicated himself to designing uniforms for the various regiments, marking the start of what would soon become a generational fascination with uniform for the Hanoverian monarchs. George did not neglect the navy; it was suggested to him that he should choose the patriotic colours of blue and red for his designs, but George instead had found himself quite inspired by the Duchess of Bedford, whom he had spotted out riding a few days previously in a deep blue riding habit trimmed with white accents. Finding the colour combination to his liking, George had the uniforms designed to that specification.[20] Proud of his creations, which were to be worn only by commissioned officers and therefore were modelled on the finest construction of fashionable male dress, George had them immortalized in a series of paintings by David Morier.

George had lofty views of his own reign, perceiving himself as one of the most successful and steadfast kings England had seen in a very long time. The previous Stuart monarchs had been reigned over by wives and mistresses, men of the cloth and men of the court alike, 'and who do they say governs now?' he once gloated to his courtiers.[21] They didn't respond, but there was a clear consensus about where the real royal power lay. One contemporary poet later put it clearly: 'You may strut, dapper George, but 'twill be in vain: we know 'tis Queen Caroline, not you, that reign!'[22] And indeed, it was true that most of the royal power lay, albeit unofficially, with George's wife, Caroline. She had begun to carefully cultivate a relationship with the British public as soon as she had married, dedicating herself to learning the English language, customs and history and introducing herself to prominent social figures and politicians. By the time George II had come to the throne Caroline was well connected and well loved, and had mastered the art of making her husband believe that her opinions were his own. Politicians would flock to Caroline for assistance in their pursuits, and George was none the wiser about his wife's ambitions.

Caroline surrounded herself with educated politicians, pioneering artists and ground-breaking scientists and at her court, which was one of the most desirable places to be, 'learned men and divines were intermixed with courtiers and ladies of the household; the conversation turned upon metaphysical subjects, blended with repartees, sallies of mirth, and the tittle-tattle of a drawing-room'.[23] It was official: her role as a patron of the sciences and arts alike made her the unequivocal figurehead of the British Enlightenment period. She was incredibly keen on botany and took a studious interest in designing the landscapes of her palace gardens, a pastime that was reflected in her wardrobe – she favoured gowns of breathable silks, typically in moody colours like dark green, garter blue or purple, interspersed with patterns of vibrant blooming flowers.[24] Her favourite style was the ever-enduring mantua, which in her early years as Queen was worn over bell-shaped hoop skirts, which, despite their size, paled in significance compared with the panniers that were introduced to ladies' wardrobes towards the close of her life. Panniers were hoop skirts that protruded from either side of the body, creating a flat, rectangular shape, effectively providing a canvas for colourfully embroidered fabrics to be displayed to fellow courtiers.

In her quest to win and maintain the favour of her British subjects, Caroline made every effort to avoid extravagance and was incredibly successful at treading the fine line between overindulgence and mediocrity in her dress. She was careful to be seen to promote the trade of her subjects: the lace that trimmed her neckline and sleeves was manufactured in the Midlands, she dressed herself and her daughters in Irish plaid, and after being made aware of a new initiative to establish silk production in the colony of Georgia, began importing and dressing in their silk organza.[25] She did, however, ensure that she kept her finger firmly on the beating pulse of fashion by regularly requesting and studying fashion dolls sent from Paris – reproductions of the latest French styles on a miniature scale which could then be passed on to a tailor to be recreated to Caroline's measurements.

Caroline made sure to shape her daughters in her image, at least during the time that she had access to them. After the christening debacle that saw George and Caroline exiled from court, King George I had insisted that their three eldest daughters remain in his care at Kensington Palace, much to the anguish of their parents who yearned for a close-knit family unit. The eldest was Anne, effortlessly multilingual, a talented painter and trained in all forms of courtly decorum – she was in every sense the perfect Princess. The public, however, saw her as the ambitious sort, and indeed Anne secretly wished that she had been born with no brothers, once lamenting to her mother, 'I would die to-morrow to be Queen to-day!'[26] Anne might also have been considered one of the great court beauties had it not been for the smallpox scars that marred her pale face, and instead the praise for beauty fell thick and fast upon the next sister, Princess Amelia. Whip-smart like her mother, 'Emily' (as she was known by her family) would host many a private party throughout her life to which only the most interesting members of society received an invite, each event breeding its fair share of gossip and intrigue. Famed for her good looks and charitable actions, she was also well known for her indelicately blunt nature and penchant for mischief, earning her the title of one of the 'oddest princesses ever known'.[27] Her wardrobe throughout her life featured tomboy-ish elements; having developed an ardent love for hunting and horsemanship, Emily would often be seen in ultra-masculine riding habits, a trend that led her to become the root of a scandal when she strode into chapel one morning 'in riding clothes with a dog under her arm'.[28] Finally there was Princess Caroline, gentle and pious, who acted as mediator when her spirited older sisters descended into argument.

When in the care of their grandfather, the three Princesses were not punished for their parents' indiscretions but catered for as befitted their status. They regularly attended balls hosted in candlelit halls or finely sculpted palace gardens, kitted out in the appropriate clothes. Their typical biannual clothing purchases saw them each receive three new dresses a year, with silk-lined hoop skirts to wear beneath, nearly 200 pairs of gloves, and a fresh set of shoes each week. There was, however, much to the chagrin of the three pretty Princesses, 'no certain allowance for ribbons or artificial flowers', an issue that was swiftly rectified when the girls returned to their mother's care after the death of George I.[29] Caroline, who personally preferred to spend a little extra for a fine lace cap, made sure to dress the trio with delicate silk flowers in their white powdered hair. Hair powder was all the rage in Georgian society, for both men and women, and was so common a feature of fashionable dress that it came to be viewed as a rite of passage for the wealthy. To appear in society with powdered hair or a powdered periwig for the first time was to appear in society as an adult.

The accession of George and Caroline also reunited them with another of their children, their eldest son and heir, Prince Frederick of Wales. Back in 1714, when the Hanoverian royals had flocked to England in their masses, George I had instructed his son to leave the seven-year-old Frederick behind. The reasons for that decision were political rather than personal, as in the absence of both George I and George II, the electoral palaces still needed a Hanoverian figurehead to rule over them, though in the eyes of a young boy like Frederick, this sort of abandonment couldn't have been interpreted as anything less than a surprise betrayal by his parents. Fourteen years came and went, and Frederick's sadness turned to resentment. On his return to the family as a young man of twenty-one, with a devilishly rakish streak and touting his fair share of mistresses, the King and Queen were wary of the man their son had become. His parents' steely reception left Frederick with a bitter taste in his mouth, and politicians were quick to capitalize upon his emotional and malleable nature, turning him further against his father in order to divide and conquer the royal family. The Hanoverians began to fracture, just as they had done during the rivalry between George I and George II, and the public resigned themselves to observing a haunting repetition of the past: 'Hanoverians,' it was said, 'like pigs, trample their young.'[30]

In 1736, Frederick agreed to marry Princess Augusta of Saxe-Gotha, for though he had inherited his mother's fair hair and eyes 'grey like a cat', he hadn't been in receipt of her intelligence, at least as it related to managing finances.[31] He hoped that Augusta (and more specifically her dowry) would help to ease the mounting debts that he had racked up as Prince of Wales. Queen Caroline, the economic proficient that she was, orchestrated the wedding and encouraged her courtiers not to purchase new clothes for her birthday celebrations that year, as was customary, so that they might instead put the money towards clothes for her son's wedding. Her plan worked: the ceremony was a most spectacular occasion, with the guests appearing in the most eye-wateringly expensive clothes imaginable. Princess Augusta, insipid but charmingly good-natured, outshone them all: she carefully balanced a sparkling crown atop her head, and wore a red velvet robe hanging from her shoulders. The *pièce de résistance* was her sparkling silver stiff-bodied gown – the typical style of wedding dress for eighteenth-century royal brides.[32] The gown was a fossilized interpretation of the styles of the 1660s, featuring the same heavily boned bodice with a low, swooping neckline and short sleeves that descended into multiple rows of intricately frilled lace. The gown was worn over a hoop skirt and, as was customary for court dress, featured a lengthy train. The royal women would turn to stiff-bodied gowns for other special occasions, such as royal birthdays or coronations, but it was almost always reserved for them alone and other ladies of the court were stuck with their typical court mantuas.

A year later a pregnant Augusta was, unknowingly, being forged into a weapon for her new husband to use in his spat against his father. In July 1737, George, Caroline, Frederick and Augusta were residing comfortably at Hampton Court, where they were often to be found during the summer months. The Princess was fit to burst with her baby, and the King and Queen were close at hand, insistent that they should be present at the birth of an heir to the throne. Petulant Frederick had very different plans and was silently plotting how he might exclude his loathed parents from the occasion. When, late at night, Augusta's waters broke, he leapt into action. With little regard for his eighteen-year-old wife's health and all the foolishness of a child in a tantrum, he wrapped her in a cloak and bundled her into a carriage destined for St James's Palace in London, far away from the sleeping King and Queen. 'For god's sake let me stay where I am!' cried the Princess, as one of her ladies-in-waiting stuffed handkerchiefs up her petticoats to stem the flow of bodily fluids now ruining her lovely silk skirts. Her pleas fell on deaf ears and the couple journeyed on. Over an hour later, the carriage rattled to a halt, and Augusta delivered her first child in St James's Palace in total darkness, lying on tablecloths borrowed from neighbours (the palace was left vacant in the summer months and was therefore woefully underprepared to host a royal birth). When the King and Queen awoke and learnt the news, they were so enraged by their son's childish antics they could not bear to lay eyes upon him. Frederick, Augusta and their new daughter were banished to Leicester House, now with a reputation as the 'pouting place' of Princes.[33] Here, the scorned Prince of Wales dedicated his time to raising his family, designing patriotic hunting uniforms to wear with his friends, and enjoying his favourite pastime: cricket.

Events in the high society calendar now needed to be arranged with expert precision so that both Prince and King could continue with their typical routines, but never have to cross paths with one another in public. One event that both father and son adored was the masquerade, which had emerged onto the social scene during the eighteenth century and positively dominated the annual calendar of events. The masquerade, with its attendees dressed as iconic historical figures or characters from ancient mythologies, afforded members of the royal family the opportunity to enjoy a brief moment of respite from court formality and allowed them to play pretend as if they were any other member of the peerage – in theory, at least. There were a few moments when a costume might successfully beguile a Duke or an Earl into thinking that an attending royal was simply one of their own, such as the time that King George, 'well disguised in an old fashioned English habit' was left giddy after an unsuspecting guest 'desired him to hold their cup as they were drinking tea',[34] but more often than not these well-known royal faces were easily identifiable beneath their masks. This could often work to their advantage, as in much the same way that brands today gift surplus items to celebrities and influencers in order to promote their business, eighteenth-century tradesmen did just the same. In 1742, for example, Princess Augusta arrived at a masquerade dressed as Mary, Queen of Scots, in a gemstone-covered costume that had been gifted to her by a local jeweller on the condition that she reveal to her fellow guests the identity of her supplier.[35]

Costumes for these events had to be decided on carefully, as a wrong choice could have catastrophic political undercurrents. For example, in the year that Princess Augusta appeared in her complimentary jewels, she was described as just one of 'dozens of ugly Queens of Scots' – evidently a popular choice for ladies that season – but just six years later, the Duke and Duchess of Queensbury were banned from court after hosting one unfortunate masquerade in which the Duke appeared in Scottish plaid.[36] In 1745, 'Bonnie Prince Charlie', a descendent of the snubbed King James II, had launched an attempt to reclaim the throne of Great Britain for his Stuart family by triggering a rebellion in Scotland. By the time of the Queensbury masquerade Scottish plaid was 'one of the things in the world that is considered most offensive' as it suggested pro-Stuart sympathies, and a rejection of Hanoverian authority. One observer who witnessed the Queensburies' political blunder could only think to blame such a naive costume choice on some form of madness on the behalf of the hosts.[37]

The years that followed the separation of the King and the Prince of Wales would be littered with personal tragedy for George Augustus. In late 1737, Queen Caroline suffered a long and painful death triggered by an umbilical hernia she had developed a few years previously, and her death left the King unable to make it through most public events without descending into tears for years afterwards. Her brilliant mind and enduring support had been his most reliable crutch as King, and George would forever insist that there was no woman alive 'worthy to buckle her shoe'.[38] In her absence, George's flame began to dim, and he would become as reserved and unremarkable as his father before him. The next disaster was the unexpected death of Prince Frederick on 20 March 1751. A few days previously, he had gone for a walk around Kew Gardens and, mistaking the clear skies for warm weather, switched into 'a light unaired frock and waistcoat' before stepping out into the cold air.[39] He had returned home a little later and fallen asleep on a couch beside an open window, and awoke a few hours later to discover he had developed a chill, one which contributed to his untimely death.

On the morning of 27 October 1760, King George II, now seventy-six years old, was found dead on the floor of his bathroom. He was survived by only three of his eight children. He was laid to rest beside his wife, Caroline, in a special coffin of his own design, which allowed the side panels of both coffins to be removed and the two connected, so that he and Caroline would remain as close together in death as they had been in life.

GEORGE III

THE THIRD KING GEORGE in our story had scarcely emerged from behind the protective barrier of his mother's silk skirts when he ascended to the throne in 1760. At just twenty-two, the first-born son of Prince Frederick and Princess Augusta was the youngest Georgian king to take the throne thus far, and his reign brought with it whispered promises of excitement and change in an ageing royal world. The court had hardly been offered the time to become acquainted with George prior to his accession; a dramatic shift in the way parenting was viewed in the eighteenth century combined with his parents' expulsion from court just before he was born had afforded him the luxury of a private upbringing that hitherto had been unheard of for royal babies. George's childhood played out before the idyllic backdrop of Kew Palace and its surrounding gardens, where under the fond guidance of his parents he would play endless rounds of cricket with his brothers and sisters, tend to his own dedicated patch of the Palace gardens, and help his father entertain guests with practical jokes and play recitals. After Frederick's death, Augusta was committed to instilling in her eldest son a high moral code and a profound appreciation for the role he was one day to inherit, ensuring that by the time George emerged onto the social scene he was on a mission to tidy up the royal circle and serve his country to the best of his ability. Shy, good-natured and quite handsome, the new King was described at the time of his coronation as 'tall and robust . . . his eyes blue . . . his hair a light auburn that grew handsomely in his face' and was still so young that he was prone to the occasional breakout of hormonal pimples.[40]

Deciding who to marry was one of George's first concerns as King. He had for some time now been enamoured with his childhood sweetheart, Lady Sarah Lennox, who was one of four famous Lennox sisters recognized in high society for their beauty, style and scandalous lifestyles. Upon his accession, it had seemed inevitable that George would choose Lady Sarah as his bride, but Princess Augusta, who found the notion of her son marrying a non-royal quite unacceptable, shut down the idea of an engagement and set about finding the next Queen of England herself. After scouring the marriage market, she picked out Sophia Charlotte of Mecklenburg-Strelitz, a minor German princess from a small German duchy. Arrangements were made, the marriage was agreed upon and, in the summer of 1761, Charlotte's measurements were sent ahead to London so that her wedding and coronation dress could be made up in time for her arrival.[41] A few months later, Charlotte would be sent along after them.

Late in the evening of 8 September, barely twenty-four hours after her arrival in England, Charlotte and George were married at St James's Palace, and their coronation was scheduled for later that month. The chapel was draped in crimson and gold fabric, with the King dressed immaculately in a finely tailored suit of frosted silver. His new Queen, however, was entrenched in a silver stiff-bodied gown that was so large on her dainty figure it slouched 'halfway down her waist' and was swamped by an equally oversized purple velvet mantle tethered precariously to her shoulders by ropes of pearls.[42] In the months that had followed the departure of her dress measurements, the seventeen-year-old Charlotte had undergone such a stressful period of change and travel that she had lost a dramatic amount of weight, and with so little time between her arrival in England and her wedding, there was nothing that could be done about the ill-fitting robes. Embarrassing slip-ups such as these would only continue throughout the wedding celebrations. The next day, as Charlotte retired from a celebratory court assembly, her train got caught on a hearth fender and pulled it out into the middle of the room, a blunder which she laughed off and downplayed with an anecdote about a Prussian princess who once set fire to her apartments after her train dragged through a fireplace.[43] It must have been clear to Charlotte from that moment onwards that the world of royal fashion was a complicated and impractical one, and the seed was planted in her mind that it was a world in desperate need of organizing.

Charlotte being plucked from relative obscurity to become consort to the British King has often been credited to a desirably meek nature. In contrast to her predecessor, Caroline of Ansbach, Charlotte posed no real threat of political involvement, and she is sometimes branded as a submissive and rather unremarkable figure. While it's fair to say that Charlotte was certainly more reserved in her ambitions than Queen Caroline had been, that's not to say that she was totally without a backbone. In the months after her wedding, her ladies tried to prompt Charlotte to dress in the English way, in styles that they believed would best please the King, but Charlotte refused to entertain these suggestions. When asked if she would like to try and style her hair in the English manner, Charlotte insisted her unpowdered and uncurled up-do looked just as good as that of her English attendants. When one of her Ladies of the Bedchamber hinted at the styles of dress that the King

preferred, Charlotte scoffed and said: 'Let him dress himself;
I shall dress as I please.'[44] The matter was swiftly put to bed.

George and Charlotte's early married life was harmonious,
largely because of their equally reserved natures and common
interest in courtly decorum. Supervising appropriate dress
amongst their courtiers was to become one of the chief concerns of the King and Queen, and this was hardly easy. The
booming London luxury trade supplied aristocrats and Palace
hopefuls with a plethora of different styles of lace, dresses,
wigs, jewellery and silks, transforming high society into a
dizzying mixture of unique and ostentatious fashions. An
epidemic craze of who-wore-what emerged in the eighteenth-
century court, and people became ravenous for a peek inside
the Palace walls, details of which were spread via newspapers
and through detailed letter correspondences. In the reign of
George III, the press transmitted information on court life
and helped to ensure its relevance, first through text alone
but later, particularly with the introduction of ladies' journals,
through images also. As primitive monochromatic prints of
fashionable ladies and gentlemen at court began to accompany
written descriptions, the birth of the fashion press was signalled – a tool which continues to be one of the most valuable
available to present-day royalty.

Of course, the prospering of the press also offered up a
platform for the monarchy to be critiqued from, and those
printed images posed a great threat to the royal reputation
when they took a satirical or downright detracting tone. All of
this prompted George and Charlotte to police with additional
rigour the collective persona that their court presented to the
world, in an image-control operation that was intense but not
so imperious that they would shy away from criticizing one
another. In 1789, when Charlotte sat for a portrait wearing
informal half-dress, the King refused to have it admitted into

the royal collection, based on a fear that her casual clothing might suggest that the Queen harboured an equally casual view of her duties to the country. The painting was left unseen in the studio of the artist, Sir Thomas Lawrence, who, ironically, had requested that the Queen should dress as she did in private so that she might seem relatable to a greater number of women in society, thereby improving her reputation. Lawrence's concept was far too radical at this stage of the royal family's existence, and while successive generations would flirt with the idea of bourgeois appeal, it was not until the twenty-first century that the royal family would fully embrace relatability as a legitimate aspect of their branding and imagery.

George and Charlotte had begun laying down fashion rules from the moment they came to the throne. In March 1762, Charlotte insisted that all ladies in attendance at court must come dressed in stiff-bodied gowns; while in Britain these had been reserved for royal use only, in the continental courts that the German-born Queen was most familiar with, they were expected of all attendees who wished to show respect to their monarch. The implementation of a court uniform was unwelcome. 'What dreadful discoveries will be made on both fat and lean!' remarked Horace Walpole, in reference to the low necklines of the stiff-bodied gown,[45] and many ladies shuddered at the thought of the money they would now have to spend on decking out their wardrobes with an entirely new style of dress. Unfortunately for Charlotte, her wishes were not followed, for she had yet to accumulate the necessary level of respect required to persuade her courtiers to part ways with their culture of style-hunting and one-upmanship. Instead, the ladies of court continued to wear their tried-and-true mantuas, or the newly court-approved sack dress – a style virtually indistinguishable from the mantua save for a deep pleat that fell from the back of the shoulders to the floor. So Charlotte insisted instead upon much smaller details such as train etiquette: the trains of courtiers had to be pinned up against the left side of the panniers whilst in the royal presence. 'The train which at Versailles trails as a mark of respect is here held up for the same reason,' remarked one visitor to Charlotte's court.[46]

All this fuss about the details of dress might give the impression that George and Charlotte were a fashionably inclined couple, that they joined the ranks of Henry VIII and Mary I as passionate subscribers to style and trend. On the contrary, vanity had never been an issue for George and Charlotte, who had both been raised to understand that their passions and whims paled in significance to their commitment to duty – for them, fashion was simply a necessary aspect of royal life. A tool, and not one that they took much of a personal interest in. George thrived when dressing for formal events, such as coronations or the State Opening of Parliament, where ceremonial clothing was a prerequisite and tradition took precedence over trendiness. In his day-to-day dress, though, the King was clearly not at all in his element, and his 'ill-made coats, and general antipathy to the fashion'[47] were frequently commented upon.

Never was George's commitment to service over style more apparent than with his wigs. The long, full-bottomed wigs of the early century had been phased out of existence by the start of his reign, replaced by a variety of shorter yet far more elaborate options. In the 1760s, however, it became fashionable amongst younger gentlemen to grow out their hair and venture into the world wigless, and being himself still only in his twenties, the King tentatively joined in. This shift in hairstyling preferences caused great distress to local wigmakers, who now watched helplessly as their business was snapped up by foreign hairdressers, and in 1765, a sizable group banded together to present George with a formal petition that they thought might reinvigorate their trade: could His Majesty please start wearing wigs again? The King found the whole thing very funny, but for the sake of helping his country's economy, cut his hair and began commissioning expensive wigs once again, even enforcing them at court and turning away at the gates those that did not comply with his wiggy wishes.[48] Wigs remained a requirement at court for most of George's fifty-nine-year reign, the most common of which was the bagwig – powdered white and curled tight around the temples, the long hair at the back of the head was then held within a black silk bag and tied in place with a little ribbon.

With his view of clothing as an extension of his royal responsibilities, it comes as no surprise that George's principal contribution to fashion history came in the form of a court uniform. Unlike monarchs before him, George III would never serve on the battlefield, but the Hanoverian obsession with military styling was certainly not lost on him. Uniforms appealed to the King in that they allowed him to convey a sense of duty as he carried out his daily tasks whilst also providing him a convenient excuse for not participating in the confusing ebb and flow of fashion. Not having a military position that would entitle him to a regimental uniform, George had to look for a new angle – and it was thus that the Windsor uniform was born. Designed by George to reflect the hunting coats created by his father in the 1720s, the new uniform was a jacket of deep blue with red facing around the cuffs and lapels, worn over buff-coloured breeches and a waistcoat. It came in two forms, half-dress and full-dress (the latter covered with heavy gold embroidery befitting the most formal of court occasions), and was worn typically at Windsor Castle, which the King had made his primary country residence in 1777 to accommodate his rapidly expanding family. George and members of his household wore the Windsor uniform with pride, and this included his wife and daughters, who donned blue and red riding habits inspired by the cut of the men's dress. Soon, through its frequent public appearances, portrait depictions and caricature representations, the distinctive blue and red uniform became the single most recognizable identifier of the King and his circle available to their public.

The latter half of the eighteenth century was a period of great instability and political unrest for the British aristocracy, as both the American War for Independence and the French Revolution brought into question the amount of power a monarch truly possessed. Fear seeped into the minds of the British elite as they watched their French counterparts being exiled and executed, and suddenly the idea of uniformity didn't seem quite as unappealing as it had when Queen Charlotte first suggested it all those years before. Upper-class ladies began adopting the uniforms worn by their husbands as part of their daily dress, and the King began to see an influx in the number of requests he received asking for permission to wear his Windsor uniform. For one royal ball, hosted at Windsor Castle in 1789, it was reported that 'everybody is to appear in a uniform, the men in the King's Hunt [Windsor uniform], which you have often seen, and the ladies in deep blue trimmed with scarlet and gold, the same colours . . . Loyalty is a most expensive virtue at present.'[49]

Dress was quickly becoming one of the most prominent means by which political allegiance could be asserted, and just as the Windsor uniform provided means to express loyalty to the King, it was also a powerful tool for voicing dissent. The Whig political party, for example, adopted for themselves a contrasting buff and blue livery in the 1780s that was nearly identical to the uniforms worn by American officers during the Revolutionary War. The Whig politicians disapproved of the King and his apparent favouritism towards the rival Tory party, and their new Independence-inspired colour scheme would have been read clearly as a message of opposition to the King.[50] The balls and courts of eighteenth-century high society quickly began to resemble a uniformed battlefield more than they did a collage of contemporary fashion – Windsor versus Whig.

In the midst of this turmoil, Queen Charlotte yet again attempted to dictate appropriate court dress, this time taking a more successful route by promoting the continuation of tradition rather than devising a new system from scratch. The key instruction laid down by the Queen was that the hoop skirt was now an unimpeachable necessity for attendees at court, regardless of the fact that fashionable society was, by the 1780s at least, beginning to move towards softer and more natural skirt silhouettes. The ladies of high society complied, but not without their fair share of complaints. In 1786, Jane Austen's sister-in-law described how distressing it had been to spend two hours in a busy court gathering dressed 'with a great hoop of no inconsiderable weight'.[51] It was positively unthinkable to sit down whilst at court, which was regulated by strict rules of etiquette, and so ladies were required to suffer in the heavy hoops without reprieve for hours on end. Soon, court dress would become a point of ridicule amongst society, for as the century came to a close and ladies' waistlines began to rise, the hoop skirt remained fixed – jutting out at a harsh angle from directly beneath the bust and transforming the body into a large, flat rectangle that was neither flattering nor fashionable.

Charlotte (and her daughters, whose wardrobes she controlled) was far more committed to the art of preserving the past through dress; rather than adopting the Empire-line dresses that came to dominate in the later years of her life, the Queen remained loyal to her antiquated court styles. It would not be until late into the 1780s that Charlotte would bid adieu to her sack dresses, and stiff-bodied gowns would not phase out of royal fashion until the final few years of the Queen's life.[52] The effect that these court rules had were varied; those who were forced to abide by them scoffed at the Queen's archaic regulations and quite tellingly chose never to be painted in court dress, lest they be forever remembered in a bizarre style that in no way reflected their personal preference or eye for trends. Outsiders who bore witness to the spectacle tended to feel quite differently and were often moved by the majesty of such a sight. Charlotte's careful orchestrations had transformed the court into a space impervious to the passage of time and by stepping into the Palace walls, you were transported to an era before revolutions destabilized the concept of monarchy, a preserved world where the Crown was still the centrepiece of society.

George and Charlotte's marriage produced fifteen children, with all but the youngest two surviving past infancy. The King was a family man at heart, always happiest when sitting on the floor playing with his children and grandchildren, and he raised his family in a close-knit environment similar to his own upbringing. Before the family had grown too large, George had used Kew Palace as one of their primary dwellings. It was private and surrounded by lush gardens which the King would regularly parade through with his family in a thin line from oldest to youngest, all dressed in matching clothes. The true appeal that Kew held for the royal family was its domesticity. Here, rules on etiquette were markedly different, with the King and Queen carrying out their business unaccompanied by the typical throng of ladies-in-waiting and gentlemen attendants. Clothing too was relaxed, with typical court dress codes set aside in favour of plain and comfortable outfits befitting the 'simplest country gentlefolks' they became whilst at the little Palace.[53] The usually image-conscious royal couple allowed themselves these moments of reprieve only because they had managed to create a sharp distinction between their private and public life, which for royals of the past had always been ceremonially blurred – laying bare the royal family for the entertainment and exaltation of their public. Invitations to private residences were reserved only for the most intimate of friends, with almost all social or ceremonial engagements now firmly allocated to the larger royal residence of St James's or the newly acquired Buckingham House (later Palace). Kew Palace was a safe space away from the public eye in which the royals could be themselves without the fear of unfamiliar faces inspecting them too closely.

This distinction between public and private life manifested itself clearly in the dressing procedure of the King and the Queen. It was a process that occurred twice a day for the royal couple, first when they woke and were helped into their 'casual' half-dress and later, after a morning spent carrying out their own personal business at Kew, when they travelled to court and were dressed in all their regal finery, ready to entertain guests for the afternoon. If not dressed in the Windsor uniform, full-dress for the King consisted of a waistcoat and breeches over which a long, slim, silk coat was worn. The thick embroidery that had characterized court dress of the earlier half of the century became localized to the cuffs, collar and hemlines of men's clothes. They were typically floral patterns made with colourful thread, and Charlotte, in particular, took great pleasure in being the hand behind her husband's neat embroidery, assisting in the finishing of his clothes on many occasions.

In 1786, the novelist Fanny Burney was appointed as a keeper of the Queen's robes, and her diary provides a detailed glimpse into the process of dressing a member of the royal family. At 7.30 a.m., Fanny would be called to the Queen, who by this time had already had her hair dressed. Then, with the assistance of a more experienced colleague, she would help the Queen to dress. The exact order in which each item should be put on or handed to the Queen was dictated by old and confusing traditions that even Fanny herself strug-gled with, and she relied upon her colleague to understand them: 'I should never know which to take first, embarrassed as I am, and should run a prodigious risk of giving the gown before the hoop, and the fan before the neckerchief!'[54] Around midday, the Queen's hair was powdered, and she would then travel to St James's, where she was helped into all of her court finery. With an annual salary of £200, Fanny's position in the royal household was extraordinarily comfortable, and she was no stranger to receiving additional perks from her royal employer, whom she often records as having a sensitivity 'that one would not expect belonged to her high status'.[55] Fanny, like many other important members of the Queen's staff, could also expect to receive second-hand clothes and accessories as a reward for their service. This long-standing royal tradition was beginning to take a toll on Palace finances, as was revealed by the Queen in a letter to her treasurer in 1792, describing a spot of financial bother: 'the bills I know are high this quarter but etiquette will have it so, for the quantity of lace and linen . . . and the clothes are far more than I want . . . and some years ago I meant and wished to have less and change seldomer but was advised against it on account of the noise it would make amongst the bedchamber women.'[56] Tradition elsewhere in court life may have been serving to reinforce the monarchy, but here, where the Queen was being pushed to buy more clothes than she ever wanted to wear just to please the expectations of her staff, it was carving out a real financial problem.

On 2 August 1786, Fanny Burney was carrying out her business at Windsor when an attempt was made on the King's life. She was present too when George animatedly recounted the ordeal to his family just a few hours later and noted his story down in her diary. As he disembarked his carriage outside St James's earlier that day, a smartly dressed woman had approached him with a written petition, only to lunge at him with a dessert knife as he reached forward to take it. The knife was snatched from her hand before it could strike, and she was violently seized by onlookers seeking to exact vigilante justice upon the King's attacker. George, who was calm despite having only narrowly avoided death, cried out to the crowd, 'The poor creature is mad! — Do not hurt her! She has not hurt me!'[57] and the woman was thankfully left unharmed. The King's assumption was correct: Margaret Nicholson, a mantua maker, was later certified insane after it was discovered she believed herself to be the rightful heir to the throne. George's reputation was indefinitely helped by his compassion towards Nicholson, though if the King had hoped that his own mental health concerns would be treated with anywhere near the same amount of care as he had shown for others, he was sorely mistaken.

In 1788, the monarchy entered one of its darkest periods, which, according to contemporary opinion, could be blamed on the King's stockings. George had experienced periods of mental instability over the course of his reign, particularly around 1765, when he was briefly removed from the public eye on account of a drastic personality change that had seen his usually pleasant nature become 'a good deal estranged'.[58] At the time, the King's brief illness had been easy to write off as a combination of both a chest infection and a depressive episode, but in October 1788, it became impossible to ignore the deterioration in his mental health. George began to oscillate

wildly between periods of hyperactivity – he would speak rapidly and nonsensically until his mouth foamed and his voice
ran hoarse, and his words and behaviour would be crude,
inappropriate or downright violent – and periods of inactivity,
before returning to his gentle and amicable self. The diagnosis
at the time was that 'humours' in his legs, caused by damp
stockings that had not been changed promptly enough after
becoming soiled, had spread throughout his body and into his
brain.[59] The King was acutely aware of this degeneration, and
the uncertainty of the situation left the court, the country and
George himself in a state of distress and anxiety.

George's treatment was nothing short of torture – involving bloodletting, blistering and long periods confined within a
'straight-waistcoat' (what we would call a straitjacket). Unsurprisingly, this did little to improve the King's troubled mind
and conversely resulted in his physical health deteriorating
rapidly too. Four months later, after the King had finally been
moved from the care of unqualified palace physicians to that
of doctors well versed in treating mental illnesses, George
seemed to make a complete recovery. Many events were held
to celebrate the King's return to good health, most of which
saw attendees make an effort to articulate their relief through
dress. At the crowded 'Grand Restoration Drawing Room',
where courtiers attended en masse to witness the King's
return to the public eye, Queen Charlotte instructed her ladies
and daughters to wear blue and orange – the colours adopted
by the politician William Pitt and his fellow members at the
Constitution Club, who had held out hope for the King's
recovery and countered calls for a regency to be introduced.[60]
At the thanksgiving service hosted at St Paul's Cathedral on
23 April, the King and Princes were dressed in full-dress
Windsor uniform, with the Queen and Princesses in purple
silk dresses trimmed with gold. The royal women, along with

many other ladies in the crowd, threaded their hair with white ribbons embroidered with the motto 'God save the King' in gold thread, a trend that remained a part of women's court dress consistently thereafter.[61] The phrase was evidently more necessary at that point than it had ever been in living memory.

The relief of the country would not be long-lived, as by 1811 the seventy-two-year-old King had relapsed, and the Prince of Wales took over his father's responsibilities as Prince Regent. Heavily satirized, George's final years as King were made increasingly harder by the onset of dementia, blindness and the heart-breaking absence of his wife. In the earlier stages of his malady, George had insisted that 'the Queen is my physician, and no man can have a better; she is my friend, and no man can have a better', though his increasingly erratic temperament later forced her to seek solitude from her husband.[62] By the time of her death in 1818, George was incapable of comprehension. According to a letter written by Rev. William Monsell (chaplain to the King's eldest son), the elderly George was only ever seen in a long dressing gown of damask satin, under which he wore a matching waistcoat with sleeves. Long-sleeved waistcoats weren't modish, but for the sick and elderly who needed additional warmth they were commonplace. King George III passed away in 1820, at the time the longest-reigning monarch in British history. According to Monsell, not long after the King's passing, he was offered a selection of his clothes including a dressing gown and waistcoat, 'which I consider rather interesting as I have no doubt it was the last article he wore in this world'.[63] The Reverend declined to take the gown on the grounds that it was much too stained, but the waistcoat was accepted and survives today in the care of the Royal Ceremonial Dress Collection, giving us an intimate glimpse into the final days of King George. The garment was clearly designed to accommodate the King's declining physical health, with puffed inserts of fabric added around the armholes to make it easier for George to be dressed. The front still bears stains of vomit or dribbled food that immortalize the difficulties he faced in the twilight of his reign.

With a legacy often watered down to that of a comedy madman, it is King George III whom we must thank for the shape of the modern monarchy, particularly in regard to their approach to clothing. Royal dress was now entirely separate from the fickle and rapid movements of fashionable society, and while there would be occasional moments of overlap in the future, it would now always be clear that the sartorial agenda of the royal family followed its own distinct path. George and Charlotte's aversion to the whims of fashion may have made them the butt of jokes of the more stylish characters of their time, but ultimately it served them and the future of the royal family very well. They had set a precedent that successful monarchs of future generations would carefully follow: the importance of royal dress was now to consider one's place in the progression of history, as opposed to one's place in the fleeting landscape of fashion.

GEORGE IV

IN 1785, THE ELDEST SON of King George III sat for one very special portrait. This was, in the eyes of the young Prince George, his final chance to win the heart of the love of his life, and what better way to do it than by sending her a miniature painting of his eye? Early the year before, the twenty-two-year-old Prince had met Maria Fitzherbert, blonde, accomplished and six years his senior, on an outing in London and found himself quite suddenly infatuated with her. The future King dedicated himself to Maria with a passion so intense he happily ignored the red flags that presented themselves. His inamorata, on the other hand, was far more level-headed and understood that their relationship could never be: Maria was a Catholic, and in accordance with the Act of Succession 1701, no spouse of a Catholic could ascend to the throne. The King would never willingly agree to this marriage, which was yet another condition that would be necessary if their union was to be considered lawful. Maria fled the country in the hope that the Prince's passion would be quelled with time, though evidently it was not as here we are at the creation of George's miniature eye portrait. The finished product was to be sent to Maria, along with a forty-two-page letter in which George proposed a secret marriage with the eye standing as a substitute engagement ring: 'P.S. . . . I send you at the same time an eye if you have not totally forgotten the whole countenance. I think the likeness will strike you.'[64]

George's final push was a success – Maria, either exasperated by the length of the Prince's declaration or charmed by his gift, returned to England to marry him in a clandestine ceremony. Not long after the wedding, the secret royal bride commissioned a miniature of her own eye, which George wore frequently, pinned above his heart and hidden by the lapels of his silk suits – their marriage was the worst-kept secret in high society. Inspired by the gesture's newfound royal pedigree, it became commonplace amongst the young and fashionable to exchange eye miniatures fixed into jewellery in an attempt to emulate some of the enigmatic charm of George and Maria's secret romance. Hundreds of these little mysteries filled the jewellery boxes of high-society ladies and gentlemen, their subjects only identifiable by the colour of the iris, the set of the eye socket, the shape of the brow. It's a deeply romantic trend, one of many that George would have a hand in igniting, being a man for whom the affairs of the heart would often outweigh the importance of duty and service.

The reign of George III, which as we have seen was governed by his measured nature and dedication to high moral standards, was underscored by the scandalous lives led by his many children. Illegitimate grandchildren born from actresses and lower nobility arrived in a steady stream, and even his daughters, most of whom never married, had their fair share of affairs and rumoured secret pregnancies. Prince George, or 'Prinny' as he was known to those closest to him, was the worst of the lot and would 'at all times prefer a girl and a bottle to politics and a sermon'.[65] Prinny's problems had started at eighteen, when he had reached his majority and was allowed to move into his own residence at Carlton House.

Growing up, he had always shown great promise, excelling in his studies and making a strong impression on courtiers for his 'engaging and distinguished manners', but now, with his own money and no one to govern him, George entered a period of his life ruled only by his pleasure-seeking nature.[66] His fatal flaw would always be his finances, for despite being offered an annual income of £50,000 the Prince of Wales was incapable of living within his means (the originally proposed figure of £100,000 had been shot down by his father, who did not wish to be complicit in what he saw as 'a shameful squandering of public money . . . to the wishes of an ill-advised young man'[67] and thought the money was better spent on charitable endeavours instead).

A great portion of the Prince's spending was dedicated to his appearance, and within ten years of moving into Carlton House he was already £31,912 in debt to his tailors alone (the equivalent of just over £5 million today).[68] George spent nearly every waking moment fussing over the contents of his wardrobe, an understandable pastime considering that his mistrusting father was wary of giving him any serious responsibilities to keep him occupied. He was jealous of the military appointments that were awarded to his brothers, but he was denied, as in typical Hanoverian style he was entranced by uniform and desperate for one that he could call his own. After much fuss, Prince George was made colonel of the 10th Light Dragoons in 1793, a role which suited his character nicely for it only required him to parade himself and his troops before the public in their sparkling blue and silver uniform, a uniform that George himself had invested a great deal of effort into designing. Privately, he continued to yearn for a more substantial position and began ordering uniforms for regiments and ranks he had no affiliation with, solely for his own private enjoyment.[69]

George's eye for detail, which led him to make poignant contributions to Britain's artistic and architectural landscape, was as meticulous as it was expensive. On one occasion, the sculptor John Rossi found himself at Carlton House waiting three long hours while the Prince tried on 'at least forty pairs of shoes' and fussed over the patterns for his clothes.[70] The time and effort that George put into developing his fashion knowledge meant that he was a trusted opinion amongst his friends and family, often stepping in to shape and fill their wardrobes too. When his brothers were stationed outside the country, it was George they trusted to organize their clothing orders, and in 1793, when the Duke of York was preparing for his wedding, Prince George was tasked with the role of sourcing jewels, accessories and even a hairdresser for the bride – his future sister-in-law.[71] After his marriage to Maria Fitzherbert, Prinny's lifestyle of womanizing and gambling calmed, but naturally he couldn't help but spend money on transforming his once-commoner bride into the glamorous wife of a Prince, spending £54,000 on clothes, jewellery and furniture for her and her new home in Pall Mall.[72]

In typical Hanoverian fashion, Prince George had a very poor relationship with his father, and the two conflicting personalities frequently butted heads. Matters were made worse by George III's stubborn refusal to cover any of his son's debts, and their familial bond quickly disintegrated. Prinny capitalized on the uniform craze that dominated the political landscape of the time to drive home his dislike of his father, announcing his allegiance to the Crown-critical Whig party by dressing his household in an 'extremely costly and elegant'[73] buff and blue uniform, and complaining or refusing to wear the Windsor uniform at events for which it was the required dress. With the King unwilling to pay off his son's debts, the Prince of Wales was forced to seek an alternative solution: marry a proper Princess so that Parliament would have to raise his allowance. In 1794, George abruptly severed his ties with 'Princess Fitz', insisting that their marriage had never been valid and declaring his intention to marry Princess Caroline of Brunswick, his German cousin of whom the King was certain to approve. Hurt and betrayed, Maria Fitzherbert retreated in shock from George's life but would always assert that their marriage had been legitimate, a sentiment shared by those closest to the couple. Many years later, after George's death, his brother would grant Maria permission to dress her household in the royal livery, and encouraged her to dress in widow's weeds, treating her marriage to the late royal with as much validity as she herself had viewed it with.[74]

Had George taken even a moment to ask after the personality of Princess Caroline, he would have quickly realized that the marriage was doomed to fail. Lord Malmesbury certainly realized the impending disaster when he was sent to retrieve the Princess from her homeland and came face to face with Caroline: short and fair, boisterous, and giddy about her future as Queen of the United Kingdom. Malmesbury was taken aback at just how outspoken she was, and quickly discovered that she possessed very few of the traits that Britain was used to seeing in their queens. Thankfully, Caroline was eager to learn and Malmesbury willing to teach: 'I preached my constant theme; Discretion, reserve, no familiarity, and less talking.'[75] The most pressing problem to Malmesbury was Caroline's lack of interest in personal hygiene, something that he tried to rectify through subtle encouragement. He had been made aware through Caroline's own boasting on the speediness with which she washed and dressed that the Princess was wholly unaware of the extent to which she was neglecting herself and tried 'as far as was possible for a *man*, to inculcate the necessity of great and nice attention to every part of dress, as well as to what was hid'.[76] It was worryingly apparent that the vain Prince George was perhaps the most ill-suited man to marry this scatter-brained Princess.

When Malmesbury felt that there was no more guidance he could provide for his royal pupil, he returned to England with Princess Caroline in tow. They arrived at Greenwich on 5 April 1795 and Caroline's new English attendants helped to exchange her 'coarse petticoats, coarse shifts, and thread stockings . . . never washed well, or changed enough' for a white satin dress and green satin mantle trimmed with gold.[77] Stubbornly, the Princess refused to wear the satin turban presented to her – which in fashionable circles was now considered the most modish headdress – and instead clung on to the beaver hat with blue and black feathers that she had brought with her from Brunswick. From Greenwich, the Princess and her cohort flocked to greet the King and Prince George, a meeting so disastrous that the Prince of Wales fled from the room in urgent search of a glass of brandy and Caroline, forgetting all of Malmesbury's lessons, announced to the room, 'My God! Is the Prince always like that? I find him very fat, and not as handsome as his portrait!'[78]

George was rattled by the behaviour of his bride-to-be. No doubt anticipating a demure and submissive Princess whom he could easily ignore in favour of his many mistresses, he was now faced with a bride who spoke flippantly and with coarse language, who was loud and did not hesitate to make her voice and presence known in any room that she found herself in. The public too were disappointed with their new Princess of Wales. 'Such a falling-off from our grand expectations!' cried one aristocrat who clearly had hoped that the royal marriage would supply her some new form of entertainment; 'the Princess of Wales, who was to afford a new model for our fashions, our manners, our pleasures – who for an instant could have supposed the bride of our divine Prince would turn out such a vulgar hoyden?'[79] Caroline's wedding dress had been prepared ahead of her arrival, first by the King, who studied documents to ensure the dress matched the requirements set by historical precedent, and then by Queen Charlotte, who personally oversaw the dressmaking process. The wedding itself was a miserable affair, with everyone in attendance acutely aware of the couple's mutual disgust for one another. The Prince and Princess of Wales would go on to live separate lives with as little interaction as they could manage, but not before the birth of their only child almost exactly nine months after their wedding: Princess Charlotte.

If Prince George had thought even for a moment that in his wife's absence he would now be free from the torment of outspoken and brash women, he was to be sorely disappointed – his daughter turned out to be an even more formidable foe. Charlotte emerged into court life during her father's regency as a relative stranger to the people and customs that made up the social world she would one day preside over. After her mother was driven out of Carlton House by Prince George's cruelty, baby Charlotte had remained in his care and was kept under close supervision throughout her childhood. Cheeky, tomboyish and rebellious at heart, Charlotte's contact with the outside world was limited and her relationship with her father strained. It wasn't until 1813 that Charlotte would be allowed to attend her first ball, dressed in a white lace gown with a plume of feathers in her hair, and not until 1814 was she presented formally at court. For this last occasion, the public clamoured outside the gates of Buckingham House to catch a glimpse of what the young heir was wearing. It was reported in the press that she wore 'an elegant petticoat of rich white satin, with a superb border of the same, and a wreath of silver laurel-leaves tastefully intermixed with white roses . . .

Headdress: a profusion of the most beautiful diamonds and ostrich feathers.'[80]

Princess Charlotte was the antithesis of her father, and the public adored her for it. Intelligent and well versed in current affairs, this Princess, who was 'rather like a young rascal dressed as a girl', also cared very little for the intricacies of fashion and was always to be seen in the slender empire-line dresses that came to define the Regency period.[81] Simple and unstructured, these gowns were inspired by the drapery of statues found at the newly unearthed sites of ancient Pompeii and Herculaneum, and perfectly complemented Charlotte's free-spirited nature. Quite often courtiers commented on her masculine behaviour – how she rode fast and with no fear, how she shook hands with everyone she met, and how she swaggered around the Palace corridors. She gravitated towards similarly practical styles, for which she was often reprimanded. In 1811, the Princess had adopted long drawers as underwear, the masculine equivalent to the chemise typically worn by ladies, popular among members of the working class but still a novel aspect of aristocratic women's dress. 'My dear Princess Charlotte, you show your drawers!' scolded her governess, Lady de Clifford, as the Princess reclined after dinner one night. 'I don't care if I do,' replied Charlotte tartly, yet the governess pushed on: 'Your drawers are too long!' With her usual unyielding resolve, Charlotte insisted 'I do not think so – the Duchess of Bedford's are much longer!' and the matter was put to bed.[82] Evidently, though her sharp nose, tall stature and chestnut hair made the Princess the spitting image of her Hanoverian relatives, it was from her mother that Charlotte developed her personality, and Prince George treated her accordingly with an icy disdain.

The Prince Regent had tried to keep Charlotte isolated from court life for as long as physically possible, but by the year of her presentation she was already showing signs of defiance that he could not control or dismiss. George employed the assistance of sisters Lucy and Charlotte Cotes to keep a watchful eye on his wayward daughter, which was, if the Prince's choice of reward for the sisters is anything to go by, a monumental task. When Charlotte left their domineering care after her wedding in 1816, George presented the sisters with an impressive set of gold and peridot jewellery as thanks for carrying out the difficult task of policing the headstrong future Queen.[83]

Charlotte's marriage to Leopold of Saxe-Coburg in 1816 (a match that she had selected and battled with her father to have approved) ushered in the first period of freedom that she had ever experienced. The couple married in a private ceremony in the crimson drawing room of Carlton House, with Charlotte wearing a court dress of silver tissue embellished with the finest-point Brussels lace, silver flowers and silver seashells.[84] Though it was her grandmother, Queen Charlotte, who had organized her trousseau, the wedding dress did not feature one of her antiquated hoop skirts, as Prince George had personally requested they be left off for this occasion. (George was not at all fond of the hoop skirt, and it was under his instruction that the unflattering item would be scrapped from court protocol in 1820.) Once the honeymoon period was over, it was time for Charlotte and Leopold to make their mark on London high society, flitting between balls, drawing rooms and theatres arm in arm and utterly besotted with one another – Charlotte in her simple dresses, wrapped in costly cashmere shawls and with her hair arranged in her signature chignon bun encircled by a wreath of fresh roses. Leopold always by her side in a sharply cut suit decorated with his insignia.

As a married woman with her own household, Charlotte was no longer trapped under her father's thumb, but that didn't stop them from making sly jabs at one another. In 1817, the now pregnant Princess invested in a vibrant blue sarafan trimmed with gold, which was to be worn over a lace blouse, a garment originating from Russian folk costume. She wore the sarafan when she sat for the artist George Dawe that same year, paired with the star of the Order of St Catherine of Russia, in what is a seemingly flattering and innocent wardrobe choice. The outfit takes a very different meaning when you consider that just a few years previously Charlotte and the Prince Regent had met the visiting Tsar of Russia, whom George had clearly not got along with. It's clear that though Charlotte cared very little for the details of her clothes, she understood their power and could hold her own on the sartorial battlefield that her father was master of, in this case utilizing the sarafan as means to express her newfound independence – of both action and mind. Later that year, Charlotte would begin a long and tortuous labour that culminated in the birth of a stillborn son on 5 November. Two days later, despite initially seeming healthy and composed, Charlotte too would pass away, and the country was thrust into one of the most intense mourning periods in living memory.

The death of Princess Charlotte of Wales brought the royal family a whole host of problems. Two heirs to the throne had been lost within a matter of days, the King was still incurably mad, and the country was being lorded over by a Prince Regent whom the public despised and who was now being blamed for contributing to the death of his only child. Upon his accession in 1820, King George IV felt he had been presented with the perfect opportunity to fix his poor relationship with the public: a coronation – the bigger the better. Immediately, the new King set about researching the famous rulers that he idolized and analysing the contemporaries that he envied, seeking to expand his knowledge of historical precedents so that he could be certain that his coronation would be the most brilliant ever seen. Beginning with the Stuart kings, George consulted Francis Sandford's *History of the Coronation of . . . King James II*, a contemporary text that documented in extreme detail the proceedings and arrangement of the controversial King's grand ceremony and was filled with illustrations depicting the regalia used. The text often formed the basis of coronation planning but George, motivated by his love of theatricality, took the instructions very literally and decided to theme the robes for his coronation around this seventeenth-century example. A steady stream of tailors and jewellers passed through the King's Brighton residence to assist him in designing the robes that he himself, his family, the peerage and attendants would be appearing in.

There seems to have been a good deal of murmuring amongst those who were privy to the plans, and a consensus was formed within the peerage that the historical costumes they were being instructed to don would likely rouse only bouts of laughter from the populace, not the patriotic respect that George was hoping for. Soon they came to appreciate the ruffs and silk slashed doublets that the King had commissioned, and praised the uniformed congregation it created, against which George stood out as its glittering apex. Costing over £240,000 (of which a staggering £24,000 was spent on George's clothes alone), the coronation was the most expensive ever seen and was only too fitting for the King of overindulgence.[85]

There was, however, one thing that was glaringly absent at the coronation: the Queen. George had tried in vain to secure a formal divorce from Caroline of Brunswick for many years, but all that this public humiliation of his estranged wife had achieved was public outrage. Now a very popular figure in society, Caroline managed to elicit sympathy from the population, which only served to further enrage her husband. When

George ascended to the throne, Caroline made it clear that she was coming to collect her title of Queen, even enquiring of her husband what she should wear to *their* coronation. George was having none of it and had her barred from the event. When Caroline arrived at Westminster Abbey, the doors were shut in her face, forcing her to climb back into her carriage and return home. A few weeks later, Caroline fell ill and passed away, her death striking a fatal blow to her husband's hope that the coronation might revive his public image.

The King was fifty-nine years old at the time of his coronation, and the evidence of his indulgent lifestyle was by now very prominent; many of George's wardrobe choices were calculated to disguise his rapidly expanding figure. Included in his coronation ensemble was a girdle corset, which, knowing he was going to be the centre of attention, he had laced particularly tight. As a consequence, George nearly collapsed in the heat of the summer sun, but it did little to put him off the practice and he wore his corset frequently from then on, spending up to three hours each day having himself cinched to a desirable shape.[86] In 1824, his corsets measured for a waist of fifty inches, which George further masked through the use of sharply tailored suits in flattering dark colours. He gravitated towards pantaloons rather than knee breeches, as they disguised the size of his legs, and chose coats with high collars and immaculately arranged cravats to conceal his prominent double chins.

George's style preferences were also influenced by the shapes and colours seen in the up-and-coming dandyism trend. In his youth, the primary fashion faction had been the 'macaronis', stylish young men who wore brightly coloured clothes with elaborate and highly styled wigs, and George had found himself surrounded by these colourful characters. Richard Cosway (a friend of the King's and the artist behind the lover's eye miniature given to Mrs Fitzherbert) was one such macaroni, always to be seen 'clothed in a mulberry silk coat embroidered with scarlet strawberries, with a sword and bag and small three-cornered hat perched on top of his powdered toupee'.[87] In 1795, the hold that powdered wigs had for so long enjoyed over eighteenth-century fashion was lost when the government introduced a tax on hair powder, and fashionable circles began the transition from sculpted artifice to natural beauty.

Figure-heading this transition was George 'Beau' Brummell, a revolutionary figure in men's fashion who argued for simple yet finely cut tailoring with reserved colours and few embellishments. Like King George, Brummell's eye for detail was precise and discerning. Often spending hours at a time tying his cravat each morning, it's unsurprising that Brummell and the King gravitated towards one another and quickly became a formidable duo in the shaping of men's fashion in the early nineteenth century. Yet Brummell's ideas on masculine self-fashioning went far deeper than the cut and construction of his chic navy-blue suit jackets; at its core it was a promotion of a more refined moral character for the modern gentleman, with sharp and sensible clothing being only an outward manifestation of the dignified behaviour he valued so highly. George's lifestyle of gambling, drinking and womanizing hardly fit Beau's archetype of the ideal man, and these differences contributed to their dramatic falling-out in 1813, putting an end to their brief period of fashion collaboration.

In 1822, George IV became the first Hanoverian King to visit Scotland. The dynasty's relationship with their Scottish subjects had been a turbulent one thus far, but with the death of Henry, Cardinal of York, in 1807 signalling the end of the Royal Stuart line, the Jacobite claim to the English throne was extinguished and much animosity quietened with it. George's trip was orchestrated by his friend the famed Scottish novelist Sir Walter Scott, who viewed his new responsibility as an opportunity to showcase and solidify Scottish national identity. Of course, dress played a key role in his mission, and in an anonymous pamphlet distributed prior to the King's arrival, Scott laid out in immense detail the importance of appearing before the King in 'the ancient Highland costume'.[88] Highland dress was an incredibly sensitive topic in the eighteenth century, with tartan and other aspects of the traditional costume having been criminalized by the Dress Act 1746 after the Jacobite rebellion. After the act was repealed in the 1780s, tartan was only tentatively readopted, but Scott hoped that the King's visit might prompt a surge in interest – and it did. The pamphlet went on to detail how ladies presented to the King intended to have their court train made of silk tartan, and that the King himself had sought a London-based tailor to create a Highland costume for his own use. The trip was a success in that it renewed interest in Scottish plaid, and George was keen to have the visit immortalized by a portrait of him wearing his new, red, highland dress. David Wilkie, the artist chosen to complete the piece, may have included the King's comically too-short kilt, but he conveniently omitted the unsightly pink stockings George wore to keep his legs warm. The artist also trimmed off a few inches from his subject's waist, though later he would compare the King to 'a great sausage, stuffed into the covering'.[89]

'I ought to have been the man and he the woman to wear the petticoats,' Queen Caroline had once announced in reference to her husband's ineptitude. 'He understands how a shoe should be made or a coat cut and would make an excellent tailor, or shoemaker, or hairdresser but nothing else!'[90] She was certainly not alone in thinking this. Two months after Wilkie's highland painting was exhibited in April 1830, when King George IV passed away at Windsor Castle, he was mourned by very few; having never realized his goal of patching up his reputation, he survived in the minds of his people as little more than a degenerate and useless ruler. The King was laid to rest in St George's Chapel and, in keeping with one of his final requests, was buried with a small portrait hung from his neck – the miniature eye of Maria Fitzherbert.[91]

Part Four

THE VICTORIA EFFECT

In July 1818, King George III and Queen Charlotte had at least fourteen living grandchildren. The death of Princess Charlotte at the end of the previous year had robbed the family of a dearly loved child and the country of a much-adored heir, but most pressingly it had left the world with one daunting question: who comes next? Given the utterly dire state of relations between the Prince and Princess of Wales, there was little use in hoping for another child of theirs, and so all eyes fell expectantly upon the Prince's many brothers and sisters. There was a plethora of potential heirs sired by these other Princes and Princesses: there was the Duke of Kent with one child, the Duke of Sussex with a boy and a girl; even Princess Sophia had a teenage son and, quite spectacularly, the Duke of Clarence had fathered ten children. Despite this seemingly limitless supply of potential kings and queens, it was a ludicrously inconceivable notion to suggest that any of them would ascend to the throne in Princess Charlotte's place – King George and Queen Charlotte may have had fourteen grandchildren but none of those grandchildren were legitimate.

For most of their adult lives, the children of George III had enjoyed relationships with duchesses, actresses and equerries as and when it suited them, but now it was time for them to commit to duty and step *up* to the task of settling *down*. Four royal weddings took place in 1818, but arguably the most important of these was a double ceremony at Kew Palace on 11 July, where Queen Charlotte's drawing room had been hurriedly transformed into a makeshift venue complete with a temporary altar and ceremonial plate transported from the royal chapels. The grooms were Prince William, Duke of Clarence, and his younger brother Prince Edward, Duke of Kent; their brides were Princess Adelaide of Saxe-Meiningen and Princess Victoire of Saxe-Coburg-Saalfeld. The brides, both significantly younger than their middle-aged fiancés, were brought down the aisle on each arm of the Prince Regent and dressed in identical gowns with wreaths of diamonds in their hair – Adelaide in silver, Victoire in gold. From the get-go, the pressure was high for these two German princesses to supply their new family with potential heirs, and it was with this wedding that a royal baby race commenced.

Later that year, Queen Charlotte passed away, content in the knowledge that she now had multiple legitimate grand-children on the way. Eventually, the aptly named Princess Victoria of Kent would become the victor of the baby race, and her reign would be one of the most significant in royal history. Before any of that, however, little Victoria had to wait in line behind her uncles – George IV and William IV.

WILLIAM IV

AT THE TIME OF HIS BIRTH, William, Duke of Clarence, was comfortably situated behind his older brothers George and Frederick as third in line for the throne. Far enough from the action for his family to assume that the dangers of active service would not imperil the immediate line of succession, William was allowed to lead the life that his brother George had always dreamed of, and at the age of thirteen joined the navy as a midshipman. Over the next eleven years the Duke of Clarence would climb steadily through the ranks, earning himself the position of rear-admiral in 1789 and the moniker the 'Sailor King' in later life. This was one of the nicer nicknames that William would accumulate, others being 'Coconut Head' in reference to his unusually pointed skull and 'Silly Billy' on account of his somewhat frazzled personality. 'What can you expect from a man with a head like a pineapple?' was the conclusion drawn by one of William's contemporaries.[1]

Long before his marriage to Princess Adelaide, William had lived a life to rival his badly behaved siblings' and in 1791 he moved in with the Irish actress Dorothy Jordan – his sweetheart and the mother of his hoard of illegitimate children. In their relationship it was Dorothy who governed their social appeal, as only the talents of a successful comedy actress such as herself could counter the mediocrity of Silly Billy, who was known to be very dull and a little dim, though incredibly well-intended. Dorothy had made her mark on the London stage with her successful stints in 'breeches roles', playing young male characters and flaunting her physique in men's clothes. The type of role had emerged as part of the gaudy Restoration entertainment scene and pulled in audiences with the tantalizing promise of popular actresses letting down their hair, exposing their legs and even their breasts. By Dorothy's time the cliché was clearly still a crowd pleaser, though breaking gender binaries was by no means a novel concept in the high-society circles that she now found herself in. After all, one of the characters in the future George IV's circle was Chevalier d'Éon, who had transitioned from male to female in the 1770s and could often be seen demonstrating her exceptional fencing skills at matches hosted in Carlton House, dressed in fine dresses with medals from her military days pinned to her silk bodice.[2]

You would be hard pressed to find William wearing anything other than his naval uniform, though on the odd occasion he went without it, he turned to his favourite plain green cloth coat and beaver hat. Unlike his father or his brother George, the Duke of Clarence's love of uniform came not from a sense of duty or an eye for fashion but from his immense sense of pride in his naval career, and he always seemed to impress people with his sharp appearance: 'He always wears his uniform and no curls and yet looks as well dressed and more of a man than any of the fashionable powder monkies!'[3] When he had first joined up as a midshipman, his clothing had naturally been dictated to him, and his trunk included: '2 uniforms, a short blue coat of the jacket make, with uniform buttons and waistcoat and breeches . . . 3 dozen shirts . . . 3 dozen pairs of stockings . . . 2 hats and 2 round ones – hats are liable to be lost overboard!' After being given command of the frigate HMS *Andromeda* in 1788, he was afforded the opportunity to style his crew however he wished.[4] Cohesive uniformity was important for his designs, and while no one could argue that they were ugly uniforms, those who had to wear and work in them found that they were not the least bit practical. 'It was his Royal Highness's pleasure undoubtedly that there should be a uniformity,' wrote one disgruntled officer, 'but the dress was of his own imagination and quite at variance from that which the Service prescribed. Old and young, tall, and short, all were to be alike; the boy of twelve years old was to be rigged out as a man, and so squeezed into a tight dress as to leave no chance of growing, unless, perchance, nature's efforts should prove more than a match for the tailor's stitches.'[5]

In contrast to the dutiful and organized man he appeared to be when commanding the seas, when at home in London, Prince William managed his finances as disastrously as his brother Prinny. He often found himself so up to his ears in debt that even the additional and sizable income of Dorothy Jordan couldn't help cover it. Dorothy herself had contributed somewhat to their financial mishaps, having spent lavishly to update their apartments with suitably theatrical decor. She had found that the benefits of high-society life were very much to her tastes and used the connections to bolster her already flourishing theatre career: '*Influence* you must have everywhere,' she wrote to William near the start of their relationship and asked if he had any power over the press to help stave off any negative criticism she was receiving.[6] The Prince helped as much as he could, though he did not have any direct control over the newspapers and was himself subject to many scathing caricatures. It was common for illustrators to rely upon the Prince's naval uniform as a visual shorthand, and they would wittily crown him with a chamber pot – the colloquial term for which was, aptly, a 'jordan'. Ultimately, it was financial issues that prompted their separation in 1811, for in order to cover his debts William had decided that he must marry an heiress. He sent a letter to Dorothy, calling her to Maidenhead so that they could say one final goodbye, and after a performance of *The Devil to Pay* (during which she burst into tears on stage), she hopped straight into her carriage to see him. Still dressed in her stage costume (a floral 'peasant' dress with a tartan scarf over her shoulders and a gigantic, frilly bonnet on her head), Dorothy said a teary goodbye to William, who vowed to financially provide for both her and her children as best he could.[7]

And so it was, after years of searching for an heiress, William ended up marrying a Princess instead. Princess Adelaide was just twenty-five when she married the Prince, and by the time of William's accession in 1830 they had conceived four children, none of which were still alive. The simplicity of neoclassical dress had now been totally eclipsed by the extravagance of the 1830s, with women's waistlines lowered to their natural place, skirts finished just above the ankle, and giant, ballooning leg-o'-mutton sleeves reinforced with wire frames to create their epic dimensions. Unlike the unwavering Queen Charlotte, Adelaide allowed the shapes and styles of contemporary fashion to bleed into women's court dress, though on occasion her conservative tastes would force her to intervene. 'The Queen is a prude,' scoffed one contemporary in reference to her dislike for low necklines, 'and will not let ladies to come *décolletées* to her parties. George IV, who liked ample expanses of that sort, would not let them be covered.'[8] Adelaide, usually so shy in public, was uncompromising with her court etiquette. It served to combat the scandalous reputation that her husband and his wayward siblings had earned the royal family, and while she accepted the presence of fashionable dress in her court, deviations from the norm had to first receive royal approval. When she began to notice a few fashionable ladies sneakily entering the palaces wearing unapproved hats and turbans, she was quick to have a notice published in the *London Gazette* clarifying that 'all ladies must appear in feathers and lappets, in conformity with the established order'.[9]

'Who is Silly Billy now?' William had announced to his Privy Council soon after becoming King.[10] It was a topical question, as many people had noticed how the shock of his accession had made William increasingly erratic – only a few days after his brother's passing, he had tried to leave St James's Palace dressed in a green coat and white beaver hat, highly inappropriate dress for a man who was expected to be deep in mourning, and had to be chased after by Lord Hereford, who persuaded him to change lest 'his Majesty's dress be taken exception to'.[11] He had also behaved with inappropriate zeal at his brother's funeral, babbling loudly and continuously to anybody and everybody who caught his eye. As the dust settled and the gravity of the situation registered with him, the new King sobered his nature. Helped by the rational influence of the wife he had grown to adore with unabashed openness, William embarked on his reign with a refreshing sense of moderation. His coronation, for example, was a matter that had caused much debate, as William firmly believed that it was an avoidable extravagance which need not go ahead. Eventually, the King caved to the pressure he was facing from traditionalists at court and agreed to a ceremony on the grounds that it was significantly stripped back and did not exceed a budget of £30,000 (a total that only just exceeded the budget George IV had dedicated to his coronation clothes alone).

It was William and Adelaide's belief that court life should strike a balance between tradition and modernity, which included certain deviations from the prerequisites of court dress in favour of accommodating the changing shapes of men's fashion – the most obvious change being the introduction of pantaloons. For the past few years, high society had striven to establish where in the pecking order of formal dress these slim-legged preludes to trousers should sit, and the consensus thus far had been far from favourable. Knee breeches, now almost obsolete in regular dress, were still considered the gold standard and the only acceptable choice for formal occasions, a precedent following in part from the strict dress code of Almack's, the most prestigious of London's social clubs. Almack's discerning owners were quick to deny entry to even the most celebrated members of society if they forgot to don their 'knee-breeches, white cravat and chapeau-bras', and even the exalted Duke of Wellington was once discreetly dismissed with the instructions: 'Your Grace cannot be admitted in trousers!'[12] During the 1830s, however, pantaloons were accepted into certain forms of court dress (and would not be parted from until the early twentieth century).

The end of the Napoleonic Wars in 1815 had opened the floodgates for French textiles and styles to return to the British market, disrupting the unobstructed business that local tradespeople had enjoyed during the period of French import sanctions. The belief held by contemporary shoppers was that French textiles were of a significantly higher quality than anything made by British hands, and this was a stigma that Queen Adelaide was personally interested in challenging. Not long after her husband's accession, she hosted a small dinner party to which she wore an elegant white dress of blond silk, of entirely English manufacture. At some point in the evening, she gathered the ladies around her and held out her skirt for them to inspect, encouraging them to compare the blond to that of the nearby Lady Mayo's dress, whose French gown was by no means as lustrous as hers. 'I hope all ladies will patronize the English blend of silk,' Adelaide concluded, and the guests were inclined to agree that the Queen's patriotic gown was far superior.[13] Soon it was reported in the press that 'the laudable example of Her Majesty has been followed by many ladies of distinguished rank; and the modists . . . are busily engaged in making dresses entirely composed of British manufacture'.[14] Adelaide was now hailed as the hero of the British textiles industry.

One young lady whom Adelaide was particularly keen to impart her love for British products to was her darling niece and heir presumptive to the King – Princess Victoria of Kent. The Duke of Kent had fallen ill and passed away just a few months after his daughter's birth, and the widowed Victoire, Duchess of Kent, had alienated herself from the King and Queen by treating them with frosty disdain. Despite the animosity that festered between the Duchess and her sovereigns, William and Adelaide's love for their niece was unwavering and they invited her to visit court as often as she was allowed, gifting her handmade dresses and attempting to nurture a preference for English textiles.

The already turbulent royal relations reached their peak when, at a banquet hosted in honour of the Queen's birthday, King William delivered a shocking speech aimed at the attending Victoire. Princess Victoria, who was also in attendance, was just a few months shy of her eighteenth birthday, and the ageing King knew that if he was to die before that day, Victoire would act as regent for her daughter, wielding her authority however she wished. It was a possibility he detested almost as much as Victoire herself, and he decided to make that very clear to his guests: 'I trust in God that my life be spared for nine months longer, after which period, in the event, no regency would take place. I should then have the satisfaction of leaving the royal authority to the personal exercise of *that Young Lady*' – he pointed down the table towards Princess Victoria – 'and not in the hands of a person now near me' – he gestured to his raven-haired and red-faced sister-in-law – 'who is surrounded by evil advisors and is herself incompetent of acting with propriety!'[15] Hauntingly true to his word, William clung on to life until his niece's coming of age and died just a month later in June 1837.

VICTORIA

IN THE EARLY HOURS of 20 June 1837, Victoire, Duchess of Kent, gently shook the shoulders of Princess Alexandrina Victoria, rousing her eighteen-year-old daughter from her peaceful slumber. 'I got out of bed and went into my sitting-room (only in my dressing gown) and *alone*,' she would later gush in her diary, recalling how she was greeted by the Archbishop of Canterbury and Lord Conyngham, who brought with them the news that her uncle, the King, was dead, 'and consequently that *I* am *Queen*.'[16] Hardly the image of regal splendour, this short young woman, with her glassy blue eyes, tiny pursed mouth and golden-brown hair hanging messily around her shoulders, now held within the confines of her 4-foot, 11-inch body the key to the future of the royal family. Under the new Queen Victoria, the monarchy would either sink or swim – there were no other options.

Victoria spent her first conscious moments as Queen unchaperoned, no doubt a thrilling opportunity for a girl who had spent almost every waking moment of her life thus far shadowed by her mother. Isolated from her royal in-laws, Victoire had pitched her camp in Kensington Palace, where she set about micromanaging her daughter's upbringing so that she might be properly poised to inherit the throne when the time came. Later in life, the overbearing attitude of her mother would cloud Victoria's view of her otherwise happy and comfortable childhood, and despite her personal hatred of the numerous long and arduous royal tours that she was sent on as a young girl, they undoubtedly succeeded in establishing a good relationship with her public, who came to view her as a refreshingly moral alternative to the raucous mess of characters who had made up the previous generation of royals.

Little Victoria had shown an interest in fashion from a very young age, one that her secluded childhood had not hindered, and from at least 1830 was painting paper dolls in the most popular styles of the time. Often the dolls were drawn by her governess, with the colours and details added by the Princess, who typically reached for pale pink and blue paints which she embellished with dainty floral designs, a prelude to her later preference for all things soft and girly in her wardrobe. A few years later, she graduated to making physical dresses for her horde of little wooden dolls, her substitute for childhood companions. They appear in an assortment of styles appropriate for a wide range of occasions, which Victoria no doubt committed to memory on her occasional outings from the Palace – evening gowns and ballet dresses from nights at the theatre, walking suits and tiny bonnets from her carriage rides around Kensington, and even an extravagant (albeit slightly inaccurate) depiction of a fictional 'Countess of Claremont' in court dress.[17]

Despite Queen Adelaide's efforts to attune her niece to the finery of British manufacture, Princess Victoria was easily influenced by the more fashionable women in her life. In 1835, Victoria first met the French Princess Louise, who had recently married her uncle Leopold and whose continental wardrobe fascinated the young Princess. Victoria's addiction to French wares began with little gifts and accessories, before eventually

Louise was supplying her with full outfits of pastel-toned silk dresses and matching bonnets, which Victoria swooned over in her diary: 'They are quite lovely. They are so well made and so very elegant.'[18] Even as Queen, Victoria would occasionally stray from the path of patriotic patronage by taking inspiration from her foreign contemporaries, particularly Empress Eugenie of France, whose signature simple and chic hairstyle she adopted for herself in the 1850s.[19]

Living a relatively sheltered existence pushed Victoria to find other means of exploration and excitement in her teenage years. This came in the form of novels the first of which that she was allowed to consume was Sir Walter Scott's *The Bride of Lammermoor* (1819), a deliciously mysterious and dark tale that enraptured Princess Victoria's vivid imagination. Scott's patriotic agenda, which had directly influenced the wardrobe of King George IV back in 1822, was now indirectly influencing the preferences of George's niece, who now craved dresses in heavy fabrics and dark colours, in contrast to the dainty gowns she had thus far enjoyed.[20] One dress from this time period survives today: a French silk velvet gown of deep blue, red and green that was woven in an imitation of Scottish tartan to reflect the Princess's growing affinity for the country she had now fallen in love with through the pages of Walter Scott's books.

Why Victoria chose to preserve this dress in particular is an interesting topic. Famous for her scrawling diaries, which she began aged thirteen and maintained for the next sixty-nine years, Victoria was acutely interested in memorializing significant events in the lives of both herself and those closest to her. Clothing was to be no exception to this, and rather than repurpose or give away pieces from important times in her life, as had been common for royals of the past, Victoria kept them close at hand for their sentimental value. The style and size of the faux-tartan dress places it firmly between the years 1835 and 1837, during which time the most significant event that Victoria would have wanted to commemorate (where a dress of this style would also have been appropriate) was the first time she met her future husband. On Wednesday, 18 May 1836, the Duke of Saxe-Coburg and Gotha brought his two teenage sons, Ernst and Albert, to Kensington Palace to meet their cousin Victoria. The two young men were handsome enough, though Albert in particular, with his tall figure and dark hair, piqued Victoria's interest. To Albert, Victoria was equally as fascinating – in her edgy tartan gown she resembled in every way a romantic heroine from the mind of Walter Scott, who incidentally was one of Albert's favourite storytellers.

These first flourishes of Victoria and Albert's relationship had to be put on pause when a year later Victoria found herself suddenly very occupied with the business of becoming Queen, and the prospect of marriage was put on the back burner. On the morning of her accession, the new Queen in her white dressing gown had been promptly whisked away to her maid's room to be helped into a black silk mourning dress that had been prepared in anticipation of her uncle's impending death.[21] It was plain yet stylish, the wide swooping neckline covered by a modest lace collar, and the asymmetrical ruffles that decorated the skirt evoked a sense of modernity and sophistication. It was in this dress that Victoria held her first Privy Council meeting, where she impressed her ministers with her composure and assured demeanour. Later that year, David Wilkie would paint the scene, though he took a major artistic liberty with the Queen's dress by depicting her in white, to contrast her radiant youth against the dour suits of her ageing ministers. At the time, Victoria had seen no problem with the change, though with the benefit of hindsight and an appreciation of how intensely scrutinized royal dress could be, she later took a disapproving stance as her fictional lack of mourning dress ran the risk of being interpreted by the public as rudeness.

On Thursday, 28 June 1838, Queen Victoria documented yet another important early morning wake-up call in her diary. Rather than the frantic shakes of her mother, this time she was roused by the sounds of a vast and quickly growing crowd just outside of her new home, Buckingham Palace, where bands were playing and gun salutes were fired sporadically to mark the special occasion. It was the day of her coronation. Under the watchful eye of the Duchess of Sutherland (her stylish Mistress of the Robes), Victoria was helped into a white satin dress decorated with gold embroidered cartouches and flowers. It was a truly magnificent gown, though it was almost entirely concealed by her red velvet and ermine-lined Parliament robe. Designed to feature a mix of both contemporary and historical elements, the robe was 'cut in the same fashion as that worn by Queen Anne Boleyn', fitting close to her body then descending from her small shoulders into a dramatic gold-trimmed mantle.[22] The finishing touches were a circlet of diamonds, a pair of silk stockings and white beribboned slippers. As soon as the shoes were tied it was time for Victoria to face her public.

The events of the day had been carefully planned to be both inexpensive (nobody was interested in a repeat of George IV's money-guzzling extravaganza, regardless of how popular Victoria had now become) and accessible, with the goal of letting as much of the public catch a glimpse of their diminutive ruler as possible. The plan of attack had been to replace the highly exclusive Westminster banquet with a long procession from Buckingham Palace to Westminster Abbey, so that the public, who had desperately packed themselves into the scaffolds that lined the journey's path, could peer through the windows of the 'golden, fairy-like' state carriage to catch a glimpse of their

Queen's little round face, surrounded by a sea of diamonds and velvet and spotty ermine fur. The sight of the Queen nearly drowning in her robes did more to endear the public to her than anything else, for in that moment she seemed 'almost like a child' and brought tears to the eyes of many as she was presented as the very paragon of innocence and hope.[23]

The ceremony, which was long and unrehearsed, was filled with a litany of errors which naturally included a fair share of costume mishaps. Victoria's train bearers, in their silver gowns with their hair encircled by a wreath of diamonds, struggled most visibly: 'our little trains were serious annoyances,' grumbled one member of the Queen's retinue, 'for it was impossible to stop treading upon them. We ought never to have had them; and there certainly should have been some previous rehearsing, for we carried the Queen's train very jerkily and badly.'[24] Once the ceremony was done, Victoria and her ladies retreated towards the robing room, where, complaining of a headache, she cast aside her orb and sceptre, unclasped her robe and threw herself down on the sofa. Victoria pried the cause of her headache – the Imperial State Crown – off her head and cast it aside. She had instructed it to be made smaller than usual to accommodate her little frame, but also so that it would remain secure and not slip during the ceremony, and though the tight band had kept it secure despite being jostled and knocked by overzealous peers it had also given her a violent pounding beneath her temples. It was then that she noticed that the Archbishop of Canterbury had squeezed her coronation ring onto the wrong finger, and with great pain and the assistance of iced water, it was tugged off and fixed.[25]

Victoria's accession had allowed her the freedom she had craved as a child, and she now found herself in the unique position of being a young, unmarried woman who by virtue of her position had no one to answer to but herself. The next few years flew by in a blur of balls, drawing rooms and public appearances that demanded a wardrobe as spirited as the woman wearing the clothes. Parliament had raised the clothing allowance supplied to the Palace, anticipating that Victoria might need a more varied wardrobe than her old and plain uncle William had done, and they were correct. The majority of this money went towards the French fashions that the Queen so adored, but she also spent money on uniforms. As a woman, she was not entitled to any of her own and instead decided to reintroduce the Windsor uniform to the royal wardrobe, which had dwindled in popularity after the death of George III and had not been seen in its feminine iteration for much longer.

Victoria's Windsor uniform was a sharply tailored jacket made to emphasize her slender physique, dark blue and double breasted with bright golden buttons displaying her royal cypher. The cuffs and collar were characteristically red, and where the jacket cut off at the natural waist, a matching blue skirt continued to the ground. The military inspiration had a profound effect on the Queen, who confided to her diary that 'I felt for the first time like a man, as if I could fight myself at the head of my troops', and the public were equally entranced by their Queen when she donned habits of masculine construction.[26] She was frequently depicted in prints and paintings on horseback – the unobstructed line of the tailoring and tall top hats featured in riding habits giving her the transformative appearance of height.

Carefree and wild, Victoria wore her riding habits frequently, for there was nothing she loved more than a brisk ride around the grounds at Windsor. She was often accompanied by her close confidant, Lord Melbourne, who had taken a paternal role in her life after her accession and offered guidance on how she should present herself as Queen. He encouraged her to turn to historical precedents, directing Victoria to a portrait of Queen Anne when she asked how she should wear her Garter order, and tried in vain to explain the importance of a monarch promoting local textiles.[27] Melbourne had noticed, where Victoria might have not, that the public were beginning to see through the glamour of the first few years of majesty and were now left wanting by the Queen they had received. In his opinion, a stabilizing presence was needed to prevent the Queen from creeping towards infamy like the previous generation of royals had done, and he raised the possibility of marriage as a way of averting this. Victoria took some convincing: 'I dreaded the thought of marrying,' she grumbled. 'I was so accustomed to have my own way,' though eventually she ceded to the advice of her trusty 'Lord M'.[28] On Tuesday, 15 October 1839, with the autumn sun shining through the windows of her Closet at Windsor Castle, Victoria proposed to her cousin Prince Albert, and plans for the most significant royal wedding in fashion history were set in motion.

Just as is the case today, all that the press could talk about in the lead up to the royal wedding was the bride's dress. The central topic was who was going to make it (or more specifically *where* it was going to be made). Conflicting reports filled the pages of newspapers for the next few months, with the most popular rumour suggesting that the Queen's wedding dress would be of entirely foreign manufacture. 'We were all led to believe, at the commencement of the reign of her present Majesty, that we should receive her exclusive patronage,' grumbled one anonymous London dressmaker, 'but I am compelled to inform you that this assertion is wholly unfounded.'[29] This complaint was published in *The Times* just a few days before the Queen's wedding and contributed to the pervasive belief that 'her Majesty's dress is to be Brussels lace' instead of the local Honiton variety. It was a sensible guess, based on Victoria's previous purchasing habits, though ultimately it proved incorrect: the Queen's wedding lace had been in production in Devon before she had even got around to proposing to Albert.

At Victoria's end of the discussion, there had been much back-and-forth about the message that the dress should put forward. The first suggestion was to take inspiration from the wedding of King George III and Queen Charlotte, for the duo had been much loved and there could be no harm done by emulating their success. On a more practical note, they also stood as the most recent example of a monarch marrying after their accession rather than before. Following in the footsteps of her grandparents would have meant Victoria wearing her velvet and ermine robes of state over a traditional court dress of silver or gold, a proposal that she struck down as soon as it was brought before her: '[We] talked of my wearing my robes at the wedding, which I wished not, and which I thought could not be necessary.'[30] Clearly the Queen was not to be swayed, and if Lord Melbourne's response to her hesitancy is anything to go by ('Oh! No, I should think not, much better white,' he assured the Queen over dinner one night), it seems as though Victoria already had a very different plan in mind.[31]

Contrary to popular belief, Queen Victoria did not invent the white wedding dress, but she certainly tore up the royal rule book by adopting it for her big day. Among the middle class, the colour white for wedding dresses had been growing steadily in popularity since the late eighteenth century; however, as proven by the shimmering silver and gold of Queen Adelaide and the Duchess of Kent's 1818 gowns, it was not adopted by royal and aristocratic circles, who still preferred the most expensive fabrics to honour tradition. By choosing white, Victoria was not only making it clear that she wished to marry as a *bride* rather than a *Queen*, she was also presenting an attainable standard of wedding fashion for a much greater majority of her subjects to aspire to. The publicity that the marriage of a young and popular Queen brought meant that reports of Victoria's wedding dress travelled far and wide, giving white wedding dresses the boost in popularity they needed to become a fixture in bridal fashion. By later enforcing the same colour upon her daughters for their weddings, Victoria ensured that subsequent generations of brides would have their own royal white wedding dress to aspire to and that the influence of the royal family on their public remained subtly intact. Queen Victoria may not have invented the white wedding dress, but she is certainly the reason why we're still wearing them today.

Victoria described her wedding dress in her own words: 'I wore a white satin gown, with a very deep flounce of Honiton lace, imitation of old. I wore my Turkish diamond necklace and earrings, and my Angel's [Albert's] beautiful sapphire brooch.'[32] In lieu of a tiara or crown she wore a wreath of orange blossoms in her hair, and rather than a velvet mantle, she opted for a detachable train around her waist. The sapphire brooch was pinned to the centre of Victoria's wide-necked dress and had been gifted to her by her husband-to-be just a few days before the wedding. It was quickly to become one of her favourite jewellery pieces. More recently it has been seen pinned to the breast of her descendent, Queen Elizabeth II, and it served as the inspiration for Diana Spencer's iconic engagement ring. It was one of many items of jewellery that Prince Albert would give to his wife as a symbol of his unwavering love and devotion; others include her favourite emerald tiara, a sapphire coronet inspired by gothic architecture, and the Oriental Circlet still occasionally worn by members of the royal family today – all of which were designed by Albert himself.

Later that year, on 24 November 1840, Prince Albert gifted his wife yet another piece of jewellery. This time it was a simple gold chain bracelet, from which a pale-pink enamel heart was hung. The heart was inscribed on the reverse with *Victoria*, the name of the Princess Royal born to the royal couple just a few days earlier.[33] Over the next seventeen years, eight more hearts were added: turquoise for Albert (known to his family as 'Bertie'), red for Alice, dark blue for Alfred, opal for Helena, emerald green for Louise, light blue for Arthur, white for Leopold and light green for Beatrice. Victoria and Albert, in an attempt to appeal to the growing middle class, placed family life at the front of their image – and it was at this point that the concept of the 'royal family' was firmly established, with public interest and royal responsibility falling not only upon the monarch and their direct heirs but on the entire family. With extra attention being paid to the growing brood of royal babies, Victoria and Albert took special care to organize their children's appearance to ensure that they exuded a sense of pleasing domestic harmony, and the royal nursery was filled with children in matching, practical clothing, often with naval inspiration.[34]

Even as the children grew older and made attempts at independence, it was difficult to escape the confines of the family unit and the sharp eyes of their image-conscious royal parents. After marrying Prince Frederick William of Prussia in 1858, Princess Vicky found that despite now living in an entirely different country, her mother was still making comments about her dress choices: 'I see by the papers you wore a green dress at the Cologne concert. Was that the one with the black lace? You must not be impatient about these details . . .' was the warning Victoria delivered to her eldest daughter, whose wedding trousseau she had personally organized.[35] Victoria herself had now come to view fashion with a different eye, having abandoned her aunt Louise as a fashion role model in favour of the carefully measured advice of Prince Albert, who encouraged sensibility over style and carefully monitored the perception of the royal family in the public eye. The effect of his influence was a quaint, if not rather eccentric appearance that featured cluttered surface embellishments of lace, ruffles and large flower motifs. During her 1855 visit to France, the Queen's homely appearance perplexed the Parisian elite, who were used to the effortless glamour of Empress Eugenie, 'the Empress born to be a dressmaker', and Victoria's curious appearance was documented with bewilderment.[36] 'In spite of the great heat she had on a massive bonnet of white silk,' began one report. 'Her dress was white and flounced, but she had a mantle and parasol of a crude green which did not seem to me to go with the rest of her costume.'[37] Finishing the outfit with a silk bag crudely embroidered with a gold poodle, Victoria had clearly dressed practically for travel, and the result was matronly rather than queenly. Albert's guidance may have helped her to avoid accusations of overindulgence and vanity, but it certainly didn't help to make her an icon of style.

The nineteenth century saw the arrival of multiple new and exciting technological innovations that the royal family were keen to adopt and promote: aniline dyes to make their clothes more vibrant, steam trains to help them to visit their subjects further afield and, most importantly, the invention of photography, which meant that their images could be broadcast to the world at large. Prince Albert, who had a keen nose for new technologies, immediately identified the advantages that photography could offer the Crown, and in 1842 he became the first British royal to have a portrait photograph taken. The royal couple quickly became key patrons in the development of the field, though Victoria, as both Queen and a woman, discovered a unique issue: '*Ah, non, madame,*' was the warning delivered to her by a portrait painter, 'the *photographie* can't *flattere!*'[38]

Most painted and print depictions of Queen Victoria had thus far presented her as a statuesque and slender young woman with conventionally beautiful facial features; the advent of photography, however, exposed to the public a very different image of their Queen. Standing at little more than five feet in a time when height was linked closely to class and health, Queen Victoria was extremely self-conscious of her diminutive stature and well aware that her shortness made any sort of weight gain seem particularly obvious. Her diaries are filled with self-deprecating criticism and frequent reports of being told off for eating too much, or too fast. 'I have such a horror of being fat,' she lamented to her diary, though with nine consecutive pregnancies (and a serious sweet tooth), there was little that Victoria could do to stop the inevitable and thus found photography to be a touchy subject.[39] In 1852, after posing for a photograph with her young children, Victoria found her appearance to be 'horrid' and subsequently scratched out her face on the negative.[40] In what must have seemed like a godsend for Victoria, who was now expected to use photography to disperse her image across the globe, the retouching process was quickly invented. This prelude to Photoshop and Facetune could slim down waists, banish flyaway hairs and smooth over wrinkles by scratching out and painting over these 'imperfections' on the negative, resulting in a final image that flattered the sitter just like a painting could. Royal photographs intended for wider distribution, such as Jubilee portraits, were discreetly retouched to present the image of a glowing, happy Queen to the world – a symbolic representation of a prosperous country. As is the case today, there were often times when retouching artists would make their influence slightly too obvious, and on the occasion of her Golden Jubilee, the elderly Queen Victoria was so heavily edited in her portraits that critics thought she resembled a wax figure more than a real woman.[41]

Queen Victoria's reign may have seen the exciting introduction of revolutionary technologies, but it was also a period underscored by brutal colonial expansion. The Great Exhibition in 1851, which provided nations around the world with an opportunity to flaunt the greatest and most glorious wares that their populace could supply, also acted as a stage upon which the British could parade their imperial victories. One of the key players in this performance was the Koh-i-Noor diamond, the largest of its type in the world, on show at the Crystal Palace and on loan from its new owner, Queen Victoria. Before the Koh-i-Noor had come to reside here, displayed in a golden birdcage as a glorified tourist trap, it had once adorned the great and legendary Punjabi kings as a symbol of their cultural and religious heritage. Its previous owner, the Maharaja Duleep Singh, had been but a child when it had first been secured to his arm, and not long after that both the diamond and the country he ruled were taken from him by British forces. The diamond was cut down into a shape that appealed to Western preferences, and under Prince Albert's supervision it was crafted into a stylish brooch for his wife to wear.

Just like the diamond, Duleep Singh was brought from his homeland, fashioned to English tastes and welcomed into the arms of high society. It was Victoria who demanded he be treated with appropriate princely decorum, though his new life in England was hardly a pleasant one. The Maharaja was himself trapped in a gilded cage; his survival in this new nation hinged upon his ability to dazzle the crowd lest he too be cut down to size.

This began with surrendering any symbols that too overtly referenced his power or culture, such as ceding his claim to the Koh-i-Noor and converting to Christianity. The exception to this was anything that the British found entertaining, chiefly his native clothes, which excited and intrigued the foreign eye. The 'easy and graceful folds' of his traditional Sikh attire, covered in 'barbaric pearl and gold'[42] were paired with sharply cut English trousers and reported upon widely by the press. Victoria, who grew to pity and care for the Prince, who was not much older than her own children, even had his dress preserved in the artwork of her favourite portrait painter, Franz Xaver Winterhalter. The Maharaja visited the royal residences often, and on one occasion even left some of his robes for the Queen's children, and her young sons posed for photographs in his turbans and their mother's jewellery. Despite his outward amiability towards the parade he was being made to endure, the Maharaja would forever resent the country that had robbed him of his culture and the woman who acted as its figurehead. His nickname for Victoria was 'Mrs Fagin', after the famous fictional pickpocket.[43]

The Great Exhibition had been the brainchild of Prince Albert, and its success marked a turning point in the public opinion of the foreign Prince Consort. He quickly became a champion of menswear for the period, representing the smart and conscientious nature of the ideal man in his serious and trim tailoring. His dark frock coats and slim trousers, the whole ensemble being made of expensive but sober-toned fabrics, signalled the final divorce from the extravagance of men's dress in previous years and Albert's personal preference for subtle luxury. Admired though he was, he would constantly perplex his adopted home nation by appearing curiously and stubbornly German. His foreignness surrounded him like an

aura, which the British public were not used to seeing their
consorts retain after marrying into the royal family, and those
closest to him reported upon it frequently: 'He is an excellent, clever, able fellow, but look at the cut of his coat, or the
way he shakes hands!'[44]

Victoria, who passionately subscribed to the contemporary
notion that the husband was undisputed head of the household, deferred to Albert in all aspects of her life and in her own
words 'didn't put on a gown or a bonnet if he didn't approve
it'.[45] Her dependence upon Albert was total, and the thought of
life without him was simply inconceivable. Unfortunately for
Victoria, it was a reality she was forced to confront far sooner
than anyone expected when, struck with an unknown illness,
Prince Albert passed away in December 1861. The Queen's
world was suddenly turned upside down, and it triggered her
historic metamorphosis into the sombre, tragic little figure
that we have come to know and remember her as. Once she
had been pried from her dead husband's body, she was helped
to bed by her ladies, but not before she collected a few pieces
of Albert's clothing to lay on the sheets with her. For the rest of
her days, Victoria would conjure her husband's spirit through
his 'dear red dressing-gown'[46] and other items from his wardrobe. It was the culmination of her curatorial instincts and
a final, desperate attempt to maintain some of the balance
Albert had provided her in life. Victoria was a changed woman;
'all, all was over!'[47]

The Queen was no stranger to mourning rituals. In an
increasingly commercial society, mortality had become an
ever more material commodity, the rituals it entailed cele-
brating not only the life of the deceased but also the wealth
of the family still remaining. Mourning dress acted as a visual
indication that the wearer was entitled to a special degree of
sensitivity, but seeing as it was comprised of various 'levels'

of grief that demanded different styles of dress for varying periods of time, if you could afford to keep up with these stylistic nuances, you were subtly conveying the heaviness of your purse at the same time. In 1860, a year before Prince Albert's death, *The Ladies' Book of Etiquette* joined the ranks of printed social guides that attempted to lay down the rules regarding mourning dress. For deep mourning, the first and most profound stage of the process, acceptable fabrics included bombazine, Parramatta cloth, delaine, barege or merino, all in black and deemed appropriate on account of their dull appearance. Surface embellishment was limited to a single fold of crepe fabric, though after a few months, lace, a white collar or a bow on a bonnet was permissible. Half-mourning was the next stage, and the *Book of Etiquette* dictated that the introduction of silk dresses, on the condition that the particular silk used had no lustrous qualities, was now acceptable. In this phase, a few new colours were approved: 'lead-colour, purple, lavender, and white'[48] were worn for the remainder of the mourning period, though some women chose to remain in this stage for the rest of their lives.

Victoria threw herself into mourning dress with a vigour that would last for the rest of her life, committing herself to widows' weeds and harshly shutting down anyone who suggested she do otherwise. 'This idea cannot be too explicitly contradicted,' she wrote in a letter to *The Times*, after they had implied that she would soon be bringing her mourning period to a close, and argued indignantly that her grief was now far more important than the act of royal dressing.[49] Mourning dress was as much of a comfort for Victoria as it was a reflection of her grief, for by committing herself to a wardrobe that had its own predefined rules and expectations, she was using the firm words of etiquette guides as a substitute for the constant guidance she had relied upon from Albert. Her wardrobe from this point onwards became several variations upon the same theme: a black gown trimmed with white lace, prioritizing practicality over style with wide sleeves and deep pockets, into which went her spectacles, her pocket watch and keys. The simple similarity of each dress meant that the Queen required far fewer fittings than before, though she kept each outfit unique with carefully planned surface embellishments. After the initial few years of mourning, Victoria traded the dull crepe fabric for more expensive silks, decorating them on occasion with tasteful gold, silver or white embroidery.

This lifelong dedication to mourning dress may have suited Victoria the *woman* very well but it had a much more complicated impact on Victoria the *Queen*. There was now no chance at all for local tradespeople to use Victoria to flaunt the most stylish fabrics that they produced, and court dressmakers suffered as a result of the Queen cancelling formal functions and court presentations, which she now viewed as a brutal intrusion upon her grief. Court presentations, the practice of eligible young women making their debut in society via their first appearance at court, had its roots in the court of Queen Charlotte, but by Victoria's time it had been refined to an art. In order to make a successful presentation and prove your eligibility for fashionable society, there were many intricate rules to follow, most of which were about dress. Evening gowns, almost always in white with long court trains, and a plume of white feathers in the hair were the approved uniform from which a dedicated industry of court dressmakers had been born. With these events put on pause by a Queen who had retreated from the public eye, these trades suffered as a consequence. Their disappointment was shared across the country by a population now left abandoned by their Queen, and within a few years cries were being made frequently and angrily by the public as a whole. If the Queen wasn't out and about fulfilling her duties, how could they be sure she was of any use at all? By delegating her public duties to her children and their spouses, Victoria bypassed the need to appear herself, unsure as she was as to how she would survive public scrutiny without Albert's guidance. This new royal arrangement suited her just fine, but there was only so much that the gaggle of young Princes and Princesses could do to keep the public entertained; it was clear that they wanted to see their Queen again.

In 1866, it was decided that Victoria would oversee the State Opening of Parliament for the first time since Albert's death, a key moment in the royal calendar that demanded some of the oldest and grandest dress traditions. Ahead of her arrival, the peerage noticed that the glittering gold throne in the House of Lords, from which the Queen was to read her speech, was draped curiously with what appeared to be swathes of white satin. Upon closer inspection, it was revealed to be the shimmering lining of Victoria's red velvet Parliament robe, the expected uniform for such an event but hardly compatible with her continued dedication to mourning dress. It was a powerful statement of her grief that even this most duty-bound of queens was casting off royal tradition in response to her emotional turmoil. This remarkable change in dress of course attracted attention and kick-started a new fascination with royal fashion. The press reported that she wore 'a black – some said a deep purple velvet robe, which, whether it were purple or black looked intensely black in the dim light of the chamber, trimmed with miniver and a white lace cap', across her chest she wore Prince Albert's ribbon of the Order of the Garter, and her head was circled by the dainty, gothic coronet that he had designed for her all those years ago.[50]

The sapphire circlet, with its tiny blue gems winking at the crowd, was one of the only pieces of coloured jewellery that

Victoria could now bring herself to wear. Even the Imperial State Crown, the central symbol of monarchical power, was off limits and sat on a pillow beside the Queen rather than on top of her head. Instead, Victoria would appear laden with brilliant colourless diamonds or smooth jet set in gold. Jet, an opaque black gemstone sourced in Yorkshire, was rare, expensive and difficult to work with, but when placed in the hands of a skilled tradesman could be transformed into delicate and impactful pieces of mourning jewellery. In 1878, Victoria found occasion to purchase more jet jewellery – a shiny black and gold locket holding the portrait of her daughter Princess Alice, who died tragically of diphtheria that year. It was joined around the Queen's neck by another locket in 1884, containing the likeness of her recently deceased son Leopold, a sufferer of haemophilia who had taken a terrible fall down the stairs of his home in Cannes and subsequently passed away.

In 1901, Queen Victoria too passed away, at Osborne House on the Isle of Wight, blind, wheelchair-bound, and surrounded by her family and pet dog. She left behind an indomitable legacy, acting as an enduring symbol of duty, morality and power for the country and empire at large. Whether that power was viewed positively or negatively varied dramatically from person to person and country to country. It was an unarguable fact that Victoria had transformed the public image of the monarchy, appealing to the virtues held by the expanding middle classes and presenting her family and their message to the world at large through any means necessary. Instrumental to this transformation was fashion, as everything from her 'simple' white wedding dress to her golden poodle reticule bag helped to transform her into a relatable figure for her subjects, a mother to the nation and a separate entity to the flock of immoral aristocrats littering society. As meticulous in death as she was in life, Victoria had left a set of very specific instructions as to how she was to be laid in her coffin. For the first time in forty years, the Queen was dressed in white, and her hair was draped with her wedding lace, which she had worn for almost all the major events in her married life, namely the weddings and christenings of her children, and for her Jubilee portraits. A plaster cast of Prince Albert's hand was slotted into hers, and his red dressing gown was laid at her side.[51] The Victorian era had finally, at long last, come to a close.

EDWARD VII

ON 1 FEBRUARY 1901, King Edward VII stood at the bow of one of many yachts now crossing the Solent. As steam from the escort of warships mingled with the clouds above, his attention had been captured by HMY *Alberta*, the little yacht just ahead of the rest, leading the fleet to Portsmouth and transporting his mother's coffin to its final destination. The yacht's standard was flying at half-mast, and the new King's brow was scrunched. Standing in his dark mourning clothes, hands perched upon his hips as he was so often seen to do in his portraits, the rather corpulent frame of King Edward was not unlike the Holbein depictions of King Henry VIII and cut an imposing figure against the stormy grey sky. He was now nearing sixty, his thick beard laced with wiry silver hair, and could boast of being the longest-serving Prince of Wales in history. He had been waiting patiently in the wings for his time to come, and with the death of Queen Victoria, it finally had. The King turned and asked why the standard was half-mast:

'The Queen is dead, Sir,' came the response.

'The King of England lives,' he corrected, and the flag was raised to its full height.[52] The Edwardian age, and with it the brief tenure of the English branch of the Saxe-Coburg and Gotha dynasty, was ushered onto the world's stage.

Growing up, Prince Albert Edward (or 'Bertie' as his family called him) had a complicated relationship with his mother; she was, of course, a Hanoverian royal by blood, and that hereditary animosity for heirs was still present in her genes, if slightly tempered. She could find nothing for which she could praise her eldest son. Slow with his studies and in her eyes painfully unattractive, the critiques came thick and fast: 'handsome I cannot think him,' she once wrote, 'with that painfully small and narrow head, those immense features and total want of chin.'[53] In many ways, Victoria was describing herself with that scathing assessment of her son's shortcomings, for the very same features that she so loathed on him could be found framed and hung in her own portraits. The Queen's all-consuming hatred of her own appearance ran strong, and with each child that emerged with her bulging blue eyes, pointed nose or receding chin, it became clear where her preferences lay. The children who best resembled her darling Prince Albert, both physically and intellectually, were saved from the brunt of her criticisms, and so Bertie was clearly, from birth, genetically at a disadvantage in the quest for his mother's approval.

This didn't stop Victoria from encouraging her son to take his place as one of the central players in the royal family. From a young age, Bertie was carrying out his role in his parents' vision for a domestic, united and socially engaged royal family, accompanying them abroad for their 1855 trip to France, a monumental occasion – the first time in over 400 years that a British sovereign had visited the French capital. They chose to dress the fourteen-year-old Prince in highland dress, now an unavoidable aspect of royal fashion that had been cemented by Victoria and Albert, thanks to their love affair with Scotland and admiration for Sir Walter Scott's patriotic prose.[54] Three years previously, they had purchased Balmoral Castle as a holiday location, decorating their furniture and their persons with Balmoral and Victoria tartan, patterns that they themselves had invented to replace the Royal Stuart variety adored and worn by King George IV all those years ago. Unlike his mother, whose flounced white dress and gold poodle purse raised more than a few French eyebrows, the people of Paris could not get enough of the little Prince of Wales in his beautifully patterned kilt. This would not be an isolated incident, and Bertie would become increasingly aware of the ways in which fashion could be used to help him take centre stage and – conveniently – to irk his mother at the same time.

For all his academic struggles, it was clear that the Prince of Wales had a creative streak. This manifested most potently in an interest in all things stylish: he would often find himself distracted by a unique hat or finely cut coat no matter how hard he or, more often, *other people* tried to direct his attention towards loftier pursuits. Prince Albert tried his very hardest to set his son on the right track, but time and time again he came back defeated: 'He takes no interest in anything but clothes and again clothes,' sighed the exasperated father, 'Even when out shooting he is more occupied with his trousers than the game!'[55] His son, Albert was forced to admit, was little more than a 'thorough and cunning lazybones'.[56] As Bertie grew up, his parents would soon have to grapple with the fact that his obsession with the fleeting intricacies of fashion was the least of their concerns. When they caught wind of a rumour that their son had taken a mistress, the royal parents, the very paragons of nineteenth-century morality, blanched at the notion that their son was freely enjoying sex *outside* the sanctity of marriage. They had gone to such efforts to present themselves as the principled outliers to an otherwise seedy upper class, but Bertie's new indiscretion was threatening to undo all of that careful stage management and thrust the family back into the infamy it had been subject to at the start of the century. Bertie's affair came to light just before Prince Albert's death in 1861, which seemed to Victoria to be too much of a coincidence to ignore. The Queen deduced that the stress of dealing with his son's continual vices had triggered Albert's premature death, and it was therefore Bertie who was responsible for her greatest personal tragedy. The mother–son relationship was drastically wounded, but Albert's death did prompt the Prince of Wales to commit to fulfilling one of his father's final wishes – that he should settle down and marry.

Just before his death, the Prince Consort had set his sights upon Princess Alexandra, one of the beautiful daughters of the impoverished Danish royal family, as his preferred candidate for Princess of Wales. Albert was informed that Alix (as she was known to most of her friends) was 'the most charming, pretty, and delightful young Princess it was possible to imagine', and he was inclined to agree.[57] Presented with her photograph, he declared to the room that based on looks alone, he certainly would have no qualms about marrying her. Hopefully his son would think the same thing. Victoria and Albert employed the assistance of their eldest daughter, Vicky, who was currently living at the Prussian court with her new husband, to investigate Alix and determine in how many ways she satisfied their requirements for a daughter-in-law: 'good looks, health, education, character, intellect, and a good disposition' were the Queen's requests.[58] Beautiful and with a sincere and perceptive nature that balanced her lack of a thorough education, Alexandra seemed at first glance to satisfy most of these requests; but the issue of health would be a sensitive topic. Vicky had noticed a tiny, virtually insignificant scar on Alix's slender neck, which she suspected to be an indication of scrofula, a form of tuberculosis that affected the lymph nodes. It was a worrying omen that through marrying into the line of succession, Alix might introduce hereditary diseases into the British royal family, and this little revelation significantly damaged the possibility of an Anglo-Danish match. Alexandra's parents immediately rectified the situation by explaining that the scar was simply the product of a clumsy doctor who had treated the Princess for a common cold as a child, and there was nothing more pressing to worry about.[59] Though the immediate threat to her future was averted, Alexandra became suddenly and acutely aware of how even the smallest indication of physical illness could send her future in-laws into a spiral of paranoia.

From that moment onwards, she did everything she could to disguise the little scar, at first wearing her hair in loose curls with a ribbon tied around her neck, and later, after coming under greater financial security, having her day dresses tailored with high, stiff necklines. For evening gowns, which etiquette dictated should expose a liberal amount of décolletage, Alix threaded her neck with diamond chokers, from which ropes of gems and pearls would descend lower and lower, spilling across her torso like crystal armour.

In 1862, Queen Victoria travelled to meet the Princess and decide for herself whether or not she was a true fit for the job. Bertie was already convinced and had decided he wanted nothing more than to take Alix, his 'rustic goddess',[60] as his bride. The young woman that Victoria met on her trip was the very antithesis of herself, willowy and well-proportioned, she was in possession of that natural elegance that the little Queen so coveted. She was hardly jealous of Alix but instead quite flattered, as the Princess greeted her in a black mourning dress devoid of all that terrible modishness that the Queen found to be so tasteless in her son. In Victoria's own words, Alix's appearance was 'one of the greatest charm, combined with simplicity and perfect dignity', falling neatly in line with her own ideas about royal dress.[61] This was not a coincidental harmony of taste; the Danish Princess had done her research, having been told in no uncertain terms that she was not to employ style as her main tool in securing British royal favour: 'fashionable dress,' Victoria had shuddered, 'anything but that!'[62] Alix's fashionable life would continue in this vein: she would always know just what to say and do to make people like her best, and there was no occasion to which she would appear garishly under- or overdressed.

Her pre-marriage research continued with a brief sojourn to England after her engagement, where she interrogated local aristocrats as to what styles the English best preferred, and particularly, what their *Queen* liked most. There was, however, another, more restrictive motivation behind the Princess's simple appearance. Her family had grown up comparatively poor, and if clothes could not be made cheaply and by their own hands, they were not ever going to make it into her wardrobe. It was a happy coincidence that her future mother-in-law adored practicality over grandeur, and the quirks of dress that her financial situation had instilled in the Princess only served to improve their relationship. 'My dear,' Victoria had enquired during Alexandra's visit, 'you seem very fond of jackets. How is it you always wear a jacket?' To which Alix replied candidly: 'I wear it because it is so *economical*. You can wear it with any sort of gown; and you know I have always had to make my own gowns. I have never had a lady's maid, and my sisters and I all make our own clothes; I even made my bonnet!'[63]

Alexandra arrived at Gravesend on 7 March 1863 aboard the royal yacht *Victoria and Albert*, dressed in purple half-mourning in accordance with the Queen's preferences. Around her shoulders she wore a sealskin cloak, one she would preserve and re-wear throughout her life, for both sentimental and economic reasons, the instinct to cherish material goods for as long as possible clearly not having faded despite coming into the fortunes of the British royal family.[64] Bertie, in his blue frock coat and grey trousers, all but sprinted down the gangway to offer Alix his arm, and together they proceeded to the train station, deafened by the clamouring crowds and escorted by a horde of young women in white dresses and red cloaks – the colours of the Danish flag.

In one of her trunks, Alexandra had brought her wedding dress. It had been a gift from King Leopold of the Belgians, a fashionable silver gown covered with Brussels lace, widely believed to be the most luxurious lace available. It was, no doubt, the most beautiful dress that the Princess had owned in her life thus far, but despite its beauty it couldn't quite win over the most important person in the royal marriage equation: the Queen. Victoria felt that a future Queen Consort of Britain should be married in a gown of British manufacture and commissioned a replacement dress from London dressmakers. Alix complied, putting the beautiful Brussels lace to one side. It seems, however, that the new Princess of Wales would find some way to wear her dream wedding dress: it has been suggested that the gown she wore to court just days after the nuptials was the very same – the eyewitness reports being so similar.[65]

The dress that Alexandra would finally walk down the aisle in was a white silk satin off-the-shoulder gown, buried in tiers of tulle and Honiton lace, wrapped in garlands of myrtle and orange blossoms and draped over a bell-shaped crinoline cage. Alix's wedding dress was a minutely updated version of Queen Victoria's, and nearly a carbon copy of those worn by Bertie's recently married sisters, Vicky and Alice. As Princess of Wales, Alexandra was now just one more aspect of Victoria's carefully orchestrated portrait of royalty and would for the foreseeable future have to resign herself to her instruction. The Prince of Wales, berobed in his blue velvet cloak of the Order of the Garter, slipped onto his bride's finger a golden wedding ring set with six precious stones. A beryl, an emerald, a ruby, a turquoise, a jacinth and a second emerald wrapped themselves around Alix's ring finger, spelling out her new spouse's name in dainty gems (the 'J' of jacinth being a common substitute for the letter 'I' in the world of gemstone initials). The appearance of the couple perfectly reflected their personalities and set the tone for how they would slot into society from this point onwards. 'Très bon gout,' declared one attendee, 'light, young, and royal!'[66]

The story of Alix's wedding dress does not end with the ceremony itself. In the wake of the wedding, William Powell Frith, the artist tasked with painting the marriage scene, requested that the clothes worn by all the guests be sent to his studio so that he might capture them in the greatest detail possible. Hats and suits, jewellery and kilts were all sent to him in abundance, but there was one key element missing: the bride's dress. Frith discovered, much to his horror, that there was not much left of the dress that could be sent to him: after the wedding was over Alexandra had asked for the gown to be cut to pieces and reconstructed into an evening dress. The skirt was slimmed, the lace and foliage cut away, and the large train was made much shorter. It was a chic transformation, an act of thrift and propagandic genius that would allow her to wear the dress to balls throughout the season, bringing the magic of a royal wedding to a much wider audience. 'I promise to send you what I can,' was the only weak assurance that her dresser could give Frith.[67]

Bertie and Alix were both intensely conscious about their personal image. They were far more sociable than Victoria and Albert had ever been and were one of the few royal couples in modern times to mingle in fashionable society. They understood that there was a demand from the populace, which they satisfied with frequent public outings and, crucially, by employing photography as part of their brand. Alexandra was herself an avid photographer and would even publish a charity book of her personal photographs in later life, but for now her appreciation for the art gave a unique perspective on how the couple could best exploit it, and they distributed their images via small *cartes de visite* – card-mounted photographs that were sold in shops across the globe. She understood what aspects of fashion appeared best on camera, identifying quickly that wearing darker fabrics allowed surface embellishments to be more clearly visible, and that wearing fabrics emblazoned with clean-cut and contrasting patterns made her the focal point of any studio scene. She adopted men's tailoring for herself, the simple lines of which meant that her style could be easily studied and emulated by those who saw her photographs, and consequently 'Alexandramania' shook the fashion world. Her high necklines, suit jackets and signature nautically inspired outfits came to shape the style landscape of the late Victorian world and situated her right alongside her husband as an arbiter of taste.

Just like his wife, Bertie was inundated by the flattery of imitation. While his mother may have found him to be ugly and disappointing, the world at large fawned over his pristine appearance. This adoration often worked in his favour, for the Prince found that there were so many people who began to walk, talk and dress like him that he could freely move about town without being recognized.[68] He was now just one of many stylish Bertie lookalikes. As he grew more confident, the Prince of Wales not only followed all of the newest trends but began setting some himself. He introduced the black homburg hat, had his trousers creased at the sides rather than the front and back, and after hurriedly dressing one morning, accidentally started the fashion for leaving the bottom button of a waistcoat undone.[69] He was also synonymous with tweed, which he made an acceptable form of dress to wear when attending races, the entertainment that he loved most of all. This ingenuity of dress was not an easy skill to master and the Prince had to dedicate a considerable amount of time and effort into studying his craft. He changed his clothes multiple times a day, strictly observing the various etiquette rules established for each type of function he attended, and it was imperative to him that others followed suit. 'He has a perfect mania on the subject of dress,' reported one exhausted soul who had hosted the Prince. 'Dr Fayrer [another guest] told me that he was quite sick of perpetually changing his clothes, as fresh orders come nearly every hour about what the suite were to wear & if a button is wrong it is at once noticed and remarked upon.'[70]

Seeing her son and daughter-in-law become a beacon to which the fashionable world flocked, Victoria was utterly horrified. 'Dress is a trifling matter,' she had once chided Bertie, 'but it gives also the one outward sign from which people in general can and often do judge upon the inward state of mind and feeling of a person.'[71] Victoria saw fastness of fashion as an indication of moral failure, and in this light it becomes infinitely clearer why she found Bertie's propensity for stylishness far more worrying than Alix's. She was satisfied that no amount of digging could ever bring up dirt on the Princess of Wales, but the Prince on the other hand was harbouring darker secrets. Though he adored his wife, Bertie was a hedonist at heart and entertained more than his fair share of mistresses. Victoria was paranoid that by appearing eccentric or vain in his approach to fashion, Bertie would attract attention towards his throng of mistresses and blow her image of royal domestic harmony right off its hinges. These mistresses, whom Bertie plucked from all different walks of life, would often leave their own stamp on fashion history: Catherine Walters, the courtesan better known as 'Skittles', was famed for her immaculately tailored riding habits that emphasized an eye-wateringly small waist, and Alice Keppel, his longest-serving mistress, made a splash when her satin oyster-coloured dress was copied by all the ladies of high society.[72]

Keppel owed the success of her oyster gown in part to the genius who had created it: Charles Frederick Worth, the Parisian-based couturier we can thank for the basic silhouettes of the late Victorian age. Having first found success collaborating with France's Empress Eugenie, Worth's revolutionary approach to style resulted in the creation of fashionable yet desirably practical women's clothing, and the ladies of high society flocked to his doorstep. The crinoline, for example, was one garment that Worth had a hand in transforming. The bell-shaped hoop skirt, first introduced in the 1850s, had seemed at the time a godsend to the stylish woman, who now had a lightweight and breathable alternative to the multiple layers of petticoats which had been the previous choice to bulk up skirt circumference. By the 1860s, Worth viewed it as an outdated piece, one that stagnated any hope of transformation in women's dress, and no doubt he would have been well aware of the many accidents they could cause. Hyperbolized though the crinoline was, newspapers and magazines were all too keen to report on stories of women setting their crinolined skirts alight; '"Another Death by Fire",' noted one of Worth's contemporaries, 'is a common heading by which modern readers are familiarized with the almost daily holocaust of women and children, sacrificed by the combustibility of their dress and the expansion of their crinoline.'[73] Perhaps the most famous of these horror stories is that of the eighteen-year-old Archduchess Mathilde of Austria, who in 1867 set herself alight after trying to hide a cigarette behind her crinoline.

Worth's solution to the crinoline issue was to gradually slim the front and sides of the structure until the bulk of the hoop expanded from the rear alone – resulting in the creation of the bustle that dominated the later century.[74] Worth swayed the women of society into accepting his transformation by simply refusing to back down, insisting that he was the authority on dress and therefore deserved the final say. It was a novel approach to fashion creation, which for the first time established the precedence of the designer over the whims of the customer, and allowed Worth to create a distinctive 'look' as a brand. One of the other transformations that the fashion world owes to his genius is the use of live models to display clothes, and many different women graced his catwalks. There was one woman in particular, whose willowy physique encapsulated the Victorian ideal, that he wished more than any would try out his clothes: Alexandra, the Princess of Wales. In the 1870s he created a new style of gown, which, rather than relying on a separate skirt and bodice, descended to the ground in one long line, clinging to the body and earning it the title of the first 'bodycon' dress. He named it the 'Princess Line', to honour the slender royal in the hope that it might capture her attention. It did, and soon Alexandra was a frequent patron of the House of Worth, bringing revolutionary fashion right to the heart of the royal world, a move that was highlighted by comparison to the independent bubble that was Queen Victoria and her mourning clothes.

Royal life was not all smooth sailing for Alexandra. The incident involving the scar on her neck was never far from her mind, and the thought that her marriage may have very nearly never happened because of her health manifested into an anxiety that constantly threatened to spill out from behind her diamond chokers and stiff collars. The year 1867 was particularly tough for the Princess, as illness and pregnancy had left her vulnerable to a terrible case of rheumatic fever that brought her close to death. It was her deep-rooted fear of displaying signs of physical weakness that prompted the still-sickly Alix to pose for a new photograph for mass distribution. She was clearly unwell: her long brown hair fanned freely over her shoulders, pulled back from her tired eyes by a simple black ribbon. Her dress was loose, and she sat slumped in her chair, protectively cradling herself with limp arms. The scene was pitiful enough to elicit public sympathy, but the fact that she had gathered the strength to pose for a photograph at all was proof enough to the population that they didn't need to fear the loss of a much-loved member of the royal family any time soon. A year later, Alix released a follow-up image, depicting her in her usual dress with her hair plaited above her head, balancing her new baby, Louise, on her back. Her skirt was hitched up at the front and secured in place by hidden ribbons, it was a walking skirt in action, implying agility and health despite the image's studio setting. Alexandra was sending a clear message that she was fully recovered and that her poor health no longer needed to be a topic of conversation, and the *cartes de visite* produced from it were among the most commercially popular that she would ever release.[75]

Card-mounted photographs and carefully selected poses may have helped the Princess of Wales to protect her public image, but there was not much that they could do to mitigate the physical impact of her period of illness. It was with great agitation that Alexandra noticed she could no longer walk with ease, for her knees were now too stiff and she had a noticeable limp. Fearing public (or even familial) disapproval, Alix tried her hardest to disguise her impediment, passing off her canes as purely decorative, or using a parasol in their place. Unfortunately, 'Alexandramania' was still in full force, and the Princess found, to her horror, that limping movements were being incorporated into ballroom dances in the society circles that she and her admirers frequented.[76] Her disability, which she had tried so desperately to mask, had become a fashion trend.

There were, however, some aspects of her physical ailments that she could successfully mask, which have only been revealed recently by displaying her dresses on standardized mannequins. When Alix's clothes are put on display there often appears to be a major tailoring error: the patterns on the back of her bodices do not lie straight. Instead, they tilt at a slight angle, indicating that the illness that left the Princess with her limp also resulted in a slight curvature of the spine – when she wore her wonky gowns, the patterns appeared to be straight, successfully disguising her condition.[77]

By the time of his accession in 1901, Bertie was fifty-nine years old and Alexandra only a few years younger. He had decided to reign under the name Edward, discarding the name Albert so as not to 'devalue' the legacy of his father, whom he thought should stand alone in the memory of his people as 'Albert the Good'.[78] The new King and Queen were certainly no strangers to royal responsibility, as for almost forty years now they had regularly been called upon to substitute for the reclusive Queen Victoria. They had managed to sustain some of the visual appeal of the monarchy during this period of royal reluctance, though with the final say inevitably lying with Victoria, there was only so much that the couple could achieve as Prince and Princess of Wales. Now that Edward was King, however, the possibilities for a royal transformation were virtually endless and, as has so often been the case throughout history, Edward saw his coronation as an opportunity to set the tone for his reign.

In a manner very similar to King George IV, whom it is often all too tempting to compare to Edward, the new King thought it best to fill the vacuum of royal grandeur that his mother had left behind with a ceremony imbued with medieval traditions. The service was littered with theatricality, but unlike George IV, Edward insisted that any practices that seemed legitimately ridiculous and had no honest bearing upon the coronation should be regulated for moderation. Alexandra also had very strong views about how the coronation might play out: 'I know better than all the milliners and antiquaries, I shall wear exactly what I like and so will all my ladies', were the strong words she sent to one of her husband's equerries during the planning process.[79] It's a statement that is clearly reflected in her coronation ensemble, which tore up the royal rule book in favour of her personal sense of style. The elderly Grand Duchess of Mecklenburg-Strelitz, one of the only court figures who had been present during the last instance of a Queen Consort, provided Alexandra with a detailed analysis of Queen Adelaide's dress and deportment for her coronation in 1831. To the Duchess's shock, there was very little from this handy guidebook that the new Queen Consort chose to implement. Most obviously, Alexandra chose a different, more vibrant shade of purple for her robes than was traditional for British Queens to wear, described as 'petunia' and thickly embroidered all over with motifs more often reserved for a reigning monarch, not a consort. Even her crown (into which the Koh-i-Noor diamond was firmly fixed) featured the four overlapping arches that were used most commonly in her native Denmark, rather than the two that are typical for British regalia.[80] She may have picked a traditional cloth-of-gold gown, but it was layered with a modern tulle that gave it a half whimsical, half modern sense of dimension and movement. The layers and lustre of the dress were intended to come alive under the electric lights that had been hidden around Westminster Abbey, which were to be activated in a blazing splendour at the moment that the King was crowned. Alexandra's express instructions that no aspect of her dress should be 'too conventional' was a tremendously successful choice on her part and inspired just the sort of patriotic response that she and her husband had hoped for.[81] 'I felt a lump in my throat and realized I was more British than I thought,' recorded the American-born Consuelo Vanderbilt, who was just one of many attendees dazzled by the new King and Queen.[82]

Consuelo was one of four ladies chosen to attend the Queen during the coronation, but she was selected not for her title as Duchess of Marlborough but rather for her appearance. All four Duchesses were tall and beautiful, with the same dark hair and aquiline features as the Queen who had selected them. It was a deliberate choice, one that allowed Alexandra to situate herself among a crowd of equally beautiful women who had no possible chance of competing with her sartorial majesty, and was reflective of a fervent vanity that underpinned many of her wardrobe choices as Queen.[83] Alexandra was highly conscious of her ageing appearance, and as a royal whose entire identity thus far had been that of the youthful, beautiful counterpart to a dowdy Queen, the fact that this was no longer the case was a very hard reality to accept. In portrait photographs, Alexandra's skin is retouched to omit all indication of age, leaving a hazy, glowing effect about her face.

This was obviously impossible to replicate in real life, and so Alexandra tried to divert attention from her face using dress. She began to blur the distinction between day dresses and evening dresses, pulling more of the chic glamour and shimmering surface embellishments out from the confines of her ballgowns and court dresses and into her daily wardrobe.

Like Victoria before her, Alexandra was breaking away from the rules of fashion in society in order to serve her own interests, and in turn created a distinctly new tone for royal style. The connotations of this change are perhaps best summarised by Cecil Beaton: 'Queen Alexandra probably started the modern tradition that British royalty can wear anything,' he wrote. 'She would wear spangled or jewelled and bead-embroidered coats in the daytime . . . These were clothes which most women would have worn at night, but the fact that she wore them during the day removed her from reality and only helped to increase the aura of distance that one associates with the court.[84]

Edward and Alexandra's approach to royal life on a wider scale was a mission to introduce modernity. They intended for the monarchy to seem more engaged with society and dedicated time and effort to better understanding the most pressing issues the country faced. They made their approach clear with the introduction of a coronation appeal, which raised £600,000 for local hospitals (roughly £47 million today). Edward was also committed to building and strengthening diplomatic relationships by making formal visits to other countries, which influenced the Queen's wardrobe as it brought her closer to the continental couturiers that she adored and dictated to the King a significant portion of his own dress choices. He now had a new excuse to expand his wardrobe in order to accommodate the various cultures, countries and climates that he was now travelling to, and brought with him on every excursion no fewer than two valets to organize and care for the contents of his travelling trunks. He also invested in a vast array of foreign uniforms that he could wear to flatter foreign leaders when hosting or being hosted, one of the few instances he expressed a Hanoverian appreciation for uniform.

The reign of Edward VII was brief but remembered fondly by many. His health was already poor at the time of his coronation, to the extent that he had to forgo wearing the heavy Crown of St Edward on account of his physical weakness. On 6 May 1910 (after delightedly receiving the news that his horse had just won at Kempton Park races), the King slipped from consciousness and passed away as a result of several heart attacks. Over the next few days, Alexandra would invite a few close friends and family to visit the late King on his deathbed. 'There she was in her simple black dress,' documented one visitor, taking in the appearance of the once-vibrant Queen, who now moved about the room as if her husband were just 'a child asleep'. Alexandra and her guest spoke for a while, and then, he wrote, 'I left her, moved just at the end to tears, and she sat down at the little chair which had been placed at the King's bedside. Round the room were all the things just as he had last used them, with his hats hanging on their pegs, as he loved them to be.'[85]

After the appropriate period was over, Alexandra would shed her mourning clothes in favour of her usual spangled ensembles, though the colour palette was more muted than before, a subtle acknowledgment of her position as a widow. Throughout the country there was widespread mourning, particularly amongst the circles that the King had frequented. At Royal Ascot that year, the royal enclosure was transformed into a sea of black, relieved only by the occasional string of pearls or a white lily fixed into a hat.

Part Five

THE WINDSORS

WHEN QUEEN VICTORIA had married Prince Albert in 1840, the British branch of the Hanoverians had come to a close. Their children became part of their father's house, the House of Saxe-Coburg and Gotha, and the reign of Edward VII marked the start of their very short tenure as a British dynasty.

There was no shock extinction of Victoria's many descendants, no replacement by a foreign dynasty, simply a need to adapt to the ways of the world. During the First World War, when Britain took up arms against Germany, a monarchy with a German name did not bode well for the royal family and would leave them vulnerable to public opinion. The name was changed by the son of Bertie and Alix, during his reign as King George V, to the thoroughly British 'House of Windsor'. I'm sure, unlike some of our previous dynasties, the Windsors need very little introduction.

GEORGE V

IN EARLY 1893, Princess Mary of Teck, the childhood best friend of the children of the Prince and Princess of Wales, was engaged. It was a picture-perfect fairy-tale route to Queenship that could have been pulled straight out of the pages of a romance novel. It was in 1886 that Prince Albert Victor, the eldest son of Bertie and Alix, first saw Princess 'May' in a new light. At her court debut, she stood beside her mother in a white silk evening gown, the low-pointed bodice speckled all over with tiny pearl flowers and her tulle-draped skirt arranged over a bustle crinoline. Her ash-blonde hair was fixed with a plume of white feathers, her neck tied with a little white ribbon, and her whole body covered in beautiful jewellery from the family collection – silver bracelets, her mother's necklace and a large star of diamonds being amongst the most noticeable.[1] Now Albert Victor saw her as not just a friend from fonder times but as a key society figure with prominent family connections.

This was the point of court presentations, to notify the world that these young debutantes were now ready to make their entry into the London social scene. It provided connections and status, making it a coveted experience that many families took a studious interest in perfecting. Many parents would rather postpone their daughter's presentation if they felt they were not adequately equipped with the funds and knowledge to commission the best dress for her debut season, rather than face the humiliation of sending her to court incorrectly dressed. May didn't have to worry as her mother, the Duchess of Teck, was a courtly style aficionado, and had been one of those British aristocrats that the young Princess Alexandra had turned to for advice during her engagement period. It's no wonder then that May dazzled despite her otherwise rather plain appearance and managed to secure the prize that most Victorian debutantes aspired towards: a socially advantageous marriage match. A few years later, Albert Victor proposed to Princess Mary.

Tragedy struck when just six weeks after their engagement the young Prince was cut down in his prime by influenza. Suddenly May found herself quite at a loss. She had already begun to settle into the life of a royal bride and had only just acclimatized to the whirlwind preparations that came with it; 'How people do bother,' she had written a few weeks previously. 'We get trousseau things sent to us on approval from all places . . . we are nearly driven mad.'[2] That trousseau of dresses and accessories for her future as a newlywed were now left to gather dust, much to the distress of her family who had paid a pretty penny for them and were quite concerned about the state of their finances as a consequence. It was during this period of turmoil that 'loving, miserable May' drew closer to Albert Victor's younger brother, Prince George, and the duo rekindled their childhood camaraderie in their shared grief.[3] It seemed obvious to everyone but the friends themselves that George was surely the only suitable new marriage prospect for May, and so it was that after much pressure from their pushy families the hesitant couple became engaged, with May still dressed in mourning for her husband that never was.

Prince George was a naval man, and though the death of his older brother had put a stop to his active service, he would never let anyone forget his time at sea. He was bolder (and a little shorter) than his late brother had been and was filled with a certain self-confidence that allowed his unique world view to shine through and compete with his many royal relatives. While his parents, Bertie and Alexandra, were characterized by their forward-thinking approach to life, fashion and the Crown, George saw the world through a much more conservative lens. He had a hesitancy, which later grew into an aversion, towards progression that manifested in all aspects of his life, including his clothing. This had relatively little impact on how his sense of style was perceived by others, as in a period where little would change for men's dress save for the size of a hat or shape of a lapel, he could comfortably hold on to times gone by without outwardly seeming too antiquated.

Princess Mary shared many of the values that her new husband held. Their marriage of duty gradually bloomed into a legitimately affectionate coupling, though with a strong internal sense of propriety dictating their every move, they would rarely ever show this to the public, or even to their children. At the time of his accession in 1910, George emerged from his father's shadow as a capsule of an age gone by, truly a Victorian thinker, both in the sense that he shared a commonality of mind with his conservative grandmother, but also in that he aligned with the character of the age to which she lent her name. He had carried himself through the electric vibrancy of the Edwardian years and come out the other side with his personal views unaffected: 'We are back in the Victorian times,' one contemporary noted of royal life. 'Everything so peaceful and domestic.'[4]

George and Mary's traditional values were a central element of their coronation. They stripped back some of the dramatics that Edward VII had infused the event with, and cast away Alexandra's stylish petunia-coloured robes, and the ceremony was a straightforward affair. They did, however, buck tradition by attending the 1911 Delhi Durbar, the coronation-style event hosted in Delhi to recognize the new monarch's position as Emperor of India. The first had taken place in 1877 when Victoria had been made Empress, and the second in 1903, but the third of these, which was to be the last of its kind, was the grandest, chiefly because for the first time the Emperor himself would be in attendance. George and Mary appeared in the same robes they had worn for their coronation, with a new Imperial State Crown designed for use by the Emperor and a new tiara for Mary – a great wall of diamond scrolls surmounted with emeralds wrapped around her frizzed up-do.

Sparkle was an integral part of the Durbar experience. Across the British Empire, the Viceroys and Governors, as well as all the wealthy Brits who had ventured abroad to make their fortunes, all felt a responsibility to adequately represent the royals and aristocrats back home for whom they were standing as substitutes. At the Durbars, this was felt tenfold, and by dressing as elaborately as possible, they could not only prove to their visiting peers that they were competent at upholding Britain's imperial interests but could also enforce their superiority over those around them, taking motifs of cultural significance, from peacocks to palmettes, to inspire their gowns and tiaras. The prominence of jewellery at the Delhi Durbar meant that it could also be used to undermine the power of the Empire: when Maharaja Sayajirao III attended wearing none of his fine jewels, it was taken as a snub to the King and a visual declaration of his disgust for British rule.[5]

At the dawn of the new reign, women's fashion had transformed significantly from the previous decade. The hyper-feminized silhouette of the Edwardian age, which had been achieved with neatly tailored gowns laced over tightly corseted bodies, had given way to a freer form inspired by Japanese kimonos and a rise in oriental influence. Waistlines were raised below the bust once more, and dress bodices were loose and airy, with artfully draped skirts tapering towards the ankles. The styles flattered the Queen, who was tall and slender, and she wore many variations on the same theme – coats and court dresses all in shades of duck-egg blue, dove grey and soft lilac. Colour was risky territory, and Mary very rarely deviated from these gentle tones; 'The Queen wore a red soft velvet dress with fur,' documented Lady Bertha Dawkins one day, 'she has never worn red before' – the year was 1930 and Queen Mary was already well into her sixties.[6]

Mary's unwavering dress sense had very practical implications. She hated spending hours at a time stood around at dress fittings and by wearing near identical clothes she rendered them virtually unnecessary. Everything from accurate measurements to appropriate prices could be procured from her immaculately kept wardrobe records; when the iconic royal couturier Norman Hartnell had nervously taken his first commission from the Queen, his proposed price for each design had been slapped down promptly. 'Her Majesty desires me to say that the price of 35 guineas for the dress is much too little,' one of her ladies-in-waiting had told him over the telephone. 'Her Majesty desires to pay 45 guineas.'[7] There was to be no deviation from her rituals, not even when it meant snagging a bargain.

The public response to the Queen's style was varied. She was not considered to be a fashionable woman; as the First World War came and went, women's dresses became shorter and far more androgenous than before, though little moves would be made on Mary's behalf to keep up with that transformation. No strict rules were enacted, even by the ultra-conservative King, to limit the impact that changing styles had on court dress, and for once even George was forced to admit that modernity might have its benefits. The shorter dresses meant that less fabric would need to be wasted in the post-war period, and limits were placed on the length of court trains, successfully avoiding criticisms that the royal world was too indulgent as they gradually re-introduced major events to their Palace schedules. The difference between Mary and the fashions of wider society was so great that it was not uncommon for women to use her as a model of how *not* to dress, the fashionable Lady Cynthia Asquith instructing her tailor that 'he must do something to my white coat and skirt to make me look less like Queen Mary', though on a grander scale her image was far more effective.[8]

During the war, the image of Queen Mary in her enduring costume, standing beside her husband in his naval uniform as they visited troops and factories, was a comforting crutch for a nation yearning for stability. Her sculptural toque hats, which were adopted for the practical purpose of keeping her face unobscured from the crowds, quickly became her most iconic feature, giving her an air of grandeur and archi-tectural elegance. 'It was like talking to St Paul's Cathedral,' was the comparison made by one of her acquaintances.[9] It may not have been achieved with the same fashion acumen, but Queen Mary was in her own unique way a continuation of Queen Alexandra's ideology that royalty can dress according to its own rules.

But there was a different side to Queen Mary. The inner workings of the royal family in this era were observed closely by one of its most constant companions, Mabell Ogilvy, the Countess of Airlie, whose long tenure as Lady of the Bedchamber to the Queen brought her into the heart of royal business, the details of which were retold in an unfinished memoir discovered after her death in 1956. The Countess was one of Mary's closest friends, and consequently was well aware of her style methodology. 'She was much more interested in fashion than most people imagined,' Mabell revealed, casting doubt on the image of a Queen who stubbornly refused to maintain a stylish appearance based on a sense of duty or even boredom.[10]

Rather, Mary's fashion choices were dictated to her by the 'conservative prejudices' of her husband, who gave instructions on every aspect of her dress, from cut to colour, to ensure they satisfied his preference for the past.[11] His criticisms were harsh and were directed at anyone who even remotely bothered to keep up with new trends: 'Now that I come to think of it,' one of his sons would later reminisce, 'clothes were always a favourite topic of his conversation. With my father, it was not so much a discussion as to who he considered to be well or badly dressed; it was more usually a diatribe against anyone who dressed differently to himself.'[12] Mabell and Mary would work together in an attempt to circumvent the King's strong opinions and find things in the Queen's wardrobe that they could change without pushing him too far: 'I think she longed in secret to get away from the hats and dresses which were always associated with her,' was the conclusion drawn by the Countess. During the 1920s, when hemlines began to shorten, Mabell and Mary conspired to make changes to their own wardrobe. Mabell volunteered to go first, 'the plan being that if His Majesty made no unfavourable comment the Queen would follow my example'. Though the change had only been one or two inches, when George confided to Mary that he thought the Countess's dress too short, Mabell let down her hemline as quickly as possible, and the Queen accepted that her fate was always to remain as a time capsule of days gone by.[13]

Stifled by outdated and dull dresses, Mary's creative impulses boiled beneath the surface before spilling out from the cracks in a stream of diamonds. Where clothing was strictly regulated, jewellery was Mary's playground, and it is to her that we owe some of the greatest and most iconic pieces of jewellery still found in the royal collection. Tiaras were not a new concept, having been drawn from antiquity by France's Empress Josephine in the early 1800s; however, it was due to Queen Mary's careful attentions that they achieved their golden age – and families went to great pains to get the designs just right. They were indicators of identity, spelling out in precious stones the family to which the wearer was born or had married into, and, according to one contemporary, 'were as much tribal insignia and cultural totems as jewelled ornament, accurately reflecting the status, ancestry and social pecking-order of their wearers'.[14] The size and design of the tiara conveyed these messages, and Mary's creations were no stranger to these symbols – her Delhi Durbar tiara is a towering three-inch wall of diamonds, and her iconic lover's knot (best known for its outings on the heads of Diana Spencer and Kate Middleton) was designed as a replica of her grandmother's tiara, referencing her family ties. Mary wore tiaras to all possible occasions, including private family dinners, and has become so closely associated with royal jewellery that the Cullinan III and IV brooch, a favourite of Mary's and cut from the largest rough diamond ever found, was referred to by her granddaughter Elizabeth II as 'Granny's Chips'.[15]

EDWARD VIII

ON 21 JANUARY 1936, the day after King George V had passed away, the declaration of his son's accession was read in the grounds of St James's Palace. It was a colourful sight, all the mace bearers and trumpeters bedecked in their fine uniforms, arranged on a balcony jutting forth from the old brick building. Just to the side, at a perfect vantage point to witness the proclamation, was the new King himself, peering through a window in a pristine suit. Beside him, a pale, chiselled face pierced through the darkness of the sea of mourning clothes – a woman, her dark hair and thick eyebrows set off against her alabaster-white skin, her head darting back and forth between the crowd and the pageant as though she were watching a tennis match. When the proclamation ended, they turned away from the window, the King raising his hat to acknowledge the crowds, and then the duo disappeared into the dimness of the Palace. Not even a year later, King Edward VIII had abdicated, leaving court life with the dark-haired woman by his side, the Crown now passed to the care of his younger brother. Edward's decision to give up the throne triggered a royal crisis on a monumental scale, fuelling the fire of British republicanism with a single, devastating radio broadcast. To understand how the monarchy reached this position,

we first have to look a little further back in the life of King
Edward VIII.

As a little boy, David, as the future King was known
(owing to the assortment of Edwards already in the family),
was subject to his father's Victorian approach to parenting.
His parents first manifested in his life as 'Olympian figures',
occasionally passing through the nursery to enquire after the
developmental progress of their heir but otherwise leaving
him to the care of his nannies.[16] Edward's own memories
of his childhood are littered with various strict instructions
from his father on the subject of dress, which even at the
age of sixty-six he could recount with regimented precision.
'We were, in fact, figuratively speaking, always on parade. A
fact he never allowed us to forget,' he wrote of his father. 'If
we appeared before him with our Navy lanyards a fraction
of an inch out of place, or with our dirks or sporrans awry,
there would be an outburst worthy of the quarter-deck of a
warship.'[17] When George noticed that his sons had begun to
stand with their hands in their pockets, a stylish pose often
featured in the fashion photography of the time, he immediately instructed their nanny to sew up the pockets of their
sailor suits.

The lack of parental approval struck deep for David; his
autobiography, A King's Story, is peppered with anecdotes of
times when he could have received his father's praise but was
instead continually deprived. These instances only increased
in number when he left home to study at Oxford and for the
first time in his life was given the freedom to control his own
appearance. 'I fancied myself a bit of a dandy – but, of course,
of the discreetest possible kind,'[18] thought David at the time.
It was during this period that he began to take a legitimate
interest in fashion, not so much for the fact that 'clothes make
the Prince', a principle that he had been made crucially aware

of by his duty-bound family, but rather as part of a search for comfort and a more genteel way of living. Part of this journey of style discovery involved adopting cuffed trousers, a trend which had first been used to keep mud and rain from ruining the fabric of men's trousers but had subsequently been adopted as a permanent fixture into the wardrobes of the voguish. Naturally, it was a style that George V detested. David first wore them in his father's presence over breakfast at Buckingham Palace, where 'instead of complimenting me on my taste, my father looked at me in a curious way and suddenly asked, with magnificent irrelevance, "Is it raining in *here*?"'[19] The young Prince David was stunned, but it dawned on him quickly that yet again he had failed to live up to his father's conservative expectations. This stifling upbringing meant that he would harbour a fierce resentment for the royal establishment and all the traditions that went along with it from a very young age; he referred to that sartorially oppressive group as the 'frock-coated enclave', in reference to the antiquated style of coat that his father insisted on wearing and would always keep close at hand in case royal duty should somehow catch him unawares.[20] It should come as no surprise, then, that one of the first things that David would do after becoming King was to ban the frock coat from court.

After the First World War, David found that the typical fashions of 1920s London were no longer to his tastes. With their emphasis on a nipped-in waist and broad shoulders, men's suits were now vaguely reminiscent of the khaki uniforms that generation of gentlemen had spent the last four years living and fighting in. But rather than finding comfort in familiarity, the young Prince found it instead through rebellion – dressing as lightly and casually as possible to break away from the rigidity of uniforms. For inspiration, he turned to America, where undergraduate Ivy League students had crafted for themselves a distinct and relaxed fashion built around drapery, and he adopted their style soon after he returned from his first American tour in 1919. David's widespread popularity during his time as a Prince can largely be accredited to the fact that he was incredibly well travelled, and this 1919 tour was one of many trips abroad that he would make on behalf of the royal family. It was David's responsibility, as one of the most sociable members of the royal clan, to bring Britain to the world, and in return he brought the world right back to Britain.

His ascent to one of the arbiters of style for his time was extraordinarily rapid, and in an age of celebrity, where Hollywood stars were dominating the pages of newspapers and magazines, it was nothing short of a miracle that he managed to hold the fort of royal relevance in the world of modern fashion. Wherever he went, he was hounded by photographers and journalists who were desperate to know where he bought his suits and what type of tie he liked to wear, the answers to which would then be dispersed to their readers post haste. He was well aware of the impact that he had on the British textiles trade, though he would earnestly insist that he never chose his clothes with the intention to have them copied. Regardless, people still went to fantastical lengths to replicate his clothes. The Prince's tailor Frederick Scholte, to whom he would remain loyal until 1959, found himself in exceptionally high demand as a consequence of his illustrious royal patron. In one of the most extreme instances, a man from Chicago established a standing order with Scholte on the condition he would receive a replica of every suit made for the Prince of Wales until further notice.[21] No doubt he would have been very confused when his deliveries arrived containing only jackets and waistcoats – David never commissioned his trousers from Scholte, preferring to source them from a different country altogether. Scholte was a talented tailor and was instrumental in helping the Prince shape his fashion sense, but he was also firmly fixed on what styles he thought were worth making and refused to cater for David's love of American trousers which used belts rather than braces.[22] That starstruck Chicagoan gentleman would be able to look much closer to home to authentically finish his royal look.

There are a great many style inventions credited to David. He's often thought to have been the man to introduce wide plus-four trousers to America and to have encouraged his fellow Brits to switch from braces to belts. Most famous is his tie with the Windsor knot, though he himself would argue that he had nothing to do with it; 'It was I believe regulation wear for G.I.s during the war, when American college boys adopted it too. But in fact, I was in no way responsible for this,' he insisted.[23] The confusion is unsurprising, as every fashion publication worth their weight in salt was desperate to declare the discovery of some new style seen on the Prince of Wales; 'Such phenomenal interest is taken in what H.R.H. wears that, as soon as he appears in any innovation, a detailed description is cabled to the ends of the earth' are the words printed in a 1935 Vogue article titled 'H.R.H. Started It'. 'And here comes the unconscious, but tremendous influence that the Prince wields. The smart sportswoman follows devotedly what the Prince is wearing,' continues the article, declaring that not only was he a trailblazer for menswear but was also a source of inspiration for the stylish, active woman, citing that the most popular tweeds, hats, coats and shoes worn by the ladies of the time could be traced back to a common ancestor – Prince David.[24]

In his memoirs, Edward cites a whole host of figures who influenced his style, referencing the colourful characters who would haunt the same jazz bars and house parties as him. They are a cosmopolitan bunch, fitting for an equally cosmo-

politan Prince, but far more notable is the figure who clearly
shaped his mindset towards fashion, whose actions and words
are brought up regularly by David to justify his choices – his
grandfather, King Edward VII. Undoubtedly, he saw an aspect
of his own story reflected in the life of his kinsman – David
was aware of the constant berating Bertie had received from
his own parents, particularly in regard to dress – and his mus-
ings on the topic of personal style often rely upon the late King
to prove that an interest in fashionable life wasn't necessarily
an indication of poor kingship, regardless of what his own
father might say. Where the two men differed quite spectacularly was in their approach to dress etiquette. Edward VII may
have relished pointing out every sartorial blunder he saw at
court, but his grandson found it to be the single most boring
affair imaginable. He despised the formality of it all, wearily
observing from behind his parents' gilded thrones as dozens
of debutantes in uninspired court dresses curtseyed and sim-
pered before them. It was at one of these dreary occasions that
David, unknowingly, first met Wallis Simpson.

Born Wallis Warfield, at the time of her presentation to
court in 1931 the American socialite was already on to her
second husband. Her family were prominent in the Baltimore
social scene but had found themselves the victims of financial
misfortune not long after her birth; Wallis had had to rely
upon the kindness of her wealthy aunts and uncles for all of
her childhood, forcing her to develop the fierce determination
that she would come to be characterized by. Her marriage to
the successful British shipbroker Ernest Simpson had seen
her make the move to Mayfair and brought her tantalizingly
close to the circles of the London elite. It was nothing too
unusual for her – she had moved in upper-class circles back
in Baltimore and had always had a drive to better her social
standing – but the ancient rituals of the British elite were a

fascinating new discovery. She took up a habit of religiously studying newspapers to find clues to crack their codes: 'There was one organ of the British press that instantly absorbed my curiosity,' she later recalled, 'the Court Circular, which recorded the movements, engagements, and appearances of the royal family.'[25] The columns of these newspapers had opened up a window into a glittering, mysterious world, the likes of which Wallis had never seen before. A few years later, she would finally get the chance to sate her curiosity when one of her new London friends offered to present her at court, providing her with a chance for a formal initiation into the London social season.

In June of that year, Wallis, like so many other budding debutantes, rose early to dress for her presentation. On went a white silk gown lent to her by her friend Connie Thaw, who had worn it for her own presentation just a few years before. Then, to satisfy tradition, she fastened a silver embroidered train to her shoulders and fixed a trio of white feathers into her short, dark hair, again all courtesy of Connie.[26] Finally, she hung a diamond cross – about the size of her open palm – around her neck on a slender chain and embarked for Buckingham Palace, ready to be presented to the King and Queen in borrowed clothes. She appeared before George and Mary and curtseyed low, then, after what many people could count on as being one of their only encounters with royalty, Wallis was swallowed up by the ocean of debutantes, court dresses and uniforms that filled the room. As she flitted around the edges of the gaggle, her ears picked up on the end of a conversation: 'Something ought to be done about the lights, they make all the women look ghastly,' griped a bored voice, a voice belonging to none other than the Prince of Wales himself, who was now trying to make a beeline for the exit.[27] Wallis took note of the remark and stood in silent amusement when at a party later that night that very same Prince gushed over the sophisticated simplicity of her dress. 'But, Sir,' she finally interrupted, 'I understood that you thought we all looked ghastly.' The Prince blanched, and a charmed smile spread across his face. 'I had no idea my voice carried so far.'[28]

And just like that, over a glass of champagne and a discussion about the pitfalls of court dress, one of the most explosive relationships in royal history was born. Over the coming years, Wallis would join David on his journeys through royal life and the world at large, becoming the latest post-holder of the position of his mistress. One fortunate by-product of being so closely associated with the most stylish man of the age was the inevitable attention she now courted from the press. By 1935 Wallis had begun to seep into the fashion lexicon, peppering herself amongst the pages of the most revered style magazines of the time. There was a distinct change brought about in Mrs Simpson by her elevated social position, which Cecil Beaton, the photographer famed for his framing of the 'bright young things' of the 1920s, picked up on when he tried to draw her portrait: 'Of late, her general appearance is more refined,' he deduced, pinning it down to her slender figure and ability to dress well. He praised her light yet immaculately tidy visage, her dedication to neat make-up, her hair – styled so pristinely 'a fly would slip off it'.[29] The likes of *Vogue* and *Tatler* could not help but print photographs of her sharp clothes, applauding her tasteful use of sportswear by day and colourful and artistic modern jewellery by night. By the time her white face appeared at the window of St James's in 1936 she was already an established figure in the world of fashion, and as synonymous with the new King Edward VIII as he was with her.

Edward's accession all but tethered him to a life of perpetual deskwork. Much to his annoyance, it was time for the new King to bid adieu to his sojourns in the south of France in favour of the piles upon piles of royal paperwork that he was now destined to flit through until the day he died. Naturally, Edward was unenthused by the monotony of it all. He tried to remedy the situation for the sake of his own sanity by culling some of the antiquated court practices that most bored him, but in doing so he attracted the criticism of those surrounding him, butting heads with some of the oldest British institutions. His experience as a much-photographed celebrity Prince had forced Edward to consider his appearance from all angles, and he had come to the conclusion that without a doubt his *left* side was his *best* side. Unsurprisingly, he was frustrated when he saw that the proposed portraits intended for use on coins and stamps featured the right side of his face in profile. He complained, and the Deputy Master of the Royal Mint attempted to explain their choice. It was tradition, he said, that when money is stamped with the portrait of a new monarch, they should always face the opposite way from the monarch who came before them; 'Your grandfather, King Edward VII, looked to the right, Sir, and his late Majesty your father looked to the left.'[30] If the new King was to get his way, he would have to battle fiercely. Edward versus institution, vanity versus tradition.

Eventually, the Royal Mint would surrender, but victory would still swoop in unexpectedly when the King abdicated before his controversial coins could even be struck. To Edward, one of his chief concerns as a new King was the woman he wanted to make Queen, Wallis Simpson. By October of that year she had divorced her husband in preparation for a proposal from her long-time beau; however, the British government refused to grant the couple permission to marry, citing Wallis's status as a double divorcee as one of their chief issues. Backed into a corner and clearly not a fan of royal life in any case, Edward decided that he could not live without

Queen Victoria's paper dolls. Drawn by her governess and coloured-in by the future Queen, these dolls show the very best of 1830s fashion – full skirts, large sleeves, and low necklines that Queen Adelaide would *not* have approved of!

Is this the most famous dress in fashion history? Queen Victoria's pale silk wedding dress changed the trajectory of royal style and put white wedding dresses on the map for good.

Queen Victoria created an iconic wardrobe that mixed mourning etiquette with royal splendour. To the left stands her son, the style-savvy Edward VII in a crisp uniform. On the right, the glamourous and willowy Alexandra disguises her neck scar with chokers and diamonds.

Dressing for the camera – Queen Alexandra (right) and her sister, Dagmar (left) pose in striking polka-dot dresses designed to stand out in photographs.

From left to right: the old-school King George V, his mother Alexandra, her sister Dagmar and Queen Mary. At the suggestion of her husband, Mary's style was traditional and conservative.

Above. After the abdication crisis Edward VIII and Wallis Simpson fled to Europe for their wedding. The soon-to-be Duchess included in her trousseau the iconic 'Lobster Dress' – a genius collaboration between Elsa Schiaparelli and Salvador Dalí.

Left. The Duke and Duchess of Windsor had a unique sense of style in later life. Relying on bold colours, daring patterns, epic proportions and eccentric jewellery, they were a fashion-foil to their family back at Buckingham Palace.

Above. Royals at war, from left to right: the future Elizabeth II in her military-style 'Princess Hat', George VI in uniform, Elizabeth Bowes-Lyon in her bright, dainty outfit and Princess Margaret.

Right. In 1969, King Charles III attended his investiture as Prince of Wales. Elizabeth II wore a sleek Norman Hartnell dress and he a set of ceremonial robes. Charles also wore his brand new, horoscope-ping-pong-ball crown.

Diana's early years as a royal were defined by her fairy-tale approach. Romance and delicacy were key to her style, crafting her into the fantasy Princess of everyone's dreams. At the State Opening of Parliament in 1984, the Princess of Wales stunned in this whimsical, Victorian-inspired gown.

In the 90s, Diana's style became cleaner and less fussy. In 1994, she wore the iconic 'revenge dress', a chic and timeless announcement of her independence from royal life.

The 'Kate effect' at work – the current Princess of Wales knows how to dress-down in royal style. With her hair loose, her no-nonsense trousers on and sporting a high-street Zara blazer, she's the royal tasked with making the institution feel down to earth.

Above. At the 2022 Jubilee celebrations, we saw the other side of Kate – the coat-dress-toting, historic-jewellery-wearing future Queen. Beside her, a classic example of Queen Camilla's style.

Left. Fashioning an exit. For their last official appearance as working royals, the Duke and Duchess of Sussex put up a united front by wearing the same shade of green in their outfits.

marrying Mrs Simpson, 'and, however painful the prospect, I shall, if necessary, abdicate in order to do so'.[31] Seeing no other option but to do just that, King Edward VIII abdicated the throne on 11 December 1936, passed the Crown over to his brother, packed his bags and left for France.

On 3 June the very next year, the summer sun beat down heavily upon the pale stone facade of Château de Candé. Men in sharp uniforms and shiny top hats were speckled across the lush green grass that surrounded the picturesque French castle, and restless at the front of the pack stood Cecil Beaton, camera in hand. He had spent the last few months patiently trekking around behind the ex-King and his lover to snap nearly every article of clothing they wore and report back to *Vogue*, who knew that now more than ever everybody wanted to know exactly what Edward and Wallis were up to. Finally, from the darkness of the castle emerged Edward, now styled the Duke of Windsor, with his new bride, Wallis, leading her down the ornate stone staircase where they posed on the final step like naturals, the Duke's left cheek turned ever so slightly towards the camera. As far as royal weddings go, the context surrounding this marriage made it one of the more curious in recent years, and so too was the bride's dress a deviation from the norm. Wallis had picked her design from the American couturier Main Rousseau Bocher, who had concocted a slender satin gown that would highlight the 'boyish' figure of his patron. Her piercing eyes were emphasized by his unusual colour choice of 'Wallis Blue' – a light and airy shade of blue created especially for the new Duchess's wedding dress.[32] The bodice resembled a draped blouse with long sleeves lined with buttons, which were one of the most enduring elements in her wardrobe; 'Buttons were always a favourite with the Duchess,' the designer Marc Bohen would later recount. 'One of the last Dior dresses I made for her was a hostess dress in ivory crepe with little buttons down the sleeves rather like that wedding dress.'[33] The bodice was cinched inwards by a heart-shaped waistband and descended to the floor in a slender flute of fabric. She wore no veil, and certainly no tiara; instead she was crowned by a small hat of blue and pink feathers, surmounted by a halo of tulle.

Wallis's trousseau had become a matter of international interest over the last few months, for her new wedding wardrobe had been carefully filled with designer pieces intended to show off her usual chicness at its most exuberant. The month before the wedding, *Vogue* had featured a spread on the soon-to-be-Duchess's new purchases, taking a particular interest in the seventeen outfits she had bought from Elsa Schiaparelli for the princely sum of £5,000. They are all tremendously formal pieces, with hints of wispy romance, but in typical 'Shiap's' style were pulled into the present day by surrealist influence.[34] The most photographed outfit in the spread (and certainly the most famous of any dress worn by Wallis) was the 'Lobster Dress', a white silk evening dress cinched at the waist by a great crimson waistband and speckled all over with printed parsley sprigs. The titular lobster was painted by Salvador Dali and arranged across the front of the skirt between the wearer's legs, invoking the sexual imagery that Dali envisioned lobsters themselves to represent.[35] Undoubtedly Wallis was making a statement when she chose the dress for her trousseau, as her sexual morality as a twice-married woman and mistress to the King had brought her under attack all throughout the abdication. The Lobster Dress represented her victory over her critics, and by refusing to tread lightly around the subject of sexuality, she proved that their remarks had not cut as deep as many of them would have hoped. If Wallis was to be known for her style and her scandals, why not marry them together?

For the rest of her life, all of Wallis's clothes would be

imbued with a sense of fantasy. You could always rely on the Duchess of Windsor to appear in a gown or suit of bold block colours, heavily laden with the most bizarre and amusing jewellery ever seen – a tutti-frutti cockerel brooch, a diamond bracelet shaped like a panther, or a chain of multi-coloured gemstone crucifixes. Edward too would become increasingly eccentric in his dress, relying on cluttered and contrasting patterns in his shirts, and jackets, and comically wide ties. It was no doubt a bid to remain relevant as arbiters of fashion even after youth had passed them by, employing an element of showmanship that fell into uncharted territory somewhere between Hollywood excess and royal grandeur. Never did they let the public forget who they were, and who they nearly could have been, with most of the handbags in Wallis's expansive collection emblazoned in gold with her monogram of two interlocking Ws, crowned by a small coronet.[36]

The Duke and Duchess of Windsor remained in the public eye for most of their lives. They would often find themselves embroiled in controversy, particularly during the Second World War, when the couple became associated with various prominent fascist figures. Publicly, the Duke would always assert that he harboured no leniency for the Nazi ideology, but many acquaintances would later insist that he had privately expressed sympathy for the party and its leader, Adolf Hitler.[37] Seeing as Hitler and the Nazi party deliberately sought to build and flaunt connections with the most stylish members of European society in order to fuel their propaganda machine, it is unsurprising that the Duke and Duchess would have been exposed to fascist ideologies in the fashionable circles that they moved in, and this explains why Hitler was so keen to meet with the couple during their 1937 tour of Germany. By the time of his death in 1972, Edward had lived a vibrant, colourful and controversial life that he would never have had the chance to experience as King. His celebrity charm and casual way of life were clearly better suited to the adventures of a socialite than a monarch, and his deviation from the typical expectations of kingship were made only more prominent when compared to his successor, the man onto whom he had thrust the Crown at the time of his abdication: his brother, Prince Albert, the Duke of York.

GEORGE VI

In 1935, Norman Hartnell received a letter from Drumlan-
rig Castle. It was a request from Lady Alice Montague Douglas
Scott, the new fiancé of Prince Henry, Duke of Gloucester, one
of the last unmarried sons of King George V and Mary of Teck,
requesting that he be the couturier entrusted with the duty of
designing her wedding dress.[38] Jumping at the opportunity to
work on such a lucrative royal commission, Hartnell created
a chic, pearl-pink gown for the future Duchess and sketched
out a design for her eight bridesmaids to wear. Not long after
the letter had been sent, Hartnell was paid a visit by three
very important members of the wedding party – Elizabeth
Bowes-Lyon, Duchess of York, and her two young daughters,
Princesses Elizabeth and Margaret Rose. The designer was
giddy with a mixture of nerves and excitement and had spent
the previous few days coaching his staff on how to curtsey to
their royal visitors.

'Not so quick and jerky,' he had instructed. 'Not like a pecking sparrow, more like a swooning swan!'[39]

The Duchess arrived with her little daughters on each arm,
she in a grey, fur-trimmed ensemble sprinkled with diamond
and aquamarine jewellery, and they in matching blue coats
with wreaths of forget-me-knots encircling their little grey

caps.[40] Elizabeth had come to inspect the bridesmaid dresses that her daughters were to be wearing and to oversee the first fitting. The dresses that Hartnell presented to her were quite different to the first sketches that he had sent to Lady Alice; he had wanted each bridesmaid, regardless of age, to match, and had drawn up a slender, empire-line gown that descended from a neckline of orange blossoms. The Princesses' grandfather, King George V, had intervened after hearing of the initial ideas, requesting that the young bridesmaids' dresses should be more traditionally 'girlish'. The new designs, short frocks with a pink ribbon sash and layers of frothy tulle, delighted the Duchess of York and delighted the royal family at large. During the wedding, the indomitable figure of Queen Mary had told Hartnell, who was on hand in case of any costume malfunctions, in full regal tone: 'We are very pleased. We think everything is very, very pretty.'[41]

The wedding of Lady Alice marked the acceptance of Norman Hartnell into the fold of royal fashion. Three months later, shortly after the death of George V, Hartnell was invited to the home of the Duke and Duchess of York, this time to discuss dresses for the Duchess herself, ones that could be quickly supplied to meet the demand of the mourning clothing that she now needed. The York family home was not one of the usual royal haunts. They did not live in one of the many official royal residences but in a rather genteel-looking mansion in Piccadilly, classy enough for a Prince and his bride but comparatively simple, to suit their reserved lifestyle.

Lady Elizabeth Bowes-Lyon was the daughter of the Earl and Countess of Strathmore and Kinghorn, and her marriage to Prince Albert had broken with royal tradition in that he, as the son of a King, had been expected to marry a Princess from another royal family, not simply the daughter of a peer. The wedding took place on 26 April 1923 at Westminster Abbey, with the Prince in his RAF uniform and Elizabeth in a gown devised by Madame Handley-Seymour. In typical 1920s style, it featured an androgynous, baggy, dropped waist and was criss-crossed with thick strips of silver lamé speckled with pearls. *Vogue's* coverage of the event, which featured an illustration of Elizabeth that accurately depicted her gown but fabricated a height that the newly titled Duchess certainly did not have, labelled the gown romantic, describing it as resembling 'a medieval Italian robe'.[42] During the ceremony, Elizabeth started a new and enduring royal wedding tradition by placing her bouquet upon the Grave of the Unknown Soldier to honour her brother, who had died during the conflict of the First World War. Ever since then, royal brides have had their bouquets sent to the Abbey to be laid at the grave, regardless of where in the country their ceremony took place. Elizabeth's bouquet contained flowers of significance to her – white roses to represent the County of York (she and Albert were now to be styled as Duke and Duchess of the region), heather to pay homage to her childhood home in Scotland, and myrtle. The trend for including sprigs of myrtle in royal bouquets had begun with Queen Victoria, but was truly cemented in tradition by her daughter, Princess Vicky, who chose to use myrtle cut from a bush at their family home Osborne House, on the Isle of Wight. From Princess Vicky onwards, each royal bride has bulked up their wedding bouquet using some of the special Osborne royal myrtle, and Elizabeth Bowes-Lyon was no exception.[43]

Married life at 145 Piccadilly was a very happy affair for the new Duke and Duchess of York. Within ten years the couple had welcomed two children and were well-liked figures in the royal family. They might not have had the same celebrity sparkle as Albert's older brother, Prince David, but they certainly knew how to balance formality with fun and charmed their way through several extremely well-received royal tours. As Prince, Albert had a propensity to fade into the background. He wasn't considered to be the most handsome, nor the most stylish of the family. Cecil Beaton, who admittedly liked to look for the fantasy in everything he turned his camera towards, found that he was entirely without 'mystery or magic'.[44] In a roundabout way this would become his appeal, as his straightforwardness assured people that he was comfortingly without artifice, and his public image was reinforced by the litany of photographs and paintings produced of the family in a state of domestic bliss. In contrast to traditional portraits of the royal family, which would often focus upon dynastic strength and inherited wealth, scenes of Albert pulling his daughters into a hug, or the family at teatime in casual day dress, made them relatable, likeable figures in the public eye, capturing something of the family values that Victoria and Albert had made their prerogative all those years before.

Elizabeth Handley-Seymour had been a dressmaker for Queen Mary long before she had come to work for the new Duchess of York. Having started out with a modest business in 1908, Madame Handley-Seymour was now an established court dressmaker, whose designs were quintessential to the period during which she operated. At the time of the York marriage, her creations pulled inspiration from Grecian drapery, Japanese kimonos and the greatest Parisian couturiers of the time.[45] She could also boast exclusive permission to replicate the creations of popular French designers such as Paul Poiret, Jenny, and the House of Decroll, marrying continental luxury with British manufacture to please the London market.[46] None of those influences are present in the wardrobe she crafted for the Duchess of York. Perhaps as a result of Handley-Seymour having spent so long designing for Queen Mary and her husband's conservative preferences, the honeymoon wardrobe supplied to Elizabeth was unremarkable, but well suited to an unpretentious country girl. *The Times* described the trousseau in detail, reporting on the high necklines and muted colours of the Duchess's day dresses and the shimmering black and purple evening gowns. 'They are very simple,' concludes the article, 'as suits a woman of small stature.'[47]

At the time, there had been no real need for either Albert or Elizabeth to aspire to anything other than smartness in their wardrobes, but with their unexpected accession in 1936, their approach to fashion would have to change radically to accommodate their new lifestyle. When King Edward VIII had told his brother that he planned to abdicate, Albert had broken down in tears at the thought of what was in store for his private little family. As Edward and Wallis embarked on their lifelong holiday around the fashion hotspots of the world, Albert and Elizabeth were left with the task of stabilizing a kingdom still reeling from the abdication crisis. There was a reverence for both tradition and continuity in the coronation robes of George VI, the name that Prince Albert chose to rule under, which was identical in composition to that of his father's. Queen Elizabeth opted to patronize Madame Handley-Seymour for her coronation dress, the design for which was also borrowed from historical precedents. The slender white gown was embroidered all over with a patriotic swirl of roses and thistles, virtually indistinguishable from the coronation dress of Queen Mary save for the sheer gold sleeves that were copied from Queen Alexandra's fairy-like gown.[48]

Norman Hartnell was offered the role of designing the coronation dresses for Elizabeth's maids of honour, perhaps as one final test to see how he would cope designing for Elizabeth the Queen Consort, not just Elizabeth the Duchess. Evidently, he passed the test as from that moment on he became a firm fixture in Elizabeth's wardrobe, battling for space alongside

Madame Handley-Seymour. In 1938, the Queen tasked him with one of the first big events of the royal couple's new reign – their state visit to France. The chance to conquer Paris with none other than the Queen of England as a model was a tantalizing opportunity for Hartnell. Immediately he began crafting a wardrobe for the tour, stuffed with day dresses and evening gowns of the most romantic variety. This was his chance to design a unique image for the new Queen, who as yet was still a little unremarkable in the wake of Mary and Alexandra's distinctive, queenly wardrobes. The unforgiving straightness of 1920s fashion had not suited Elizabeth and her girlish softness, and Hartnell's Paris wardrobe was filled with his signature shimmering, voluminous grace, which he believed would help transform the Queen in the eyes of the public. 'I had to visualize the stage on which the Queen would be the principal figure,' he thought to himself, and, drawing upon his experience designing for theatre, he meticulously researched the colour palettes of the locations these dresses were to be worn in and the uniforms they would appear beside.[49] Each colour was carefully selected with the intention to make the Queen the central figure in each scene that she performed in.

Just three weeks before the tour was due to commence, Elizabeth's mother passed away and the court was thrust into a period of mourning. The departure was put on pause until, at the Queen's insistence, it was rescheduled for a few weeks later. The chaos had sent Hartnell into a spiral as the beautiful, coloured gowns that he had so carefully devised were now entirely inappropriate for a woman in mourning. Even more crushing was the possibility that his first major opportunity to transform Elizabeth's royal image was now ruined, as the regulation black and purple mourning dress had no place in the vision of this royal British rose that he had been concocting. He was summoned to Buckingham Palace to discuss what could be done. As designer and client pondered over the best course of action, Hartnell suddenly remembered that it had been traditional in the French royal court to wear white for mourning. Nervously, he suggested it, and the Queen agreed, sending him back to his studio with a new mission to fulfil. 'I was to pass, as it were, a magic wand over the whole collection and transform all the dresses into white in the fortnight that was left to us,' and off he went to design a collection fit for a fairy Queen.[50]

'Today France is a monarchy again. We have taken the Queen to our hearts. She rules over two nations,' declared one Parisian newspaper at the height of the state visit.[51] Elizabeth had taken the capital by storm, passing through each scheduled event like a wispy memory of a time gone by, her charm pulling in crowds unlike anything Paris had seen before. The summer sun shone through the layers of her tulle skirts like light through a fairy's wings, the lace trimming her bodices evoked a romanticized nostalgia for the Victorian age, and the silver sparkles of her eveningwear twinkled as she moved through ballrooms and opera halls. *This* was the transformation that Hartnell had hoped for, one that was achieved by playing into the Queen's natural softness, not hiding it beneath uncompromising harsh lines. It was not only the Queen that won the hearts of the French but Hartnell too; he received praise from some of the harshest fashion critics on the scene. So successful was the France trip that the Queen instructed Hartnell to handle her clothes for the next few state visits. Once that initial flurry of foreign excursions was over, Elizabeth called Hartnell to Buckingham Palace once more, procuring from her dressing table a little leather box. Inside was a thank you gift, a pair of gold cufflinks enamelled in blue and red with the Queen's initials: 'E.R.'

The novel element of the Queen's white wardrobe had been the inclusion of a crinoline under her skirts. They would come to be a fixture in mid-century women's style, cemented more famously in fashion history through Dior's 'New Look' of the late 1940s. Later, Christian Dior would inform the world that the 1939 white wardrobe was one of his greatest inspirations; 'Whenever I try to think of something particularly beautiful, I think always of those lovely dresses that Mr Hartnell made for your beautiful Queen when she visited Paris.'[52] Hartnell and Dior's designs shared a romantic fullness – borrowed directly from the silhouettes of the Victorian period. This was no coincidence: when Hartnell was first commissioned by the royal couple, King George had taken a keen interest in assisting his wife to acclimatize to her new role and had offered to help Hartnell find inspiration for his creations. Cigarette in hand, he had taken the designer on a personal tour around Buckingham Palace, pointing out to him the most beautiful royal portraits that hung on its walls.

Frequently, George had stopped at the works of Franz Xaver Winterhalter, one of the painters most loved by the aristocratic elite of the mid-nineteenth century. Over on one wall was the Duchesse de Nemours in a white silk gown, just to the side was Queen Victoria in her sprawling parliament robe, and in another room, a quartet of oval paintings of Victoria's four eldest daughters in white dresses covered in tulle and ribbons. Each of these paintings had been made between the late 1840s and the early 1860s, just as the bell-shaped crinoline was emerging onto the fashion scene, and when Hartnell left the Palace, his mind was filled with images of Elizabeth Bowes-Lyon as a Winterhalter Queen. In his memoir, Hartnell would credit this moment as his inspiration for the white wardrobe, stating plainly, 'it is to the King and Winterhalter that are owed the fine praises I later received for the regal revival of the romantic crinoline,' and so, while he might not be known as a revolutionary of men's fashion, King George VI certainly played his part in the transformation of women's style in the mid-century, influencing some of the greatest minds in fashion, whether they knew it or not.[53]

The outbreak of the Second World War put a halt on Hartnell's journey of style discovery for the Queen. Just like his parents before him, King George was keen to get his family involved in the war effort and turn the Crown into a symbol of national stability. When visiting the most devastated areas of the country, dress was a simple issue for George. All he had to do was don his uniform and suddenly he was part of a network of his fellow countrymen; his camaraderie with the nation and participation in their struggles were obvious and established. On the odd occasion, Elizabeth would appear in a similar, muted olive coat with a hat styled in mimicry of her husband's military cap, but there was only so much that the fairy Queen in khaki could achieve like this. For Elizabeth, wartime dress was a more nuanced issue, and both she and Hartnell pondered long and hard over the best approach to take. Instinctively, the mind went to sombre colours, but Hartnell felt a gut resistance: 'In black? Black does not appear in the rainbow of hope.'[54] Instead, the Queen appeared in the bombsites of London dressed in gentle, soothing colours – soft pinks and blues that were not extravagant but transformed her into a beacon of comfort and possibility.

Elizabeth did not see herself to be above the strict rules of government-enforced 'austerity' dress, intended to help ration the raw materials that were in scarce supply. There were limits on the amount of fabric a dress could be made from and the number of seams it could have, and Hartnell bemoaned the stifling restrictions placed upon surface embellishment, right the way down to how wide a belt or collar could be.[55] Evening dresses were the most complex issue, as while most court functions were put on pause during the conflict, there was still the rare diplomatic engagement that Elizabeth would be expected to dress finely for. The royal family were acutely aware of the need to unify the country and felt that flaunting austerity regulations would tarnish their strong relationship with the public. For these more formal occasions, Hartnell dressed the Queen in pieces that had been made before the outbreak of the war, painting them by hand with floral designs as a substitute for banned embroidery. From a more practical position, Elizabeth convinced Hartnell to accept a request from the Board of Trade to make utility clothing for the public. 'You have made so many charming things for me,' she had told him, 'that if you can do likewise for my countrywomen, I think it would be an excellent thing to do.'[56] Hartnell had also crafted a black velvet case for her gasmask, and a special gown to preserve her modesty when she and the rest of the family had to run across Windsor Castle to reach their dugout.[57]

In the years after the war, the King's health began to decline. His premature death in 1952 rocked the nation as well as his family, and as his eldest daughter ascended to the throne in his place, his wife assumed the position of Queen Mother, a role she would play for the rest of her extraordinarily long life and the one she is best remembered for in public memory. In her final years of Queenship, and through into her widowhood, Hartnell and Elizabeth had devised a constant, iconic wardrobe that followed its own unique rules. During the day, she always wore a matching coat and dress, which in the designer's vision must always be in the same light, bright colours – brown and navy, which he found to be dour and uninspiring, were never to be used.[58] To add stature to an otherwise diminutive figure, Hartnell included statement collars of thick fur or finished the look with one of Elizabeth's signature capulet hats, the front brim of which would sweep up and away, keeping her face visible at all times. For white tie events, Elizabeth exchanged her hats for some of the largest tiaras at her disposal. The Greville Tiara, an imposing lattice of diamonds and platinum, was her favourite and added a few extra inches to her height. To best showcase her favourite double string of pearls, her necklines were typically low and V-shaped, and her evening gowns were always pale, providing a clean, clear backdrop for her colourful insignia and jewels. The Queen Mother's wardrobe made her an enduring figure of both comfort and smartness, but now, for the latter half of the century, the eyes of the world would not focus entirely on her. Now they turned to her daughter, Queen Elizabeth II.

ELIZABETH II

BRITAIN LOVES ITS QUEENS, that much is certainly true. When Elizabeth Alexandra Mary Windsor was born on 21 April 1926, she was named after the three iconic queens of the twentieth century. Queen consorts, yes, but symbols of female royal majesty none the less. From the moment her birth was announced, the matter of how the little York Princess was to be raised became a matter of national interest, and parenting debates raged through newspapers and magazines for the first few months of her life. Would the Duchess adhere to traditional parenting tactics? Or was she well versed in the suggestions now being put forward by innovative childcare experts? Generally speaking, Elizabeth Bowes-Lyon was an engaged mother who rejected the trifles and impracticality associated with many old-school parenting rituals, but there were some new suggestions she just couldn't get behind. One of the most heated debates of the time was which fabric it was best to dress a baby in – in the traditional camp, cotton was the go-to, but the nurses of the day had begun to suggest wool as a softer, warmer alternative. No amount of reasoning could convince the new royal mother to dress her baby in wool; she had recently visited a welfare centre where wool was regulation for their babies, and with her usual witty charm had quipped that the infants had all looked 'rather like little gnomes'.[59]

So cotton it was for Baby Elizabeth. Her mother may have admitted it was 'frilly babies' that she liked best, but she was also acutely aware that her daughter had been born amidst a time of unrest, when the workers of major industries across the country were having their pay cut and their hours increased. Tastelessly flaunting a pampered and beribboned little Princess at a time of national crisis was not on the Duchess's agenda, and so all the clothes made for her baby were simple yet sweet. Together she and her mother, as well as Queen Mary herself, had sat down to hand-sew the little cotton baby clothes themselves, also employing the help of seamstresses from some of the hardest-hit areas of the country. 'Many poor gentlewomen,' the press reported glowingly, 'have profited by the Duchess's order for fine lawn and muslin frocks, little bonnets and jackets, and all the delightful accessories of a baby's toilet.'[60]

On the morning of 29 April 1929, the chubby, rosy-cheeked face of Princess Elizabeth gazed daintily out from the shelves of newsagents and corner shops all across the globe. Framed in red, her first appearance on a *TIME* magazine cover labelled her 'Princess Lilybet', in reference to her charming familial nickname – Lilibet, the product of a toddler struggling to pronounce her own name. A year later, Lilibet was joined by a younger sister, Princess Margaret Rose, and the York family at 145 Piccadilly was complete. Marion Crawford was the Princesses' nanny, and her controversial memoir gives us an unorthodox glimpse into their first experiences with fashion. Even as a child, Lilibet liked to be hands-on and proactive. 'She was never happier than when she was thoroughly busy and rather grubby,' wrote Crawford, and explained that as a consequence the little Princess had no time to care about fashion, being happy to wear whatever anybody put on her.[61] Princess Margaret, on the other hand, was instinctively drawn to clothing. According to Crawford, her favourite pastime was to sit on the hill at the end of their garden and admire the clothes of the ladies walking past on the other side of the wall, before scurrying back to the nursery to sketch her own designs.[62]

The little Princesses may have differed greatly in their approach to fashion, but in practice they were styled identically. There was nothing regal in the way that they dressed, and at first glance you might have mistaken them for any other 1930s schoolgirls kitted out in matching tweed coats with jaunty little berets. The wardrobe choice was a conscious one and was intended to teach the Princesses a valuable life lesson: that deeds, words and a commitment to duty were far more important to the modern royal than looks alone. They didn't own anything very fancy, particularly in terms of jewellery. All they had to fill their trinket boxes were a matching string of pearls and coral, made from a broken-up necklace of their mother's.[63] Aside from that, it was toy brooches and beaded necklaces made in their own spare time. The simplicity of their early years made their move to Buckingham Palace after their parent's accession far more significant. It was a monumental shift in responsibility, and their new royal roles meant a new royal wardrobe was in order for everyone – even for the nannies. For Marion Crawford, life at Buckingham Palace meant budgeting and planning her clothes at least a year in advance, but both her preparations and her finances could be instantly put to waste when a sudden death would plunge the court into mourning. At the turn of the century, Palace staff had received their mourning clothes from their employers, but Marion was gutted to discover that this courtesy had long been out of practice by the time of her service.[64]

Long gone were the days spent playing in the gardens of 145 Piccadilly and the evenings sat quietly around the fireplace. Now, Elizabeth's family were occupied with courtly functions, the first of which was her father's coronation in 1938, which saw the two Princesses sporting their first long dresses. Floor-length lace lined with golden bows, they were, as was expected, identical for both girls. The only point in which the ensembles differed was that Elizabeth, as the older child, had a small train on her skirt, which Margaret did not, causing her to descend into a jealous meltdown.[65] Both girls were introduced here to the more impractical elements of royal ceremonial dress, having to manage a heavy velvet robe lined with ermine fur and a dazzling gold coronet on their heads. For Elizabeth, this was the first of many historic moments in which her shoulders would carry such a robe but for now, as far as was possible, her parents tried to keep the grandeur in her life to a minimum.

Other events in the royal calendar were State balls, and while Elizabeth and Margaret did not get to attend, they nonetheless took great interest in discovering what everyone was going to wear. Margaret in particular made it her business to visit everyone – from her parents to her nanny – to admire their beautiful evening clothes and jewels. Of all the regular guests in the Palace ballroom, it was their aunt Marina, Duchess of Kent, who most excited the Princesses. Having married into the British royal family in 1934, the glamorous Grecian Princess was widely considered to be the most elegant of royal women, and her slender frame and aquiline features encapsulated the beauty standards of the 1930s. Each one of her outfits was obsessed over by the press and the little Princesses alike, and at the age of ten, Margaret was already vowing to follow in her footsteps; 'When I am grown up,' she told her nanny, 'I shall dress like Aunt Marina does.'[66] Little Margaret would have been very proud to have been told that one day she would make that a reality and become a key style icon for her generation.

While balls may have been off limits to Elizabeth, she made frequent appearances at the many garden parties hosted at the Palace during the summer months. Dressed in matching white gowns of light, floaty fabric, the Princesses followed their parents as they weaved through the crowds seeking out persons of distinction to greet or outstanding members of the community to congratulate. The whole time, Elizabeth policed her younger sister on her behaviour: 'If you do see someone with a funny hat, Margaret, you must *not* point at it and laugh.'[67]

Only a few years later, the outbreak of the Second World War forced Elizabeth and her sister into seclusion; they were kept safe at Windsor Castle whilst their parents journeyed back and forth between wreckage and bombsites. The girls may have been far from the action, but they still sought ways to contribute to the war effort. It began with pantomimes, little comedy performances of classic stories in which the Princesses and their friends starred as the main roles – dressing up and acting before an audience of local schoolchildren in order to raise money for the Royal Household Wool Fund, which supplied wool to make blankets for soldiers fighting on the front.[68] In these shows, which included the likes of *Cinderella* and *Aladdin*, Margaret would typically play Princesses and more often than not Elizabeth would play Princes.

After turning eighteen in 1944, Lilibet traded her theatrical breeches for khaki uniform and joined the Auxiliary Territorial Service, the women's part of the British Army, where she trained as a mechanic and driver in order to be of a more practical use to the war effort. Cecil Beaton was commissioned throughout the war to produce images of the

royal family, showing the King and Queen as sympathetic figures adhering to wartime austerity measures. Amongst these
images were photographs of Elizabeth in her new uniform;
they are iconic but were not unfamiliar to the public. In 1942,
Elizabeth had been made Colonel of the Grenadier Guards
and Beaton had commemorated the moment with a series
of photographs of the Princess in a military-inspired suit and
hat. The hat, a tall and simple fabric cap, was modelled on
those worn by men in the service and caught on as a trend for
women during the war years. It was closely associated with
Elizabeth and came to be known as the 'Princess Hat'.[69] On
Europe's Victory Day, not long after Elizabeth had joined the
ATS, the royal family appeared on the balcony of Buckingham
Palace as part of the countrywide celebrations. In the centre
stood Winston Churchill in his typical suit, flanked on either
side by the King and Queen in uniform and a pale-blue frock
respectively. On the fringes of the group stood Margaret in a
girlish blouse and skirt ensemble and Elizabeth dressed in her
smart military uniform. She looked striking, as the sharp lines
of the tailoring suited her figure much better than the dresses
and cardigans that her mother liked to dress her in, and her-
alded the neat coat dresses she would later settle upon as her
queenly wardrobe.

Soon it was time for Lilibet to pick her first 'grown-up'
clothes. Over the last few years, clothing had had to serve an
entirely practical purpose and followed closely the austerity
regulations put in place by the wartime government. During
the war, ration coupons were brought into effect as a way to
prevent wasteful purchases of fabric. The public were allocated a certain number of coupons per year, which could then
be used to purchase clothes for a fixed quantity determined by
the amount of material and labour used to create each item.
In 1945, the allowance was twenty-four coupons a year, and no

exceptions were made for Elizabeth or Margaret. Generally, the family survived on hand-me-downs; her eighteenth birthday photographs show Lilibet wearing her mother's sparkly crinoline gowns from before the war, and for sportswear she borrowed her father's plus-four trousers.[70] Now, however, she had the chance to pick clothes that were entirely her own. After inspecting designs sent from Norman Hartnell, the future Queen chose which clothes she would like to have made up. In amongst this new wardrobe was a cherry-red dinner dress – a far cry from the dainty pastels her mother had always dressed her in.[71]

In 1946, Lilibet triggered a ravenous media frenzy when, at the wedding of Patricia Mountbatten, she was photographed fondly chatting with the bride's cousin and casually handing him her fur coat.[72] This was Philip Mountbatten, and Princess Elizabeth had been giddy about him ever since their first meeting in 1939. He had jumped in and out of her life in the intervening years, appearing as a front-row spectator at one of her Windsor Castle pantomime performances, by which point her family were all well aware of her infatuation. The image of Philip helping the Princess with her fur coat, however, was the first time the country had any inkling of her attachment. At the Palace, he had become a familiar face, pulling up at the gates in his small sports cars, ready to take the Princess out for the night, much to her parents' apprehension. He stuck out amongst the formality of court life, walking with Elizabeth through the halls dressed always in flannel trousers ('not always very new or creased,' noted a member of Palace staff[73]) and a tennis shirt casually buttoned low with his sleeves rolled up. Fashion was changing and so was the world, and this was something that Elizabeth embraced fully and encouraged those around her to accept also. She was never shy about informing her parents when their views became outdated, and when the ladies-in-waiting at the Palace gave up on wearing hats, it was Elizabeth who informed her shocked mother that 'these days girls simply don't have a hat' and that she shouldn't be so old-fashioned![74]

Philip was born a Prince of Greece and Denmark, though his family had been dethroned and exiled not long after his birth, leaving him in the care of his uncle, George Mountbatten, in 1930. His foreigner status, plus the ties that some of his sisters had with the Nazi Party, made him an unpopular prospective consort in the eyes of the British public, but Lilibet was not to be swayed. As a legitimate relationship flowered between the royal duo, Philip denounced his Greek and Danish titles and became a British citizen. In July 1947, Philip and Elizabeth's engagement was announced to the public. The ring he had given her was made using diamonds from one of his mother's old tiaras.

It was Elizabeth Bowes-Lyon who got the ball rolling for her daughter's wedding dress. As was typical amongst high society families, Princess Elizabeth usually patronized the same dressmakers as her mother, which unsurprisingly included the much-loved Norman Hartnell. The couturier was thrilled when the Queen invited him to submit potential wedding dress designs for her daughter, but he was understandably rather daunted when he discovered he would only have three months to whip up one of the most important dresses of his career. Lost, Hartnell wandered through the halls of London's art galleries, hoping to stumble across a new historical inspiration for the Princess. What would be Lilibet's equivalent to her mother's Winterhalter wardrobe? Suddenly he stopped before a Botticelli painting and everything seemed to fall into place. The woman he was designing for was almost certainly going to be known as Queen Elizabeth II, so where better to find inspiration for her wardrobe than in Renaissance art, from a period when Queen Elizabeth I was one of the central figures? Hopefully, with a dress of such significance, Hartnell could give Britain its own sense of rebirth as it battled through the tumultuous post-war years.[75]

The dress that Hartnell crafted for his Renaissance Princess was one of lustrous white satin that he had to ensure was made from silk produced by the appropriate worms. He had to double check with his supplier that the silkworms were from China, and not Japan or Italy, which had been Britain's adversaries in the Second World War. 'Was I so guilty of treason that I would deliberately use *enemy* silkworms?' recounted an amused Hartnell in his memoir.[76] The dress itself fit neatly against the Princess's body, curving gently over the plains of her torso, with long, closely fitted sleeves. Just below the natural waistline, the dress spread out into ripples of white satin – a sort of conservative fit and flare gown. All across the dress and its 4-metre-long train was a pattern of floral motifs taken directly from the canvases of Sandro Botticelli. With the windows of his shop whitewashed to keep out prying eyes, Hartnell worked with his embroiderer to place the designs across the fabric, spreading orange blossom, syringa and jasmine across the satin in constellations made of ten thousand seed pearls.

Even for this most important occasion, ration coupons still applied. For such an elaborate dress, the amount necessary was staggering, and despite the fact that the Princess had been saving hers for quite some time now, she still did not have enough. Feeling sympathy for their Princess, fellow brides-to-be came together to donate their own ration coupons, but as touched as Elizabeth was, she had to return them all, as gifting them was illegal. The remaining 200 coupons were provided by the government instead.

When Princess Elizabeth walked down the aisle of West-minster Abbey on the morning of 20 November 1947, she paired the dress with earrings from her grandmother, Queen Mary, and two strings of pearls owned by the eighteenth-century Queens Anne and Caroline of Ansbach. Queen Mary also provided Elizabeth with a headpiece to wear for the ceremony: her architectural and iconic Fringe Tiara, though just hours before the bridal party had left Buckingham Palace for the Cathedral, disaster had struck – the tiara had snapped. Elizabeth's mother tried to reassure her. 'We have two hours and there are other tiaras,' she had said, and the Princess tried to distract herself by focusing on the make-up she was putting on.[77] The court jeweller and the broken tiara were whisked away to his workroom under police escort and later he emerged, with just moments to spare, holding the Fringe Tiara in one dazzling piece.

Elizabeth Windsor married Philip Mountbatten at 11.30 that morning. The groom was dressed in his navy uniform, not an uncommon choice for royal weddings, but particularly poignant for Philip. Rumours had continued to swirl about his family's Nazi connections in the lead up to the marriage and stressing his time in the Royal Navy during the Second World War was a sure way to set the record straight. He saw himself as a Brit through and through and had done for many years now. Just before the wedding, the King had made him the Duke of Edinburgh, and that was how the couple were known for the first few years of their marriage: Elizabeth and Philip, the Duke and Duchess of Edinburgh. They made Clarence House their family home and filled it with two happy, chubby royal babies, Prince Charles and Princess Anne.

On 7 February 1952, Queen Elizabeth II was sitting quietly on a plane home to London. She and Philip were returning from Kenya, where they had been staying in their tranquil retreat, Sagana Lodge. Forty-eight hours ago, they had left the lodge for Treetops, a hotel in the branches of a giant fig tree, overlooking a picturesque watering hole. They had stayed up all night talking, photographing animals and admiring the scenery, entirely unaware that during the night Elizabeth's father had died in his sleep. *She* was now the Queen. By the time the couple returned to Sagana Lodge they seemed to be the last people in the world to learn of the King's death. They left Kenya in a hurry, packing and leaving so quickly that Elizabeth had no time to change into fresh clothes before boarding the plane. So, what was the outfit that this smart little Queen first faced the public in? A pair of dusty blue jeans, designed for exploring the Kenyan treetops.[78]

As soon as Elizabeth returned to England, the coronation preparations began. Norman Hartnell had already been invited to join the team long before the Queen commissioned him to make her gown; he had been tasked with the role of updating the red velvet robes that the peeresses would wear in order to make them more economical. His changes were the first to be made to the robes since the days of Queen Anne, and naturally he had to run the ideas past the monarch for approval. Maybe it was Hartnell's ability to seamlessly modernize tradition that had convinced the Queen to offer him the job. Off he went to dig into royal fashion history to unearth precedents and inspiration for his masterpiece. He started with Elizabeth I, but where her epoch had proved such a goldmine of inspiration for the 1947 wedding dress, Hartnell found that the epic proportions and busy surfaces of her royal gowns were not quite appropriate for the unpretentious woman he was currently designing for. Next he stumbled across Queen Anne, who was crowned in gold tissue and lace, and Queen Victoria who appeared all in white.

By now Hartnell had identified a theme. If his creation was to follow in the footsteps of its forebears it would need to be devoid of all colour, made of some sort of lustrous white fabric and decorated only with silver or gold. The design he submitted to the Queen was for a full-skirted silk gown with a dainty sweetheart neckline and short embroidered sleeves. All across the skirt scalloped garlands of gold beads were framed by the emblematic flora of England, Wales, Scotland and Ireland: roses, leeks, thistles and shamrocks were all subtly depicted by tiny clear crystals. The Queen adored the dress but had a few suggestions of her own. In her opinion, it looked slightly too similar to her wedding dress, and she asked if Hartnell might want to introduce some colour to the skirt.[79] He was hesitant to buck tradition after having spent so long researching but at Elizabeth's insistence began drafting samples with pale-pink, green and purple beads to brighten up the emblems. At a later meeting the Queen mentioned that it would only be appropriate to include *all* the representative flora for the Commonwealth nations, and Hartnell depicted them with similar vibrancy all around the hem of the skirt. It was, without a doubt, the most important dress that he would ever create, and he was justifiably nervous about how it would be received. Realistically, he knew that whatever anxiety he was feeling could only be a fraction of that which the Queen must currently be experiencing and, for his benefit as much as Elizabeth's, decided to embroider a single, lucky four-leaved clover in amongst the patriotic shamrocks.

The first decade of Elizabeth's reign was a continual case of trial and error in the quest to establish her independent dress sense. Hartnell had already witnessed the beginnings of her fashion journey when he first began supplying her wardrobe as the Duchess of Edinburgh, noting in his memoir that 'this was the first occasion upon which I was asked to design clothes of a darker colour'.[80] In this assessment, 'darker' did not necessarily denote sombre or even dimmer colours, but rather an unusually saturated wardrobe that Hartnell was not used to crafting for royalty. All through her childhood, Elizabeth had been styled in the gentle pastels that her mother had adopted as her own royal uniform. They served to help her stand out from the crowd and increase visibility, but now, with her requests for clear-blue and holly-red dresses, Elizabeth was hinting that vibrancy rather than lightness was her preference.

Many of Hartnell's existing royal fashion clichés remained in place, however. He used dainty hats and full-skirted frocks to create a girlish look for his youthful Queen, and historical inspiration was never far from his mind. A sense of fairy-tale majesty was created by dusting each evening gown with a smattering of beads, diamonds and pearls in meticulously hand-sewn patterns. This complexity of craftmanship was essential to Hartnell's understanding of royalty and what a royal should look like. It was his opinion that the clothes he supplied for the Queen should help to reinforce the inherent unattainability of royal life, and the intricate surface embellishments kept these dresses out of mass-market production. Hartnell had learnt this lesson early on when, in 1953, Elizabeth stepped out before the cameras at the Empire Theatre in Leicester Square for the Royal Film Performance dressed in an incredibly simple gown. A black silk halter neck faced with a wide panel of white, it was undoubtedly the chicest that the Queen had ever looked, and the movie-star glamour of the whole ensemble made it headline news. It was a hit from a publicity perspective, but part of this success was owed, much to Hartnell's horror, to the fact the dress was remarkably easy to replicate. The simplicity of the gown meant that within twenty-four hours copies were available to buy from high-street retailers and paper patterns were being sold for only a few pence – giving hundreds of ordinary women the chance to dress like a Queen.[81] Hartnell never dressed the Queen in a gown that simple ever again.

Another designer to join Queen Elizabeth's retinue early on was Hardy Amies, who had first dressed her as a Princess in 1950. Like Hartnell, Amies had a specific agenda about royal fashion and believed firmly that the Queen's clothing should be unattainable. *Unlike* Hartnell, he felt that this should be achieved through luxury materials and craftmanship rather than regal embellishments. Throughout the 50s and 60s, Amies crafted a sleek image for the Queen that prioritized structured coat dresses and simple lines. Under Hardy Amies's careful eye, the foundations were laid for the iconic image of Queen Elizabeth and her bright and colourful coat dresses; he even began to do away with the enduring light-blue royal colour palette that she had rarely been seen without, introducing a more liberated variety of tones into her wardrobe.

As Queen, Elizabeth's schedule was more hectic than it had ever been. Such a busy year dictated an equally busy wardrobe, one that needed to be stocked by many couturiers. The contributions of Norman Hartnell and Hardy Amies were joined by those of many of Britain's brightest stars of fashion, who each in their own way contributed to the image of the young monarch. With so many creative minds directed at one lone muse there was potential for chaos in the wardrobe department, yet Elizabeth was blessed with a guardian angel (and the designers faced with a great adversary) in the form of Margaret MacDonald, the Queen's personal dresser. 'Bobo', as she was fondly referred to, managed the designers and the details of the Queen's wardrobe, making it her business to provide the brief for each outfit and ensure that royal tradition was not sacrificed in the name of fashion.[82] Bobo's word was final, and it was she, not the couturier, who got to decide the accessories that finished an outfit. This was particularly frustrating for the designers, and they came together in disapproval over this interference with their vision, taking particular issue with the practical (and in their opinion unsightly) black handbags that the Queen always paired her custom outfits with. It became commonplace for the Queen's designers to gift her fashionable bags for Christmas in the hope she might use those instead. She never did, and the Queen's iconic black bags became a staple in her wardrobe for the rest of her reign.

Of all of the events in the royal calendar, the most challenging occasion for a designer is a royal tour. Queen Elizabeth II was one of the most widely travelled monarchs in British history, and as the representative for the United Kingdom on the world's stage she needed a profoundly spectacular wardrobe for each foreign visit. The designer also had to ensure that the host nation was honoured; for a trip to the Vatican City, for example, the Queen would need plenty of black lace outfits for audiences with the Pope, as the strict Vatican dress code is non-negotiable, not even for monarchs! (That being said, Catholic queens are granted the privilege of wearing white lace instead, and currently only six women boast this exception, from, for example, the Spanish, Belgian and Monegasque royal families.) The wardrobe must be prepared well in advance and compiled into a pocket-size booklet known as 'The Blue Book', in which each event of the tour is documented down to the minute, with each corresponding outfit noted beside it, a simple 'T' denoting when a tiara will also be worn.[83]

Elizabeth made her first foreign tour as Queen in 1954, a seven-month trip around the Commonwealth with Australia as the first stop. It was a historic event in that it was the first time a reigning monarch had set foot in the country, and both Elizabeth and Norman Hartnell were keen to include as many sartorial references to the host nation as possible. Green and gold, as the colours of Australia's Commonwealth Coat of Arms, featured heavily in the wardrobe, and so too did the wattle, the national flower. On the first night of the tour, Elizabeth dazzled the crowds in a sunshine-yellow gown speckled with golden wattle flowers. 'I was never more impressed than when I saw her wearing her wattle gown. It was regal and it was Australian,' wrote the artist William Dargie, who later commemorated the dress in the official Australian portrait of the Queen. 'I knew I had to have that wattle gown.'[84]

From then on, nearly every wardrobe curated for a foreign tour included references to the host's national or flag colours, as well as associated emblems. During her 1961 trip to Pakistan, the Queen sported a simple white dress with a rippling emerald train that formed the colours of the Flag of the Star and Crescent, and on her 1983 visit to California, she visited an aircraft carrier in a blue-and-white ensemble that matched the uniform worn by the US Navy officers who received her there. On the same trip, she attended a reception and banquet at 20th Century Fox's Sound Stage 9 in a rather conservative white gown, the bodice of which was covered with vibrantly embroidered Californian poppies. Diplomatic dressing was not introduced to the royal family by Elizabeth (Queen Alexandra had donned a bronze gown smattered with shamrocks for her visit to Ireland, and we have already seen how George IV adopted tartan for his trip to Scotland) but it was an art that she certainly refined.[85] With the Queen having limited political power of her own, the state visits were mostly symbolic, and strengthened diplomatic ties. Dressing to compliment the host nation helped fulfil this mission and pandered to the camera – from one quick glance at the Queen's outfit in the pages of a glossy magazine, the public could tell immediately where Britain was sending its favour.

At the same time, the Queen's sister was also beginning to explore the world of fashion. The austerity of the post-war years had stifled Princess Margaret's creative instincts, and while at home in the United Kingdom regulations would not be lifted until 1949, the royal family's visit to South Africa in 1947 had opened her eyes to all the excitement she had been missing out on. Dressed in her war-appropriate simple frocks, the sixteen-year-old Princess had looked on in resentment as the women of Cape Town received them in their stylish, regulation-free clothing. Next to them, Margaret had complained, 'we look like housemaids'.[86] The tour was pivotal to her public image, and on her return the British press hounded Margaret with a newfound interest in her fashion, which the Princess was happy to indulge.

That same year, the couture titan Christian Dior had debuted his very first collection in Paris. It was a monumental break from everything that women's fashion had become during the war years, eschewing thrifty, short hemlines and utilitarian construction in favour of a glamorous and hyper-feminine silhouette that borrowed heavily from nineteenth-century style – *this* was his legendary 'New Look'. Through Dior, the corset made a return to prominence; small waists were emphasized by the use of padded hips below tight-fitting jackets. Skirts were his forte, and his attachment to long, calf-length skirts that ballooned over frilled crinolines earnt him the title of 'the hemline dictator', and a liberal dose of criticism over the wastefulness of his sumptuous designs. The acclaim and controversy of Dior's collection helped its reputation to travel fast, and his ideas trickled down into the work of other designers and dressmakers. Eventually it reached the attention of Princess Margaret, who was instantly infatuated with the New Look, but with Britain still embroiled in post-war hardship she would have to accept that the designs were needlessly wasteful. Instead, she commissioned the usual roster of royal dressmakers to revamp and restyle her existing clothes to give them the illusion of volume.

In 1950, Princess Margaret received an invitation from Christian Dior himself to attend a private viewing of his latest collection at the French Embassy in London. In his autobiography, Dior backdated the presentation to the autumn of 1947, implying that it only took a year for his relationship with the British royal family to flourish. A self-proclaimed Anglophile, the French designer also harboured an obsession with nobility that drew him inexplicably towards British royalty. As a Princess of the blood, Margaret embodied the type of woman he wanted his clothes to be seen on; having taken inspiration from the likes of Franz Xaver Winterhalter, Charles Frederick Worth and Norman Hartnell's white wardrobe, the designer had the glamour of royalty at the core of his creative vision. Dior was keen to airbrush the fact that many of the royal women had already adopted elements of the New Look by 1950, as they had done so not by wearing *his* clothes but through the efforts of those he had inspired. Disguising the true date of the showcase created a much neater storyline for his brand. Margaret arrived at the embassy with her mother, Princess Marina and Marina's sister, Princess Olga of Yugoslavia, and the connection between designer and royal was instant. Dior found Margaret 'delicate, graceful, exquisite', the picture of royal elegance, and was full of praise for her 'Titania-like figure'.[87] His fairy princess was equally enchanted and jumped at the chance to add the couturier's creations to her wardrobe.

Margaret and Dior were a formidable partnership. Self-assured and self-confident, the Princess had the mind of a qualified designer and knew exactly how best to style herself. In 1951, she ordered a new Dior gown to wear for her twenty-first birthday portraits. The designer famously enquired: 'Does

Your Highness feel like a gold person or a silver one?' 'A gold,' Margaret had decisively responded, and the work began.[88] The gown that the Princess received was a beautifully pale organdie creation with an asymmetrical neckline and a swirling, voluminous skirt spilling out from a belted 22-inch waist. The gold that Dior had expertly woven into the design was actually a mixture of mother-of-pearl, raffia, and beads that twisted across the front of the skirt. When Margaret sat for Cecil Beaton's camera, the photographer had been underwhelmed with the dress, but Margaret adored it. 'It's got bits of potato peel on it,' she said happily, running her hand over the twisting gold designs.[89]

Cecil Beaton's photographic eye might not have been satisfied with the Dior dress but the public certainly were, and with each public appearance that the dress made (first at her birthday party in August, later to a November charity ball in Paris) her popularity as an arbiter of style only continued to grow. Margaret's position in the royal family gave her privileges that were denied to her sister; unlike Elizabeth, Margaret never had to restrict herself to patronizing British brands and could explore whatever international designer took her fancy. Nuances like diplomatic dressing and crowd visibility didn't dictate her wardrobe, and she was rarely seen without a dramatic fur cape, Hollywood-style cigarette holder and large, glamorous sunglasses. Her involvement in the world of fashion saw her style change continually throughout her life, and by the 70s she had already moved on to a more simple, bohemian shape, but whatever changes she made to her wardrobe, there was always one constant: 'What she wears is news.'[90]

In Hardy Amies's studio, a special mannequin just for the Queen was established. Its measurements fit hers precisely, and over the many years it spent hosting the clothes of the monarch its dimensions were minutely altered with each inch she lost or gained. The clothes that were built around it fell into a comfortable rhythm; the sleek lines of the 60s had compounded Amies's fantasy of simplicity, and the vibrancy of the 70s and 80s had helped him to firmly move on from uniform blue. He continued to design for Queen Elizabeth right up until 2003, playing a pivotal role in her life by dressing her through one of the most difficult decades of her reign – the 90s. With three of her children undergoing messy and public divorces, the devastating Windsor Castle fire in 1992 and finally the death of Diana, Princess of Wales in 1997, the close of the twentieth century was a particularly disastrous period for the royal family. A fixed, dependable silhouette of prim coat dresses and matching hats made fresh with a random cycle of bold colours became the great hallmark of Elizabeth's style in later life, underscoring each royal appearance with a sense of stability, regardless of whatever turmoil might have been occurring behind Palace walls. Being such a reliable dress formula, it became usual for bets to be placed on the colour of the Queen's hat for Royal Ascot each year, with bookmakers and gamblers alike taking solace in the fact that Elizabeth could always be trusted to appear in one of her impressively vibrant outfits (though in 2008, when fascinators were made acceptable headgear in the Royal Ascot dress code, it was rumoured that the Queen might eschew tradition for once – she did not). With the stakes so high in a very literal sense, it was important for the specifics of the Queen's outfits to be kept a surprise. The Queen's dresser often left decoy hats visible in the workroom at Windsor before each Ascot appearance, to prevent any Palace insiders making informed bets, a system which was brought into effect after a member of Palace staff caused a scandal by doing exactly that.[91]

In 1994, Angela Kelly was hired as an assistant dresser to the Queen. She was soon to be promoted to the role of Senior

Dresser, and before long her role had expanded to include the positions of curator, wardrobe and in-house designer, and Her Majesty's personal advisor. There was nobody who knew quite so much about the Queen's day-to-day life and the demands of royal fashion than Angela Kelly, except for maybe Queen Elizabeth herself. It was Kelly who applied the final flourishes to the royal image that had been established by Hartnell and Amies, constructing a neat rubric that would serve the Queen as she continued to serve her country into her old age. Clearly priding herself on predicting every challenge, every adversity and every possible moment to shine that might confront the Queen in her daily life, Kelly organized her clothes, arranged millinery commissions, sourced fabrics for coat dresses, maintained ceremonial robes, and even personally wore in Her Majesty's shoes to prevent the Queen from hurting herself during long engagements.[92] Comfort was key, and it was vital that nothing that Kelly sourced or designed could hinder the Queen's ability to perform royal duties. Dresses fit loosely, as was the Queen's preference, and sleeves were no shorter than three-quarter length. In the evenings, white dresses continued to be standard and functioned as a background upon which jewels and insignia could flourish. Beading and crystals were often essential for these formal dresses, but they could often cause discomfort, and to prevent this Kelly would insert a few extra layers of lining to make them more tolerable.

As part of her role as curator, Angela Kelly was also entrusted with the task of caring for and organizing the Queen's expansive jewellery collection. Among the most impressive pieces are the tiaras, particularly those that the Queen was often seen wearing. Her reliable favourites included the beautifully delicate Girls of Great Britain and Ireland Tiara, the distinctive interlinking circles of the Vladimir Tiara, the vibrant Burmese Ruby Tiara, and the impressive Fringe Tiara worn on her wedding day. Despite the grandeur of these shimmering headpieces, they are not the jewellery for which Elizabeth II is most fondly remembered, rather it is her collection of particularly expressive brooches. A focal point for any royal-watcher looking to understand the Queen's mindset, Elizabeth used them to send clear sartorial messages that could be both diplomatic and personal. Elizabeth's silver fern brooch was gifted to her in 1950 by Lady Allum, who was, at the time, the wife of the Mayor of Auckland and subsequently the brooch appeared whenever the Queen visited New Zealand. For her televised Diamond Jubilee speech in 2012, she opted to wear a pair of matching aquamarine brooches that had been an eighteenth birthday gift from her father, a reminder that each accession day celebrated was also a time of remembrance for the royal family. Perhaps one of the most touching brooch moments came with the diamond wedding anniversary photographs taken of the Queen and Prince Philip, for which Elizabeth donned the same necklace and brooch (a chrysanthemum made of sapphires and diamonds) that she had worn for their honeymoon photoshoot all those years before. The Queen later wore the brooch again to celebrate her seventy-third wedding anniversary in November 2020.

As a particularly diminutive woman, the Queen relied heavily on her clothes to provide visibility for herself and by the twenty-first century this had become an art form. The choices made varied from engagement to engagement, and as Angela Kelly has revealed, also considered the specific people who were going to see the Queen. For a visit to care home, for example, a 'strong, well-defined colour, with a structured hat' was selected to help those with visual impairments 'see her and feel part of the visit'.[93] If the engagement was to be outside, and if there was a chance of rain, a regular umbrella simply would not do. For the same reason that the width of the

Queen's hat brims was carefully regulated, an opaque umbrella was off the table, as it would obscure the Queen's face and head far too much. To solve this, the Queen's wardrobe was equipped with a selection of clear umbrellas, each trimmed with a band of colour to match whatever she happened to wear for that particular walkabout. The cohesive colour scheme allowed for accessories such as the hat or umbrella to become an extension of the Queen herself, allowing those further back in the crowd to feel as though they had seen the monarch, even if they had only caught a glimpse of a fuchsia umbrella or sapphire hat.

The death of the Duke of Edinburgh on 9 April 2021 profoundly affected the make-up of the royal family. An enduring presence, his ties to both Greek and Danish royalty saw an international community converge upon his 2022 memorial service, where respects were paid by attendees wearing both black and green. Green, or more specifically 'Edinburgh green', was the colour that Philip and Elizabeth chose for their family livery after their marriage. In the time of the Tudors, household livery colours were used to identify which servants attended which master, but today it is more commonly used to denote which vehicles belong to which member of the royal family. Upon her accession, Elizabeth graduated to the use of the royal red (sometimes claret) livery, but in private both the Queen and Prince Philip retained the use of Edinburgh green, making it a particularly apt colour to wear for his memorial service. No one was more affected by the loss of the Duke than the Queen herself, though despite his absence Philip continued to provide support in a much more personal way. Throughout the final year of her life, as the Queen began to develop mobility issues, she was often seen relying on the support of a walking stick – one that eagle-eyed royal-watchers recognized as having belonged to the late Duke of Edinburgh.

The death of Queen Elizabeth II on 8 September 2022 was a monumental event for the global community. With the vast majority of the British population having only ever known one monarch, the transition from Queen to King triggered a variety of mixed emotions. The outpouring of grief was reflected tenfold by members of the royal family, who each wove touching symbols of remembrance into their mourning clothes. The Duchess of Sussex repeatedly wore a set of understated earrings that had been gifted to her by Queen Elizabeth, and Catherine, Princess of Wales, opted for pearls as a reference to the late Queen's favourite jewellery. At the funeral itself, all eyes were on Princess Charlotte, who wore a dainty horseshoe brooch that had been gifted to her by her great-grandmother and had once been in the collection of Elizabeth Bowes-Lyon. While many of the royal women had repurposed dresses they had worn previously, Sophie, Countess of Wessex, sported a custom Suzannah London coat dress embroidered with flowers from Elizabeth's wedding bouquet and lily-of-the-valley, her favourite flower.

CHARLES III

ON 14 NOVEMBER 1948, Charles Mountbatten Windsor was born. On 26 July 1958, he was created Prince of Wales, and on 12 September 2017, he broke royal records by becoming the longest-serving Prince of Wales in history. On 8 September 2022, he broke records yet again by overtaking William IV as the oldest British monarch to ascend to the throne when he became King Charles III at the age of seventy-three.

At a first glance, there is very little about King Charles's fashion that is particularly exciting, at least not in the way we have come to understand fashion in the twenty-first century. In a world where trends come and go in micro-doses of rapidly oscillating aesthetics, the enduring constancy of King Charles's wardrobe is far from the overstimulating eye-candy that we have become accustomed to seeing. By contrast, his style seems fixed in a bygone era, epitomized by his refusal to part ways with his faithful double-breasted suits, despite the single-breasted variety having taken over in popularity. Is it stubbornness that has kept King Charles so fixed in his ways? Perhaps it's a certain nonchalance about the topic of fashion. He certainly likes to insinuate the latter, describing his own style, in a speech in 2012, as somewhat like 'a stopped clock', implying some sort of defectiveness with his approach to dressing, a style that lags behind and is only successful by fluke. But an indifference to fashion doesn't earn you a spot on any best-dressed list, and King Charles has certainly appeared on a fair few of those throughout his life. In 2019, he featured in *GQ* magazine's '50 Best-dressed Men' list, scoring a place just below David Beckham and Harry Styles but beating the likes of Timothée Chalamet and Donald Glover. Connoisseurs of fashion and expert journalists all agree that what King Charles brings to the table is a confident, proud presentation of excellence in British tailoring, which studies painstakingly the intricacies of traditional craftmanship and balances it with a constant concern for what is yet to come. Like the Janus of the fashion world, King Charles looks to the past and future with equal verve, and there are lessons to be learnt from his approach to style that will be invaluable to any twenty-first-century fashionista, regardless of their personal style.

King Charles has spent the majority of his life as the Prince of Wales, and his association with the title was so firmly established that by the time of his accession the switch to monarch caused a considerable number of Prince-Charles-related faux pas. The Prince of Wales title is awarded to the reigning monarch's eldest son, symbolizing their position as heir to the throne. It is not an automatic title and must be bestowed upon the heir (as it was for Charles at the age of ten) by the reigning monarch, before being compounded in a ceremonial investiture. Charles's investiture was held off until 1969 and took place at Caernarfon Castle in Wales; in the ten weeks leading up to the event Charles studied Welsh history, language and culture in preparation for the role. For the event itself, Charles wore the uniform of Colonel-in-Chief of the Royal Regiment of Wales, over which a velvet ceremonial mantle edged with powdered ermine fur was draped. The investiture functioned like a coronation and, as a consequence, required the monarch to 'crown' the new Prince of Wales with a coronet. The specific coronet used had historically been passed down from one Prince to the next, and as each small crown became too old and fragile, it was retired and a new one created. In 1902, a new coronet had been made for King George V (then the new Prince of Wales), to be worn in lieu of the coronet of Frederick, Prince of Wales, which had been in use since 1728. This *should* have been the coronet used by Charles at his investiture, but the last Prince of Wales, King Edward VIII, had stolen the piece when he abdicated, forcing the royal family to commission another new crown.

The newly created coronet followed closely the historical precedent set by its forebears, but since its creator was the talented and experimental British artist Louis Osman, the final result was imbued with plenty of 1960s anachronisms. It comprised the traditional purple velvet cap trimmed with ermine and encircled with a base of Welsh gold, from which futuristic fleur-de-lis sprouted, and a profusion of sprinkled diamonds and emeralds represented Wales's national colours. A single gold arch rises over the cap, denoting the status of the prince as lesser than the monarch, whose crown always boasts two overlapping arches. Resting at the top of the arch sits a monde, a small sphere traditionally representing the 'world' a monarch rules over – in this instance made using a ping-pong ball dipped in gold and engraved with the Prince of Wales's insignia.[94] Hovering on a frame around the monde are an orbiting set of diamonds arranged as the constellation of Scorpio, Charles's star sign, completing what is a stunningly inventive work of retrofuturism that will be worn by Princes of Wales for years to come.

Moments like the investiture have been a rare occurrence in royal life over the past few decades. It was the first major ceremonial event since Elizabeth II's coronation, and the last until Charles's own in 2023. In the interim, high-profile events such as state banquets have filled the void, but save for a few choice photographs, they are rarely opened up to public view. Royal weddings, however, are a much more public affair, mixing sparkle and ceremony with a dash of romantic fantasy, and in 1973, Charles's sister, Princess Anne, became the first of the four royal siblings to walk down the aisle. Her dress leaned into the ceremonial aspect, with the Princess personally contributing to the design of her medieval-inspired Maureen Baker gown that featured dramatic trumpeted sleeves and a sleek high-necked silhouette.[95] If the public thought they were going to be seeing another tiara-toting royal bride anytime soon, they were to be heartily disappointed, as Charles was more than content with life as a bachelor and spent the rest of the 1970s establishing his career as a working royal.

His personal taste in fashion was also gradually establishing itself, though perhaps it's more correct to say his affinity for anti-fashion was growing. We've seen throughout the course of this book the power that the elite have historically held over the world of fashion, in many instances being the only demographic with the means to form and reform popular styles at a semi-regular pace. Fashion was their playground, the consumption of styles and aesthetics (and their subsequent disposal) just one of the many tools utilized to establish their social dominance. By the twentieth century, however, that monopoly over fashion had faded, replaced by a system of more accessible means. Suddenly, it became a far more radical statement of distinction to *reject* the mainstream standard of fashion, even on a luxury level, and replace it instead with an entirely individual, relatively unchanging uniform of dress.[96] Charles has been an avid follower of and indeed one of the central shaping figures behind this lucrative art of stealth-wealth dressing. Its staples include high-quality knitwear, sturdy tweeds, and powerful overcoats, all of which feature prominently in his wardrobe.

Maintaining such a specific personal style throughout his life has brought many advantages to the King, particularly in that it has created a stand-out look for him to be associated with, much like the coat dresses adopted by his mother. Like the late Queen Elizabeth, Charles has also used colour in order to distinguish himself from the pack and lighter, softer colourways have found themselves at home in his wardrobe. He has never shied away from and has in fact become intrinsically associated with the beige suit, partnered with a lilac or blue shirt, and grounded with a muted jewel-toned tie. These are the things he freely admits to caring about; 'I mind about detail and colour and things like that,' he confided to *Vogue* with faux nonchalance,[97] though the details he cares for are hardly casual points of dress. Cufflinks stamped with his royal cypher, shoelaces allegedly steamed straight by his valet, a wardrobe containing coats worn by King George VI, and shoes made with leather from an eighteenth-century shipwreck all form part of his commitment to the finer points of his style. There's an undeniable Edwardian twang to Charles's sartorial expression, as from both Edward VII and Edward VIII we see a manifest desire to dress sublimely but with little visible effort, and to always be dressed correctly for the task at hand. There lies the second benefit of Charles's personal style: he can never be considered 'unfashionable', as he very clearly has no intention of being fashionable in the first place. It's a nifty trick to avoid media scrutiny on a superficial level, but it does of course run the risk of allowing the wearer to be eclipsed by those who do choose to subscribe to changing trends.

In September 1980, the press uncovered a juicy royal secret: Charles, the Prince of Wales, had begun a relationship with Lady Diana Spencer, and instantly they were ravenous for photographs of the woman they had a hunch might just become the next Princess of Wales. Within days, photographers had tracked down her place of work, Young England Kindergarten in Pimlico, and laid siege to the little brick building. It was impossible for anyone to work in peace, and Diana's boss began looking for a solution. 'Do you think if you go and have a photograph taken, then they'll go away?' she suggested, and off Diana went, taking two children with her for support.[98] For her impromptu first photoshoot, on the grass outside her place of work, the future Princess of Wales sported a homely lilac blouse under a purple sweater vest and a conservative long, blue skirt. Around her neck she wore a sizable gold 'D' necklace, letting everyone know that *this* was the woman they had come to photograph. The photographs were heartwarming, but at the most unfortunate moment the sun peeked out from behind a cloud and shone straight through Diana's billowing skirt, showing off her slender legs. The cameras snapped away eagerly, while Diana was none the wiser.

It was the start of a constant and fatal obsession, but for now the worst damage that the press had done was to leave their subject extremely embarrassed. When the see-through skirt photographs appeared in the *Evening Standard* that afternoon, Diana and her boss both realized their mistake. 'I remember her standing there with her hands over her face going bright red,' recalled Kay King, the owner of the nursery, 'and me thinking, "Oh, dear. I think I've rather blown the romance." Knowing how sensitive the Palace was about things like that.'[99] Queen Elizabeth's indomitable reputation for neatness and professionalism had left no room for mistakes like that; her daytime outfits were made of stiff fabrics with weighted hems to preserve her modesty. Diana was extremely nervous about how the royal family might now view her; 'I don't want to be known as the girlfriend that had no petticoat,' she is alleged to have said.

All was not lost, and Diana would have the chance to present herself to the press on her own terms when her engagement to Prince Charles was announced. The announcement itself was pencilled in for 24 February 1981, with a coinciding photocall. In planning what outfit she would wear, Diana's mother advised her to visit Belville Sassoon, one of the most popular fashion houses amongst the more conservative circles of the British elite. She wanted her daughter to pick something she genuinely liked and so dropped her off alone at the store, where she mooched around for a little while and quietly admired the clothes. The sales assistants didn't recognize Diana and came to the conclusion that this shy nineteen-year-old was probably lost and went over to tell her that she'd have better luck visiting some more affordable stores. Embarrassed and with an entirely non-confrontational nature, Diana left without complaint, and by the time David Sassoon had realized his employee's mistake she had already made it to Harrods down the road and bought her famous cobalt-blue suit from off the rack.

When the husband-and-wife duo David and Elizabeth Emanuel were commissioned to create the wedding dress for Diana Spencer, it was a dream come true. They were young, fresh faces in the design world, who had been in the running against some of the most established industry names. Diana was already a fan of theirs and had already made a few post-engagement outings in their evening gowns, trusting them entirely to guide a complete fashion novice into one of the most brutal terrains in the industry – the world of royal fashion. Her first few dresses of theirs were typically girlish and delicate, princessy in every sense of the word, but during one fitting at the Emanuel salon she had spotted a slinky ink-black gown with a daringly low-cut sweetheart neckline.[100] In Diana's eyes it was the most sophisticated dress she could imagine herself wearing, with the colour being a particularly 'grown-up' choice. Despite it having already been worn by another client, Diana decided to wear the dress to her first official public outing. The reviews were mixed: on the one hand, everyone agreed that the soon-to-be Princess of Wales looked incredibly chic, but many thought that chicness was not a quality a Princess should aspire to. Most of the grumbling centred around the neckline, decrying Diana's bare shoulders and décolletage as inappropriate, and there were murmurings that black, as a mourning colour, was much too sombre for the occasion.

When the Palace confirmed just a day later that the Emanuels were to be tasked with creating the wedding dress, many speculated that the special gown might mirror the frothy black dress from the charity do; perhaps it would be tight-fitting, or might they rip up the royal rule book by opting for another low neckline? In the end, Diana and the Emanuels stuck firmly to the 'Princess' theme, though they did their best to keep this a surprise! Press scrutiny around the designs was intense, with the Emanuels even catching reporters digging through their bins in the hope they might discover discarded designs, fabric or even parts of the paper pattern.[101] To ensure that the dress Diana married in would remain a secret no matter what, they left scraps of decoy fabric in the bins outside their studio, and a second, entirely different design was drafted just in case the original dress was leaked to the press.[102]

Thankfully for both designer and client, the dress remained a complete secret until it appeared on the steps of St Paul's Cathedral on 29 July 1981. It's one of the most visually striking royal wedding dresses in history and certainly the most famous, passing Victorian elements through the machine of 1980s excess to create a gown as dramatic as it is iconic. A fitted, boned bodice of ivory silk taffeta exploded into a crinoline-style skirt that was hidden in part by a detachable train at the waist, which at 25 metres was the longest train ever used for a royal wedding. Thousands of sequins and pearls decorated the bodice in heart motifs, complementing the romantic diamond scrolls and hearts that formed her tiara, the iconic Spencer Tiara. The bodice took its inspiration from the nineteenth century, with puffed gigot sleeves that had been popular both in the 1830s and the 1890s and a wide ruffled neckline reminiscent of Queen Victoria's penchant for Honiton lace. The finishing touches were a golden horseshoe sewn into the back of the dress for good luck and a panel of lace that had once belonged to Queen Mary, used to embellish the torso. The dress referenced royal history, was made of royal history and *became* royal history. It was an overnight sensation, and every bridal shop worth its weight was soon providing its own, more affordable version of the dress.

The fairy-tale quality that imbued Diana's wedding dress began to diffuse into her regular royal style. Long gone was the tweedy little nursery assistant with her very practical jumpers and skirts, and in her place was the Princess of Wales, someone whose historical position demanded she provide some sort of style inspiration for the nation. A historical approach was a safe route for Diana to venture down as there was really no present-day example for how a woman in her position should dress. Much like the Queen, she was expected to maintain a certain dedication to British designers and a professional mode of dressing that alienated her from other celebrities of her time, but she could hardly copy the Queen exactly. Elizabeth was well into her fifties and Diana barely out of her teenage years, so there was already a disconnect between what had been established as acceptable royal uniform and what would suit the family's newest addition. Diana's sartorial insecurity was clear in these first few years, and she quickly became labelled a dowdy dresser.

Her mother decided to step in. She arranged a meeting with *Vogue* fashion editor Anna Harvey and asked her to direct Diana towards designers who would understand the unique challenges that came with being Princess of Wales.[103] Diana's fashion education began by teaching her to dress for the camera, getting her to play with textures, patterns and high-contrast colour schemes. The severe lines of her day outfits compared with the shimmering lustre of her evening gowns harkened back to the time of Queen Alexandra, who had pioneered the royal art of dressing for the camera and had clearly passed the baton on to Diana. She learnt quickly and with vigour, and soon Diana was making her own unique requests to her designers. Gloves were absolutely off limits in her eyes, as she felt the need to make real, physical, skin-to-skin connection with the people that she met, and hemlines needed to be long, so that she could crouch to greet children without endangering her modesty. For Diana, dressing for the camera might have been important, but dressing for the people was essential.

A dress designed by David Sassoon (who had quickly made up for the embarrassing engagement dress mishap) encapsulates this best, one that Diana herself labelled as her 'caring dress'. This blue crepe-de-chine dress was covered in a pattern of vibrant pink, purple, and yellow flowers, and she wore it repeatedly for hospital visits. She had found that the bright colours made children in particular very happy, and with each subsequent appearance of the dress she would style herself more and more with children in mind. The original design had included a matching wide-brimmed hat, but Diana had done away with it on the grounds that it prevented her from getting closer to people. She would also pair the dress with statement necklaces, which gave children something to play with when she carried them. Diana knew that the press were fed up with the dress but she couldn't care less. If the children were happy, then so was she.

The social capital of the modern royal is attention. Wherever they visit, whatever cause they are seen to support, that particular institution is granted the opportunity to share the royal limelight for a moment or two. The value that these hosting organizations now place upon the members of the royal family are no longer strictly limited to their order of precedence in the line of succession but rather their potential to spark media coverage for the event. Of course, the line of succession plays some role in this, as the press are far more likely to take an interest in one of the Queen's children than one of her second cousins. Generally speaking, it is the younger, typically female members of the family who spark the most interest. A huge deciding factor in this is fashion. The attendance of a Princess, Duchess or even the Queen meant a new outfit was going to make its debut at your event, photos of which would be distributed not just in newspapers but magazines and fashion publications all across the globe – with the name of your organization written proudly in the description beside it. It offered publicity to a wider audience that might not usually be interested in what specific charities the royals chose to patronize and teased the possibility of going down as part of royal fashion history. What if the gown worn to your movie's premiere, the hat worn to your hospital visit or the new necklace debuted at your fundraising gala made it into a list of best royal fashion moments of all time? You could guarantee then that your event would remain in the public consciousness for much longer than it ever would have without your stylish royal attendee.

As one of the younger central members of the royal family, Diana ranked high in this new, semi-celebrity valuing of the monarchy. She worked with the top designers of the time, and it was almost a certainty that each event she attended would be hounded by photographers desperate to see what she wore. In this sense, fashion was Diana's trump card within the royal institution, and it allowed her a sense of autonomous power in the system, even as her relationship with Prince Charles began to deteriorate. Famously, as the 80s became the 90s, Diana's wardrobe took a sleeker approach. She shrugged off the romantic flounces and beribboned blouses in favour of mature, chic suits and after her separation from her husband in 1992, began to employ the genius of foreign fashion designers to enhance her look. Instrumental in this transformation were the designers Catherine Walker, who had been designing for Diana since her marriage but who is best known for revolutionizing the suits in her wardrobe, and Gianni Versace, whose body-conscious silhouettes and bold block colouring gave Diana an air of modernity and prioritized the woman, not the adornments that covered her.

One of Diana's dresses from this time, which has become so famous that it rivals her wedding dress for the number-one spot, is the 'revenge dress'. On 29 June 1994, an interview with Prince Charles was broadcast, in which he dropped the bombshell that he had been unfaithful to Diana during the course of their marriage. It was a shocking and embarrassingly public admission that the Princess of Wales knew would make headline news the next morning. That same night, she was scheduled to make an appearance at the Serpentine Gallery and, as usual, a dress had been picked out well in advance – a conservative gown that ticked all the boxes a working member of the royal family was expected to satisfy. This was no longer a possibility for Diana, who now more than ever wanted to distance herself from her in-laws, and she decided to buck tradition by wearing a short, tight-fitting, off-the-shoulder Christina Stambolian frock. It was old, as she had bought it three years earlier but had never worn it on the grounds that it was far too daring to be considered royal.[104] Now, however, that was the exact reason why she wanted to wear it and, knowing how taboo the choice was, she had her lady-in-waiting telephone ahead to warn the organizers about the dress change. Diana's plan worked spectacularly, and she appeared the next day right alongside her husband on the front pages. She had successfully inserted herself into an otherwise one-sided narrative and gave herself a little bit of agency in the situation.

After her divorce from Prince Charles in 1996, Diana's overall approach to fashion radically changed. During her time as part of the royal family, it had been her major appeal, and the element of her brand that generated the most value. As an independent figure, still set on carrying out her charitable endeavours, Diana wanted to prove that she as an individual had enough influence to bring attention to important causes, not just her clothes. Of course, she still dressed spectacularly for any event she attended but it's poignant to note that her most famous looks from this time are often her casual outfits, with her biker shorts, oversized sweatshirt and Reeboks combo still regularly featured in magazines and Pinterest boards to this day. Nowhere is this change better epitomized than in the 1997 Christie's auction of dresses from the Princess of Wales's collection. Comprising seventy-nine lots, the auction served the practical function of raising money for charities that were near and dear to Diana's heart but also allowed her to wipe the slate clean. She was no longer restricted by the rules set forth for royal fashion and this allowed her to embark on a brand-new journey, led by her own initiatives. Her tragic death later that year cut the adventure brutally short.

With Diana standing at the forefront of royal fashion throughout the 80s and 90s, it's no wonder that her husband was swallowed up by the background, but that's not to say he wasn't doing anything revolutionary. Sometime in the early 90s (the sole recounter of this story, the King himself, is frustratingly vague with his dates), Charles turned to the companies that applied for his royal warrant and laid down a set of basic sustainability requirements they needed to meet if they wished to retain his patronage.[105] It was a shock to the businesses, but in Charles's eyes it was hardly an outlandish proposal. An environmentally conscious mindset was one he had been raised with as his father, Prince Philip, who was one of the founding members of the world's largest conservation charity, the World Wildlife Fund (now World Wide Fund for Nature), had also been particularly committed to causes of sustainability. With a great deal of resentment, the various companies complied, and later found to their astonishment that not only did they get to keep their royal warrant but by improving the ethics of their supply chain they were actually saving money.

In early 2005, it was announced that the then Prince of Wales was engaged to Camilla Parker-Bowles, his long-time partner, having proposed with a family heirloom ring once belonging to Queen Elizabeth Bowes-Lyon. The context of the marriage was wrought with friction, as many people still viewed the relationship with distaste because it had begun when Charles was still married to his first wife, Diana. The wedding comprised a civil ceremony at the Windsor Guildhall, followed by a blessing at St George's Chapel, within the confines of Windsor Castle. For the civil ceremony, Camilla chose a cream chiffon silk dress that descended into overlapping disks of fabric before stopping just below the knee. She wore a matching coat, on the lapel of which she fastened a brooch of black pearls and diamonds, arranged in the shape of the Prince of Wales plume, gifted to her by Charles. It was reported at the time that the brooch had been created for King Edward VII as a gift for his mistress Alice Keppel, who happened also to be Camilla's great-grandmother. For the blessing later that day, she changed into a more formal dress, one that was more fitting of the grand chapel setting though made a point of being markedly less bride-like. A pale-blue chiffon dress peeked out from behind a matching floor-length coat, embroidered daintily with shimmering gold. It was undeniably regal, and the contrast of the light dress and structured coat cast a dramatic silhouette that was completed with a Philip Treacy headdress of feathers dipped in gold and tipped with small diamonds. The unconventional nature of the wedding proceedings, which did not include a religious ceremony, prompted the bride to avoid a tiara for the big day, despite the fact she had two of her own to pick from.

When entering into the life of a working royal, Camilla, as the new Duchess of Cornwall and later Queen Consort, has chosen an understated approach. Happy to commit quietly to the causes that concern her, showy fashion is not a priority, but even with her jam-packed schedule she still finds the time for some well-thought-out self-fashioning. With the help of her dresser Jacqui Meakin (former dresser to the Queen Mother), Queen Camilla has crafted for herself a neat wardrobe teeming with understated glamour: coat dresses with her favoured mandarin-style collar fit neatly into the standard of royal fashion established by Queen Elizabeth, but Camilla's look is rejuvenated with subtle emphasis on the waist using darts and panels to cinch or draw attention to her figure. Queen Camilla is extremely conscious of how ageing fashion can be and has purposely banished colours from her wardrobe that she has deemed frumpy, 'menopausal mauve' being the nickname she has given to her least favourite shade.[106]

Charles values longevity in his clothes and has spoken with distaste of the 'throw-away' society we have developed, in which we have become accustomed to taking from a seemingly limitless pool of resources with little regard for where things have come from or where they will go when we are finished with them. He is a keen promoter of a circular economy, a central element of which is repurposing rather than replacing objects and garments. For Charles, this process begins with conscious shopping, seeking out suppliers that utilize high-quality materials and craftmanship to ensure the longevity of the garment. A loyal patron of Savile Row, the King favours suppliers such as Anderson & Sheppard, who provide his suits, and Turnbull & Asser, who provide his shirts. The second aspect of this process is to discover a personal style, to ask the question: 'Am I buying this because it's what I love to wear? Or is it just popular now?' and purchase accordingly. Charles's timeless personal style has allowed him to continue wearing his clothes for decades; the pearl-grey morning suit that Charles wore to his son Prince Harry's wedding in 2018 had actually been bought in 1982 and did not look out of place on him at all. It fit perfectly with what we have come to understand as his style. Finally, as wear and tear is inevitable, it is important to mend and not replace garments, and Charles certainly makes no secret of the fact that he will happily patch an overcoat if it means getting a few extra years out of it.

This sort of fashion mindset, though beneficial for the environment, is unfortunately inaccessible to most people, as even without the Savile Row price point just the act of making a garment last is a difficult affair. At the beginning of our story, in the time of the Tudors, repairing and repurposing clothes was standard practice for people in all walks of life, and the skills necessary to do so were common knowledge. Nowadays, a lack of information seems to be one of the biggest deterrents to a sustainable, circular economy, and this is something that King Charles has identified as his primary focus. In 2007, the future King headed a consortium that purchased Dumfries House, an impressive Scottish estate from which he now runs many of his environmental initiatives. Its focus is on providing education for young people on topics that align with Charles's own interests, and the curriculum offers sessions on farm education, animal welfare, horticulture and, of course, textiles. The main goal is to make people aware of where their food, their clothes and their everyday objects come from, with the intention of encouraging them to evolve into more mindful consumers. Many high-profile names in the fashion industry have aligned themselves with the mission of Charles and Dumfries House; the likes of Christopher Kane and the brand Alexander McQueen are official supporters of the Future Textiles education scheme, though the latter is certainly a surprising collaborator as McQueen himself once claimed to have stitched the words 'I am a cunt' into the lining of a jacket he made for the future King Charles.[107] In collaboration with the luxury brand Net-a-Porter, the Prince's Foundation launched The Modern Artisan, a course at Dumfries House that equips young adults with high-quality garment constructions skills, with a focus on sustainability.

It was there, at Dumfries House, that Charles was informed of his mother's declining health on 8 September 2022. By the time of his arrival at Balmoral Charles had acceded to the throne, and Camilla had become his Queen Consort. It was a moment of profound change for the country and in particular in the lives of the new King and Queen. As they looked towards their coronation, a new generation of royals were preparing to take centre stage.

Part Six

THE NEXT
GENERATION

THE WORLD OF royal fashion is a closed circuit. As members of that unit, the royal family have marginal amounts of freedom of expression, but with the final say often coming from the same monarch for ten, twenty, thirty, even seventy years at a time, that environment runs the risk of stagnating. We've seen that there were certain royals who dipped their toes in and out of fashionable society, revelling in its entertainment and style but never staying long enough to be labelled as anything other than a tourist. Alix and Bertie may have frequented the theatres and balls of their stylish peers, but they never allowed people to forget that they were royal. Princess Margaret may have explored a wider scope of fashion than her sister, but no one would suggest that she was anything but a quintessential Princess. Even Diana Spencer, 'the People's Princess', had a carefully maintained royal wardrobe that was intentionally unattainable and immediately marked her out as a member of the royal institution. As Cecil Beaton so clearly put it: 'Since royalty by its very definition is above the crowd, it stands to reason that the fashions of kings and queens should be individual and unique.'[1]

Royal fashion may be a closed circuit, but it is not an inflexible one. The British monarchy owes its longevity to its ability to adapt to changing landscapes, movement that is more noticeable when one ruler replaces another but that in recent years has begun to occur more prominently in other branches of the family. With Queen Elizabeth II providing such an unwavering sense of continuity, change occurred most prominently when the royal circle opened itself up to welcome somebody new into the fold. Transformation in modern royal fashion has come to be defined not by the monarch but by their younger relatives, children, grandchildren, in-laws and so on.

An article on royal tiaras that appeared in the official Platinum Jubilee programme informed that Queen Elizabeth II did not wear them for vanity, rather they functioned to support her diplomatic missions by denoting the importance of state visits. It's certainly fair to say that tiaras have taken a backseat in recent years, with the most commonly associated headwear for the late Queen having been her distinctive hats rather than any state crown or platinum sparkler. It's a far cry from the time of Queen Mary, who would rarely release a portrait photograph that didn't feature one of her beloved tiaras sitting pride of place in her coiffure. The outbreak of the Second World War put a halt to this, and in response to the conflict and hardship faced by the majority of the country, the tiara fell out of style as a vulgar and pretentious display of wealth. Tiaras returned to the royal fashion lexicon in the post-war years, making appearances at a whole host of events in the royal calendar, from the State Opening of Parliament to Hollywood movie premieres. We've even seen new tiaras enter the royal collection. For her marriage to the Duke of York in 1986, Sarah Ferguson was given a diamond tiara by the Queen and Prince Philip, and in 1999, Sophie Rhys-Jones was gifted a new tiara, refashioned from one of Queen Victoria's old circlets, to wear for her wedding to Prince Edward. As Countess of Wessex, Sophie received yet another tiara in 2005, the Wessex Aquamarine Tiara. It was probably given to the Countess in order to help meet the demands that came with making regular appearances at foreign royal events, as Edward and Sophie tend to be the go-to ambassadors for British royalty in other European kingdoms.

This influx of modern royal tiaras can be attributed to the sudden uptake of commoners into the family. Wedding-tiara etiquette stipulates that the bride should wear the tiaras of their own family at the ceremony, before adopting the jewels of their in-laws for the rest of their married life. Diana Spencer may have been a commoner from the perspective of the royal family, but she came from one of the most established aristocratic families in England and had her own hereditary tiara to wear. For her first marriage to Captain Andrew Parker-Bowles in 1973, Queen Camilla had worn her hereditary Cubitt-Shand Tiara. Had she been able to marry Prince Charles in a formal ceremony rather than the civil ceremony that her divorcee status had restricted them to, she may have opted to wear it again in 2005, or perhaps her Keppel Ruby and Diamond Tiara instead. Sarah Ferguson and Sophie Rhys-Jones were the first brides to join the immediate royal family with no family jewels of their own, but they certainly would not be the last.

On 16 November 2010, the engagement of Prince William of Wales and Catherine Middleton was announced. It had been anticipated for years; the duo had met at St Andrew's university and had been a semi-consistent couple ever since. Kate had joined William as a guest at many formal functions and had hinted at the seriousness of their relationship by committing to a quasi-royal wardrobe even then. In late 2006, Kate had joined William for his passing-out ceremony at Sandhurst, which marked the completion of his army training. It was the first event at which both she and senior members of the royal family would be present, and though she was seated far from the monarchal flock, an extremely fortunate fashion choice singled her out as part of the inner circle. Kate opted for a statement red Armani coat, which almost entirely obscured her black dress beneath. She wore tights and a pair of knee-high suede black boots, pulling together an outfit that also featured black leather gloves and a wide-brimmed black hat. It was a modern answer to the Queen's signature coat dress and hat combination, the colours of which were undoubtedly chosen to match the black and red of William's uniform and offered up her interpretation of a twenty-first-century royal to both the press and her future in-laws. Kate's choice to create a sartorial link between herself and William coincidentally worked a little too well, as the Queen had also opted for red, quite possibly to highlight William's ties to the Crown. A few eyebrows were raised, as one speculative royal fashion rule often cited is that nobody in the family should dress in the same colour as the Queen when appearing as a collective. It says something about Kate's understanding of fashion symbolism that even though she was in no way formally affiliated with the royal family at that point, the very fact that the press dubbed it a 'protocol catastrophe' was proof that the Middleton and royal entities were already beginning to merge in the public consciousness.

Making such a strong debut meant that her wardrobe choices during their brief break-up period the following year were far more significant. Kate was very clearly not dressing for a royal role any more. She was pictured in a revealing handkerchief-style dress for a club night in London and a shimmery lingerie-inspired dress for a book launch not long after. It was a wardrobe typical of an in-demand young socialite, certainly not a future royal bride. This brief style stint was erased when William and Kate rekindled their relationship, and by 2010 it was time for the engagement photocall. Kate's dress choice immediately evoked the feeling that the world was looking at the new Princess of Wales. They were not, of course, as the title was held (albeit not formally used) by Queen Camilla and was not granted to Kate until after the accession of King Charles III. Regardless, she seemed to embody the role as it has historically existed – she was a young, attractive, future Queen who offered a balance to the older women of the royal family who were expected to abide more firmly to rules about dress propriety. The glossy, wraparound style of Kate's Issa dress contrasted the conservatism of its hemline and sleeves with the chicness of its rippling fabric, and its deep-blue colour recalled images of the previous Princess of Wales, who had worn blue for her own engagement photocall. The most obvious Diana similarity was, of course, Kate's sapphire and diamond engagement ring, the very same ring that Diana had worn all those years before.

The speculation regarding who Kate might opt to use as designer for her wedding dress was heavily influenced by this initial glimpse at semi-royal dressing. So far she had shown a very real respect for the conservative values that tend to encapsulate royal style, and a keen interest in harmonizing with previous or current members of the family. The top candidates for the wedding dress were then drawn from a list of well-known and well-loved royal designers, with the leading suggestions being Elizabeth Emanuel or Catherine Walker & Co. When Kate stepped out in front of Westminster Abbey on 29 April 2011, she revealed her choice of Sarah Burton, creative director of Alexander McQueen, as dress designer. She was not one of the typical royal designers, but she did have some more quiet links to the family. In 2005, Kate had been a guest at the wedding of Queen Camilla's son, and Burton had been the designer behind the bride's dress. Together, Kate and Burton had worked on a look that would honour fashion history but with a modern twist, opting for a traditional white satin and lace combination that borrowed heavily from late Victorian styles. The lace-covered bodice was padded slightly at the hips to create the illusion of a corseted waist and a semi-bustle at the back of the skirt added to the traditional feeling of the gown. These antiquated elements were countered by a sharp, plunging neckline and an informal semi-chignon hair-style framed by the Cartier Halo Tiara, a favourite of Princess Margaret, whose own wedding dress had also served as inspiration for Kate's look.

The wedding dress was met with widespread critical acclaim, but there were others at the event who fared less well in the wake of the royal wedding. In late 2012, stylist Mary Fellowes met up with her second cousin Sarah Ferguson, the Duchess of York, who had a request to ask the celebrity fashion expert. Her daughters, Princesses Beatrice and Eugenie of York, who were both barely in their twenties at the time they attended their cousin William's wedding, had made headlines for all the wrong reasons. Perhaps hoping to use the occasion to make their own debuts, they had both opted for bold looks that featured very eccentric hats. Eugenie wore a cobalt-blue Peter Pan-esque cap fixed with a purple flower, and Beatrice had sported a bizarrely architectural beige 'pretzel' hat. The mockery they were subject to in the wake of the wedding was extraordinarily intense, coming from the press and social media alike, likening them to the two evil stepsisters from Cinderella's story. The pressure had reduced them to tears on multiple occasions, and with Queen Elizabeth's Diamond Jubilee now fast approaching, they were terrified of a repeat. 'I think it might be a good time for the girls to have some help,' said the Duchess, and Fellowes agreed to assist in transforming their look.[2] She opted to strip back their style to a simpler, cleaner silhouette and directly borrowed from the Queen's 1950s style. It was effective at helping the sisters avoid further abuse, and the inspiration was clear enough that it even caught the attention of the muse. 'Granny gets the reference. And loves it,' confided one of the sisters.[3]

In recent years, Beatrice and Eugenie have attracted great praise for their unpretentious and stylish fashion choices. They aren't working royals, and so only appear in the public eye on limited occasions, but each time they do, they attract a significant amount of positive attention from the fashion community. Their wedding dresses are particularly worth noting. In early 2020, it was announced that Princess Beatrice was to marry Edoardo Mapelli Mozzi in a May ceremony at St James's Palace. The outbreak of the Covid-19 pandemic put a halt to these plans and the planned nuptials were replaced by an extremely private ceremony at one of the small chapels on the Windsor estate. In the spirit of keeping it a small affair, Beatrice made the decision not to commission a wedding dress but instead borrowed from her grandmother Queen Elizabeth's expansive collection – repurposing an ivory taffeta and diamante-encrusted Norman Hartnell gown worn by the Queen to the 1967 State Opening of Parliament as an alternative.

Back in 2019, Princess Eugenie also imbued her wedding dress with a heartfelt message. Her silk Peter Pilotto gown was intentionally designed to expose the long surgical scar running down the bride's spine – one she has had since undergoing a surgery for scoliosis as a child. Eugenie's decision to make her scar part of her wedding look brings to mind one of her not-so-distant ancestors, Queen Alexandra, who felt such pressure to hide her own scars and spinal curvature that she transformed fashion history masking them. 'It's a lovely way to honour the people who looked after me and a way of standing up for young people who also go through this,' the Princess said, 'I think you can change the way beauty is, and you can show people your scars and I think it's really special to stand up for that.'[4]

The presence of social media, which had made 2011 so miserable for the York Princesses, is one of the main challenges faced by the modern royals. If television brought the royals into our homes, social media put them in the palm of our hands. Never has it been easier for us to keep up with them and their fashion; it's given them infinitely more power to influence trends but also opens them up to a whole host of new critics. It's also fundamentally changed our expectations of celebrities, making relatability one of the most highly valued assets. The royal family, by nature of their social position, are impossibly unrelatable, and while they may not be celebrities in the typical sense, they are public figures nonetheless. How, then, are they supposed to maintain relevance in the popular mindset? That is where Kate Middleton steps in.

As a member of the core royal family, Catherine Elizabeth Middleton is two different women: Kate Middleton and the Princess of Wales. To this day, Catherine is still referred to by the press as Kate Middleton. This makes sense, as it's the name she was first introduced to us by, but times have changed. She's not the twenty-something uni student and possible girlfriend of one of the world's favourite Princes any more. She's not being papped as she dips in and out of London nightclubs, she's a titled woman with three royal children, totes tiaras at state banquets and poses with antique brooches for portrait paintings of herself. It's an entirely unrelatable life that she leads, but that's exactly the reason why she needs to be two different women at once. It's born from the social-media-driven need to appear accessible, to be of value in the modern world of celebrity, to prove to the public that ancient though the concept of royalty might be, they can still, in some way, represent the everyday person. It's *Kate Middleton* who wears Gucci mini dresses to open a new wing at the V&A. It's *Kate Middleton* who puts her hair in a ponytail to make a hospital visit and wears a Zara blazer for a trip to a Lego factory. Kate Middleton is 'one of us', and her wardrobe is crafted to reflect that – giving us affordable style options or dressing to more accurately reflect the current world view of celebrity style.

The Princess of Wales, however, is the woman who represents tradition. The Princess of Wales (or as she was previously titled, the Duchess of Cambridge) wears coat dresses and bespoke hats to church services. She's the woman who dresses her children in clothes that their father or even grandfather wore and pushes them around in prams from the 1940s. The Princess of Wales inherited the Lover's Knot Tiara from Diana Spencer and the Lotus Tiara from the Queen Mother's collection, and wears them with sashes and insignia that date back hundreds of years. It's an entirely foreign world to the majority of the population, but it is made agreeable, even accessible, by the presence of Catherine in those situations. After all, it's the 'Kate effect' not the 'Princess of Wales effect' that is her sell-out power.

The 'Kate effect' is the popular term used to describe the specific instances when Catherine makes the world go *crazy* for something. Usually this applies to fashion, typically of a more affordable variety, that she either wears herself or dresses her children in. Knitwear seen on Prince George or Princess Charlotte will sell out within hours, especially if they come from high-street retailers like John Lewis and Cath Kidston. She took the British label Goat to a global level and made Reiss a household name. 'There is no question that Kate wearing Reiss has impacted our brand,' said David Reiss, the brand's managing director, recalling that after Kate first wore one of their dresses in 2011 there was so much traffic to their website from across the globe that it crashed.[5] A royal so close to the core of the family unit choosing to wear high-street brands for public engagements was an entirely alien concept.

Anna Harvey, recounting her time shaping Diana Spencer's wardrobe, insisted that affordable fashion was such an absurd suggestion that it was not even discussed. Diana's royal wardrobe may have been crafted with the intention to foster human connection, but it still needed to represent fantasy – an unattainable fairy-tale existence that was only available to princesses.

So, if Kate Middleton's sartorial superpower is the 'Kate effect', what about the Princess of Wales? For this we can look back to the red Armani coat dress from 2006. Ask anyone what colour they associate with the Wales family clan, and most likely they'll say blue. Starting with her Issa engagement dress and sapphire ring, Catherine has carefully cultivated a link between herself and the colour blue. Her first official portrait in 2013 featured her in an inky-blue blouse, followed by a second in 2022 in which she wears a teal-tinged dress by The Vampire's Wife beside Prince William in a suit and blue tie.[6] For their ten-year wedding anniversary photos, Catherine wore a floral dress and William a blue jumper, and for the 2022 Easter Service at Windsor, William, Catherine, George, and Charlotte were all dressed in various shades of blue. In much the same way that the Armani coat had helped to merge Catherine with the rest of the royal family, the 'Wales blue' marks the five young royals out as a distinct unit within a wider familial network, emphasizing their unity and suggesting a commonality of values.

Why the colour blue in particular? We know that blue has been a favourite amongst modern royals; it was Queen Alexandra's favourite colour, was a frequent feature in Queen Mary's wardrobe and was undoubtedly a personal favourite of the Queen Mother. Elizabeth Bowes-Lyon adored dressing herself and her two daughters in pale blue, particularly when they made public outings, as it contrasted nicely with the typically muted colour palette of day clothes at the time. It became such a fixture of their identity that their nanny, Marion Crawford, felt she needed to stop wearing it herself: 'Blue of a certain misty shade was always the Duchess's favourite colour, and it happened to be mine as well. More than once upon coming down to lunch I found we were all dressed in the same colour. After that I tactfully adopted brown.'[7] So blue day clothes have a historical precedent as a modern royal uniform, almost a contemporary answer to George III's Windsor uniform, but how fair is it to say that Catherine is personally aware of that, or even that she is personally making the choice to pick a colour scheme and not her dresser? I would argue that it's quite possibly her own directive. We've seen with her wedding dress that she is interested in seeking out and recreating moments in royal fashion history, and her background as an art history student has undoubtedly given her an appreciation for the symbolic value of colour. Blue is a more palatable alternative to the colours traditionally associated with royalty, being far less aggressive than red and significantly more conservative than purple. It has associations with peace and also modernity, making it a perfect representation of the Waleses' quest to appeal to both traditional and progressive values in society.

None of this is to suggest that Catherine is being two-faced or intentionally deceptive, but rather it serves to show the extent to which she has had to bear the brunt of the issue of modern celebrity culture. Older, more senior members of the family are able to use their age to avoid confronting the issue of social media head on, but the Prince and Princess of Wales physically cannot. Their marriage coincided with the rise of Twitter, Instagram and Facebook, meaning that they, as young and in-demand royals, had to consider the ways that they could pander to that particular audience from a very early stage. Relatability is not entirely Catherine's cross to bear; both Prince William and Prince Harry have made approachability a key aspect of their public image and have imbued it into even the most formal of royal occasions. In the centenary portrait of the royal family by John Wonnacott, Prince William stands with his sleeves rolled up and his hands stuffed into his pockets, watching as Prince Harry, in a polo shirt, leans over the back of a chair. Later, in 2009, Nicky Philipps captured the two brothers in a casual, off-duty pose that contrasted sharply with their crisp uniforms and colourful insignia, summing up on a canvas the dichotomy of trying to make such an ancient institution seem accessible.[8]

This bleeds into their fashion as well. It's not entirely uncommon to see either of the Princes sporting a shirt, jumper and jeans combination for official portrait photographs, which are some of the most widely distributed images of the duo. It's quite telling that these particular outfits tend to make their real-life appearances at more casual engagements, indicating that the image the Princes want to project the most is their ability to separate themselves from the formality of tradition as and when it works best. Generally speaking, their fashion is still very conservative, involving various uniforms and very similar dark suits. This is much more indicative of the current climate of men's formalwear than anything else and makes it a lot harder for us to decode any personal branding messages that William and Harry might want to project. In the wider fashion world, again facilitated by conversations on social media, there has been more of a push to redefine what constitutes men's formalwear, to which the Princes have occasionally contributed. For the 2021 Earthshot Prize Awards, Prince William sported an emerald velvet suit over a black polo-neck top, not particularly radical when compared to the likes of Billy Porter and Harry Styles (who tend to be the front-runners in conversations about masculinity in fashion) but borderline revolutionary for an institution that tends to praise conservative fashion and bristle at innovation.

In 2016, when California-born actress Meghan Markle stepped out in public wearing a dainty, handmade necklace strung with the initials H and M, the world got their first hint that her relationship with Prince Harry was getting serious. The prospect of a new, major royal wedding is always exciting, as it hints at significant changes not only to the family dynamic but also to the world of royal fashion. No royal bride knows what's in store for them when they take up royal duties, but they have an idea of what to expect based upon their own personal understanding of what their new role entails, and more often than not this is echoed in the style they bring with them. For Diana Spencer, this meant embodying the fairy tale that her marriage was supposed to represent with whimsical, soft fashion. For Catherine Middleton, it was about showing that royalty can still be relevant to a younger generation, that it has one foot on the ground and can be an 'attainable' source of inspiration. So, what was Meghan Markle going to bring to the table?

Meghan's path to the royal family was quite unusual when compared to other stories. She was thirty-six at the time of her marriage and had spent nearly two decades already in the public eye, working as an actress and activist. As a consequence, she had already developed a sense of personal style that was tailored to a specific public profession, one that has less established rules than the monarchy, and that was governed mainly by her own personal preferences. During her pre-royal days, Meghan kept a lifestyle blog called *The Tig*, which chronicled her thoughts and experiences about fashion in the mid-2010s. It gives us a rare and refreshingly personal insight into the mindset of a future royal, and whilst in a world of fast fashion and micro trends it is occasionally painfully 'of its time', the pieces that she gravitates towards are still indicative of her personal style. She was quick to praise the statement overcoats spotted up and down the runways of New York Fashion Week in 2015, and regularly suggested switching a dress for a pantsuit at parties. While these might be key elements of Meghan's wardrobe today, at the time she was discussing them in *The Tig*, they were not fully reflected in her public style. You were much more likely to see the *Suits* star sporting a smart-casual outfit, typically a knee-length dress with heavy texture and patterns, not something we often see her in today.

Why then did Meghan Markle enter the royal family with such a distinctly different working wardrobe? Again, this comes from her personal interpretation of what the role meant to her. Generally speaking, Meghan's royal style borrows from the aesthetics of American female politicians, or politically adjacent figures, particularly from the democratic side of the scale. The First Family is often considered to be America's answer to the British royal family, and so it's a case of Meghan having looked to familiar figures to shape an understanding of the demands that would be made of her after her marriage. All you have to do is follow Meghan's gaze to the outfits worn by the Biden and Obama families at the 2021 Inauguration to get an understanding of the fundamentals of that style. Monochrome colour palettes, wide-leg trousers as opposed to skirts or dresses, and large, statement coats that cut a powerful silhouette. There's a business-like quality to the outfits, suggesting that Meghan felt her new role would present her with the opportunity to continue the social work she had already been committed to, this time on a global scale. Large, statement bags trump clutches and purses in her outfits, with the likes of her trustworthy Strathberry tote and colourful Mulberry pieces giving her a dynamic, business-like feel. Stylish and practical, Meghan fits somewhere in between the celebrity and political style brackets. Fitting, really, once you consider that the monarchy itself has ricocheted between those two camps throughout history.

Meghan's wedding dress perfectly encapsulated not only her personal style but her international background too. She chose Clare Waight Keller to be the mastermind behind its creation, who as the British creative director of the French brand Givenchy honoured tradition whilst introducing a foreign element. The plain silk boat-neck gown was made with absolute simplicity in mind. It was intended to be both royal and casual with its slightly relaxed fit and impressively long veil, perhaps testament to the success of Catherine and the other young royals at establishing an approachable group identity. Meghan's 5-metre-long veil was undoubtedly the most impressive part of her wedding ensemble and took longer to complete than even the dress itself. It formed a picturesque halo pinned in place by Queen Mary's art deco Diamond Bandeau Tiara and was painstakingly hand-embroidered with each of the Commonwealth flowers, along with California poppies to represent her home state. Interwoven with the flora were crops of wheat, a popular royal symbol denoting peace and love, and wintersweet, a flower that grows in the gardens of Kensington Palace, particularly outside Nottingham Cottage, which was where the royal couple were living at the time of the wedding.

Meghan, like so many brides, followed the 'something old, something new, something borrowed, something blue' tradition for her wedding look. The dress itself was the 'something new', Queen Mary's tiara was the 'old' and 'borrowed' aspect all conveniently rolled up into one, and the 'something blue' came in the form of a tiny piece of blue fabric sewn into her veil – taken from the dress she had worn on her first date with Prince Harry. Unlike the Princess of Wales, as Duchess of Sussex, Meghan would not continue to use blue as an identifying colour. The Sussexes certainly don't use colour in the same way that William and Catherine do, at least not to the same extent, but they seem to have picked a colour to call their own, nonetheless. Green seems to be a common theme in their wardrobes and has made appearances at many of the key moments in their marriage. At their engagement photocall, Meghan opted for an emerald-green dress by P.A.R.O.S.H., which she revealed for the interview after removing her beige coat. Journalists (who were perhaps so used to seeing a set colour scheme emerge for young royals) were quick to note that in the months between the engagement and wedding, Meghan gravitated towards outfits that framed a single green article of clothing with neutral accompaniments. Two of the most obvious instances of a green colour scheme came with their exit from life as working royals in 2020. For their final engagement at the Commonwealth Service, Meghan opted for a vibrant green Emilia Wickstead cape dress, which Prince Harry emphasized by wearing a suit lined with the same shade. In 2021, the couple posed for a *TIME* magazine photoshoot in which they both wore monochromatic outfits of varying shades of green, Harry in a casual, pared-back suit and Meghan often in wide trousers and a sturdy coat.

What meaning does the colour green serve the Sussexes? Practically, it fits very nicely with the other symbolic aspects they've chosen to align themselves with. The Duke and Duchess like to pose for official portraits outside: it's far less alienating than a grand palace interior might be and neatly complements their personal interests in environmental causes, something that both Prince Harry and Prince William take incredibly seriously. The colour green features heavily in the scenery that the Sussexes enjoy appearing in, and wearing the shade helps them to complement their surroundings but also to bring it with them into other environments. There is another colour of significance that has begun to creep more prominently into Meghan's wardrobe specifically, one that also featured heavily in the *TIME* magazine photoshoot: white. She's worn it for two of the major public engagements that she has attended since the highly controversial *Oprah* interview in early 2021, and I believe that it too has a political inspiration. Her first appearance at the Invictus Games in 2022 saw her sporting an oversized Valentino pantsuit, and later, for the Thanksgiving Service for the Queen's Platinum Jubilee, she wore a sleek Dior coat dress. Both were white. Over the past few years, female democrat politicians in the USA have committed to wearing white to mark key feminist issues and achievements, paying homage to the Suffragettes who used the colour as an emblem of their movement. It has essentially become a sartorial shorthand for female strength and group identity, making it a poignant choice for Meghan to wear at what are likely to be some of the toughest occasions in her public life.

One of the central wardrobe innovations to enter royal life in recent years has been repetition. Both the Princess of Wales and the Duchess of Sussex have championed the royal art of re-wearing outfits for public occasions. Generally speaking, these royal women will opt for a new ensemble for the most important events in their calendars but frequently rehash outfits for other engagements. Norman Hartnell had neatly outlined the reasons why he could never fathom the thought of anything other than a new outfit for each royal outing when he recounted the challenges of designing the Queen Mother's touring wardrobes.[9] If one state received a new dress and another did not, was the Queen not implying that she thought her hosts to be second-rate? Rather than fall into the trap highlighted by Hartnell, these young royals primarily use re-wears as a way to avoid offence. In the early years, Catherine opted to bring out old dresses when she was attending a wedding as a guest, so that she would not steal press attention from the bride herself. Similarly, she would often don a familiar outfit when carrying out engagements with more senior members of the family, so as not to detract from their initiatives.

In more recent years, the royal recycling revolution has had less to do with etiquette and more to do with social issues. The Wales and Sussex units both express keen interest in environmental conservation efforts and patronize multiple charities and organizations that seek to make a positive impact on the environment. Following in the footsteps of King Charles, Catherine and Meghan have shifted their focus towards consumer awareness, with emphasis being placed upon the longevity of an item of clothing as opposed to its stylishness. Catherine, with her timeless pieces, and Meghan, with her versatile capsule wardrobe, are champions for the aesthetics of this eco-friendly push. Yet it is not enough to simply *represent* the movement, they need to embody it, which is an entirely impossible goal if with each royal engagement a new outfit is being crafted just to gather dust afterwards. These outfits need to be re-worn, often and over a long period of time, to prove it is possible to remain stylish whilst rejecting fashion fads. It is one of those rare instances in which royal tradition, in this case the pressure to maintain a wardrobe that speaks not too directly to the time, harmonizes with contemporary conversations about fashion without the need to change.

Throughout our story, we have seen how royals have imparted their own agendas through dress codes. From Jane Seymour's gable hoods to Queen Adelaide's English blond, encouraging adherence to a set style has often proved a successful method of making royal prerogatives more impactful. Attendees to the inaugural Earthshot Prize Awards, an initiative established by the Prince of Wales, were asked to consider the environment by not purchasing a new suit or gown for the event. Sure enough, William and Catherine's directives led to their guests wearing environmentally conscious re-wears on the green carpet.

We have also seen, particularly since Princess Beatrice's mid-pandemic wedding, that royal fashion has changed to avoid criticisms on the subject of overindulgence in a period of severe financial uncertainty for most of the United Kingdom. In yet another instance of royal life going against the grain of the everyday experience, the historic Platinum Jubilee celebrations of Queen Elizabeth II coincided rather awkwardly with this intense cost of living crisis. Any Jubilee is a cause for celebration, but for this milestone landmark – the first Platinum Jubilee to be celebrated by a British monarch – there was set to be a particularly exuberant affair. There was understandable tension in the lead up to the event. The question 'Is this really the best time?' hung on many lips, but this was certainly not the first time that the royal family had faced a challenge such as this. Casting our minds back to 1831, we will remember how William IV argued against a lavish coronation on the grounds that the nation was still reeling from the double financial devastation of a war with France and a spendthrift King. His pared-back ceremony served the royal cause well and restored some semblance of faith within the public that their monarch was attuned to their situation. Just like King William's coronation, the Platinum Jubilee celebrations were not cancelled but there was certainly an element of awareness, at least on a sartorial level, of the financial difficulties facing the country. For the Trooping the Colour parade, the first major event of the celebrations, the future Queen

Camilla and the Princess of Wales both opted for dresses that they had worn before, and even Prince Louis was dressed in a hand-me-down sailor-style suit that had been his father's. Ever since, more and more royal engagements, particularly those helmed by the Princess of Wales, are treated to a royal re-wear.

Modern royal fashion is not at all about personal enjoyment. If it were, perhaps we would see a little more variation, understand a little more about the people wearing the clothes, rather than simply seeing ourselves reflected back through the prism of this strange and mysterious institution. After the departure from royal life of Princess Diana, a protective barrier was built around royal bodies. Its defences are tailor-made in Savile Row stores and Fashion Week catwalks, polished to the high heavens in the hope that no fault will be found in this impenetrable armour. We can read into what each little embroidered detail on one of Anne Boleyn's linen shirts may have meant or why certain styles of jewellery were adopted by each monarch, as it was a relatively safe pursuit for these historical monarchs to be so intensely outspoken. By and large the Tudor court could control who got to look at them, who got to ogle at their brocade and murmur about their headdresses. They were surrounded by a complex network of courtiers who typically shared their social, cultural and religious views on life. It was easier to control what message your clothes were putting out when everyone who had the chance to view them was within touching distance of the Crown. It's telling that as fashion illustrations began to be included in the printed press, King George III became suddenly quite dependent upon a simple, matching royal uniform for his family. Then too, as photography reached its maturity, Victoria and Albert became increasingly concerned with how their son's sartorial self-expression might reflect poorly upon the family. The vulnerability that social media has exposed modern royalty to is easily the most extreme example of this media exposure. With the pinch of a finger, each and every outfit worn publicly by the royal cohorts can be examined on a minute level. With one quick Google search we can discover how much money was spent on each look and the potentially controversial provenance of each ancient jewellery piece can be unearthed.

Rigid uniformity, occasionally masquerading as celebrity style, gives the modern royals a perfectly consistent cookie-cutter mode of fashion. It's repetitive and predictable, to the point that even the most minute deviations can have significant impact, before snapping right back to the regular program. That daunting exposure of internal flaws that Queen Victoria so passionately believed fashion could reveal is now entirely beyond the parameter of royal dressing. Their neat and polished appearances are intended to reflect the world they live in and the institution to which they belong – representative of the role whilst being entirely unrepresentative of the person within. Today, we learn an awful lot more about the royal point of view through their fashion, but frustratingly little about their persona. It is a uniform that is at its most effective when we can't tell that it's a uniform, when it seems to reflect the everyday experience. When it doesn't, it's painfully obvious, and the dissonance prompts us to wonder just how socially aware the royals truly are.

Just what path royal fashion will take in years to come is impossible to predict. The story up until now has been far from a linear trudge towards conservativism; rather, with each passing monarch we have often somersaulted back and forth between extravagance and banality, stylishness and severity. We can't be certain that subsequent generations of royals will adhere to the cultivated uniformity of the modern royals, or even that their current images will remain constant. Images of Queen Elizabeth II in ceremonial gear were commonplace, an accepted truth, but how will the public image of the younger royals fare when we see them in velvet robes and regalia? That's hardly a visual that sits coherently with the creation of a set of people who are supposed to be 'just like us'. It will be the ultimate test, to see just how successful their personal branding has been, if they can continue to make over 500 years of complex, ceremonial traditions seem 'relatable' to the modern eye.

Acknowledgements

Writing this book has been one of the most surreal adventures I have ever experienced. It's also been exhausting, and occasionally draining, but it has always been incredibly rewarding. I want to start by thanking Katie Packer and Holly Purdham, my wonderful editors at Headline. Thank you for believing in me and thank you for your guidance! This whole process was entirely foreign to me, and I cannot imagine having better guides. I would also like to thank the entire team at Headline Publishing; your enthusiasm for this book has been all the motivation I have needed to push through my writing slumps!

I never thought I would get an opportunity like this so soon in my career and I owe this, as well as so many other opportunities I have had lately, to the continual support of TikTok. When I first created @theroyalwardrobe (originally @lavenderstages, after a ghost story from the Bristol Old Vic Theatre) it was to give me something entertaining to do during lockdown. This little 'hobby' has turned into a following of nearly half a million people, and I want to thank each and every one of you for stopping to listen to my history rambles. I would also like to thank Natalie Lyddon and the whole TikTok team for their continual support. I cannot thank you enough for all you've done for me.

ACKNOWLEDGEMENTS

Thank you to Polly Putnam, Elizabeth Thompson and Matthew Storey from Historic Royal Palaces. I greatly appreciate the time you took to discuss the collection with me; and Claire Robinson at the University of Saint Andrews, thanks also for your input on Charles II's wig. The work of Valerie Cumming, Joanna Marschner, Eleri Lynn and Aileen Ribeiro has been pivotal to the writing of this book, and I would like to take the time to give extra credit here. Thank you also to Charlie from @notaroyalexpert for your feedback on my modern royal commentary!

Throughout this process I have lost my mind and my confidence on multiple occasions. My friends and family have been the ones to help me find them again each time, and for that I am especially grateful. Mum, Dad, Dee, Callum and Chloe (and Rocky too), I love you so much. Thank you for being so supportive, and for being the unconsenting victims to my many history rants. I'll need a break after this, so you'll be safe from museum trips for a week or two. Verity, Sarge, Jess, Grace and Sophie, you are the reason this book even exists. You have kept me focused, you've kept me sane and you've kept me happy, and I would not have made it through the last three years without you. Every time I read a line from this book I can't help but think about each tuna melt from the library café, each episode of *Gilmore Girls*, each trip to Woody's and each indie rock night that went along with it. Three years just isn't enough.

Image Credits

First Plate Section

page

1 Henry VII, Elizabeth of York, Henry VIII and Jane Seymour, oil on canvas by Remee van Leemput, 1537 (Royal Collection Trust/© His Majesty King Charles III, 2023/Bridgeman Images). Anne Boleyn, oil on panel by an unknown artist, 1534 (Hever Castle/Bridgeman Images).

2 Edward VI, oil on panel by William Scrots, c.1546 (Royal Collection Trust/ © His Majesty King Charles III, 2023/Bridgeman Images). Elizabeth I, 'The Rainbow Portrait', oil on panel by Oliver Isaac, c.1600 (Universal Images Group North America LLC/Alamy). The 'Chequers Ring', mother of pearl, gold, rubies and enamel, c.1570 (Album/Alamy).

3 James I & VI and Anne of Denmark, engraving by Renold Elstrack, 1610–1615 (Chronicle/Alamy). Henrietta Maria, oil on canvas by Anthony van Dyck, 1636 (Metropolitan Museum of Art, New York. Bequest of Mrs. Charles Wrightsman in honour of Annette de la Renta, 2019).

4 Catherine of Braganza and Charles II, engraving by an unknown artist, after 1662 (© National Portrait Gallery, London). Wedding suit of James II, 1673 (© Victoria and Albert Museum, London).

5 Mantua, silk and metal, c.1708 (The Metropolitan Museum of Art, New York. Purchase, Rogers Fund, Isabella Shults Fund and Irene Lewisohn Bequest, 1991). *His Royal Highness the Prince of Orange says goodbye to his wife Mary as he leaves for England to help the Protestants,* mezzotint by Jacob Gole, 1688–1702 (Royal Collection Trust/© His Majesty King Charles III, 2023/Bridgeman Images).

6 Caroline of Ansbach and her son, oil on canvas by Herman Vander Myn, c.1727 (Orleans House Gallery, Richmond Borough Art Collection).

7 Court dress, silk and metallic thread, c.1750 (Metropolitan Museum of Art, New York. Purchase, Irene Lewisohn Bequest, 1965).

Image Credits

A View of the Ball at St. James's on the King's Birth Day, June 4 1782, engraving with etching by an unknown artist, 1782 (Royal Collection Trust/© His Majesty King Charles III, 2023/Bridgeman Images).

8 *Her Royal Highness the Princess of Wales in her Court Dress on the 4 of June 1807*, from *La Belle Assemblée*, 1807 (© Museum of London/Heritage-Images/Alamy). George IV, oil on canvas by David Wilkie, 1829 (Royal Collection Trust/© His Majesty King Charles III, 2023/Bridgeman Images).

Second Plate Section

page

1 Page from Volume of Miss Victoire Conroy's paper dolls (Royal Archives/© His Majesty King Charles III, 2023). Queen Victoria's wedding dress, silk satin with Honiton lace, 1840 (Royal Collection Trust/© His Majesty King Charles III, 2023).

2 King Edward VII; Queen Victoria; Queen Alexandra, half-plate glass negative by and after Alexander Bassano, 5 May 1881 (© National Portrait Gallery, London).

3 Princess Alexandra and her sister Dagmar, photograph by Maull & Co., 1873 (© Historic Royal Palaces/Bridgeman Images). George V with Dowager ex-Empress Maria Fyodorovna and members of the Royal Family, 1923 (Fine Art Images/Alamy).

4 Wallis Simpson wearing the 'Lobster Dress', photograph by Cecil Beaton for *Vogue*, 1937 (Cecil Beaton/Condé Nast/Shutterstock). The Duke and Duchess of Windsor, photograph by Patrick Lichfield for *Vogue*, 1967 (Patrick Lichfield/Condé Nast/Shutterstock).

5 *The Royal Family*, postcard published in the 1940s (Glasshouse Images/Alamy). Investiture of the Prince of Wales at Caernarfon Castle, 1969 (Keystone Press/Alamy).

6 Diana, Princess of Wales arriving at the State Opening of Parliament, 1984 (Colin Davey/Hulton Archive/Getty Images).

7 Diana, Princess of Wales arriving at the Serpentine Gallery, June 1994 (Martin Keene/PA Images/Alamy). The Princess of Wales (then Duchess of Cambridge) in Copenhagen, February 2022 (Doug Peters/Alamy).

8 Camilla, the Queen Consort (then Duchess of Cornwall), the Princess of Wales (then Duchess of Cambridge) and Prince George attending the Trooping of the Colour, June 2022 (Doug Peters/Alamy). The Duke and Duchess of Sussex at the Commonwealth Day Service, Westminster Abbey, March 2020 (Anwar Hussein/Alamy).

Bibliography

Arch, Nigel, and Marschner, Joanna, *Splendour at Court* (London: Unwin Hyman, 1987)

Arnold, Janet, *Patterns of Fashion 3* (London: Macmillan, 1985)

Aronson, Theo, *Princess Margaret* (London: Michael O'Mara, 2001)

Aspinall, A. (ed.), *The Later Correspondence of George III, Vol. I* (Cambridge: Cambridge University Press, 1966)

Aspinall, A. (ed.), *Mrs Jordan and Her Family* (London: Arthur Barker Ltd, 1951)

Battiscombe, Georgina, *Queen Alexandra* (London: Constable, 1984)

Beaton, Cecil, *The Glass of Fashion* (London: Weidenfeld & Nicolson, 1954)

Beattie, John, *The English Court in the Reign of George I* (Cambridge: Cambridge University Press, 1967)

Bellany, A., 'Mistress Turner's Deadly Sins: Sartorial Transgression, Court Scandal, and Politics in Early Stuart England', *Huntington Library Quarterly*, 58:2 (1995), pp. 179–210

Bendall, Sarah, *Shaping Femininity* (London: Bloomsbury, 2021)

Bentley, S. (ed.), *Excerpta Historica* (London: S. Bentley, 1831)

Boaden, James, *The Life of Mrs Jordan* (London: E. Bull, 1831)

Boreman, Tracy, *Crown and Sceptre* (London: Hodder & Stoughton, 2021)

Brendan, Piers, *Edward VIII: Uncrowned King* (London: Penguin, 2018)

Brett, Maurice V. (ed.), *Journals and Letters of Reginald, Viscount Esher, Vols. I & III* (London: Nicholson & Watson, 1934)

Brooke, John, *George III* (London: Constable, 1972)

Brown, Rawdon (ed.), *Calendar of State Papers and Manuscripts Relating to English Affairs in the Archives of Venice, Vol. 5, 1534–1554* (London: HMSO, 1873)

Bucholz, Robert, *The Augustan Court: Queen Anne and the Decline of Court Culture* (Stanford, CA: Stanford University Press, 1993)

Burnet, Gilbert, *Bishop Burnet's History of His Own Time* (London: Henry G. Bohn, 1857)

Burney, Fanny, *Diary and Letters of Madame D'Arblay, Vol. I* (London: Henry Colburn, 1842)

Bury, Charlotte (ed.), *Memoirs of a Peeress, Vol. I* (London: Henry Colburn, 1837)

Campbell, John, *V.R.I.: Queen Victoria, Her Life and Empire* (London: Harmsworth Bros, 1901)

Campbell Davidson, Lillias, *Catherine of Braganza* (London: John Murray, 1908)

Carlton, Charles, *Charles I: The Personal Monarch* (London: Routledge, 1995)

Carlyle, Thomas (ed.), *Letters and Memorials of Jane Welsh Carlyle, Vol. I* (London: Longmans & Co., 1883)

Carter, A. J., 'Mary Tudor's Wardrobe', *Costume*, 18:1 (1984), pp. 9–28

Carter, Sarah, and Nugent, Maria (eds.), *Mistress of Everything: Queen Victoria in Indigenous Worlds* (Manchester: Manchester University Press, 2016)

Cathcart, Helen, *The Queen Mother Herself* (London: W. H. Allen, 1979)

Christopher, Prince of Greece, *Memoirs of H.R.H. Prince Christopher of Greece* (London: Hurst & Blackett, 1938)

Churchill, Winston, *Marlborough, Vol. I* (London: George G. Harrap & Co., 1947)

Cokayne, George Edward, *The Complete Peerage of England Scotland, Ireland, Great Britain and the United Kingdom, Vol. VII* (London: St Catherine's Press, 1910)

Coward, Rosalind, *Diana: The Portrait* (London: HarperCollins, 2004)

Cowles, Virginia, *Gay Monarch: The Life and Pleasures of Edward VII* (New York: Harper, 1956)

Cowper, C. S. (ed.), *Diary of Mary, Countess Cowper* (London: John Murray, 1864)

Crawford, Marion, *The Little Princesses* (London: Cassell & Co., 1950)

Cressy, David, *Charles I and the People of England* (Oxford & New York: Oxford University Press, 2015)

Cumming, Valerie, *Royal Dress* (London: Batsford, 1989)

Cunningham, Peter (ed.), *The Letters of Horace Walpole, Vol. II* (London: Richard Bentley, 1857)

Curzon, Catherine, *Queens of Georgian Britain* (Barnsley: Pen & Sword, 2017)

Dawson, Elizabeth, '"Comfort and Freedom": The Duke of Windsor's Wardrobe', *Costume*, 47:2 (2013), pp. 198–215

Dennison, Matthew, *The Last Princess: The Devoted Life of Queen Victoria's Youngest Daughter* (London: Hachette, 2010)

Dimond, Frances, 'Queen Victoria and Fashions for the Young', *Costume*, 22:1 (1988), pp. 1–12

Dior, Christian, *Dior by Dior*, trans. Antonia Fraser (London: V&A, 2018)

Doebner, R. (ed.), *The Memoirs of Mary, Queen of England, 1689–1693* (London: David Nutt, 1886)

Dolce, Joe, 'Cullinan', *Quadrant*, 64:4 (2017)

Duff, David, *Alexandra, Princess and Queen* (1980)

Dyer, G. P., *The Proposed Coinage of King Edward VIII* (London: HMSO, 1973)

Eastoe, Jane, *Elizabeth: Reigning in Style* (London: HarperCollins, 2012)

Edwards, Anne, *Matriarch: Queen Mary and the House of Windsor* (New York: William Morrow & Co., 1984)

Ellis, Jennifer (ed.), *Thatched with Gold: The Memoirs of Mabell, Countess of Airlie* (London: Hutchinson, 1962)

Elyot, Sir Thomas, *The Boke Named the Governour*, ed. H. H. S. Croft (Kegan Paul, Trench & Co. 1883)

Emanuel, David, and Emanuel, Elizabeth, *A Dress for Diana* (London: Pavilion, 2006)

Entwistle, Joanne, *The Fashioned Body* (Cambridge: Polity Press, 2015)

Everett Green, Mary (ed.), *Letters of Queen Henrietta Maria* (London: Richard Bentley, 1857)

Fisher, Saint John, *The English Works of John Fisher: Bishop of Rochester* (London: Early English Text Society, 1876)

Forsberg, Laura, *Worlds Beyond: Miniatures and Victorian Fiction* (New Haven, CT: Yale University Press, 2021)

Fraser, Antonia, *King Charles II* (London: Weidenfeld & Nicolson, 1979)

Fulford, Roger (ed.), *Dearest Child: Private Correspondence of Queen Victoria and the Princess Royal 1858–1861* (London: Evans Bros, 1977)

Gairdner, James (ed.), *Letters and Papers, Foreign and Domestic, Henry VIII, Volume 12* (London: HMSO, 1891)

Ginsburg, Madeleine, 'The Young Queen and Her Clothes', *Costume*, 3: Issue sup 1 (1969), pp. 39–46

Gold, Claudia, *The King's Mistress* (London: Quercus, 2012)

Gregg, Edward, *Queen Anne* (London: Routledge & Kegan Paul, 1980)

Greig, James (ed.), *The Diaries of a Duchess: Extracts from the Diaries of the First Duchess of Northumberland* (London: Hodder & Stoughton, 1926)

Giustinian, Sebastian, *Four Years at the Court of Henry VIII, Vol. II*, trans. Rawdon Brown (London: Smith, Elder & Co., 1854)

Hall, Augusta (ed.), *The Autobiography and Correspondence of Mrs Delany* (London: Richard Bentley, 1861)

Hall, Edward, *Hall's Chronicle* (London: Richard Grafton, 1548)

Hall, John (ed.), *250 Royal Speeches* (Charleston, SC: Nabu Press, 2011)

Hardman, Robert, *Queen of Our Times* (London: Pan Macmillan, 2022)

Harris, Carolyn, *Queenship and Revolution in Early Modern Europe* (Basingstoke: Palgrave Macmillan, 2016)

Harris, J. H. (ed.), *Diaries and Correspondence of James Harris, First Earl of Malmesbury, Vol. III* (London: Richard Bentley, 1844)

Hart, Kelly, *The Mistresses of Henry VIII* (Stroud: The History Press, 2009)

Hartley, Florence. *The Ladies' Book of Etiquette and Manual of Politeness* (Boston, MA: G. W. Cottrell, 1860)

Hartnell, Norman, *Royal Courts of Fashion* (London: Cassell, 1971)

Hartnell, Norman, *Silver and Gold* (London: V&A, 2019)

Hatton, Ragnhild, *George I* (London: Thames & Hudson, 1978)

Hayward, Maria, *Dress at the Court of Henry VIII* (London: Routledge, 2007)

Hayward, Maria, 'Dressed to Impress' in *Tudor Queenship: The Reigns of Mary and Elizabeth*, ed. Alice Hunt & Anna Whitelock (Basingstoke: Palgrave Macmillan, 2012), pp. 881–94

Herbert, Thomas, *Memoirs of the Last Two Years of the Reign of King Charles I* (London: G. & W. Nicol, W. Bulmer & Co., 1815)

Hervey, John, *Memoirs of the Reign of George the Second, Vol. I* (London: John Murray, 1855)

Hervey, John, *Some Materials Towards Memoirs of the Reign of George II, Vol. II* (London: Eyre & Spottiswoode, 1931)

Heylyn, Peter, *Aerius Redivivus: Or, The History of the Presbyterians* (London: Jo. Crosley, 1670)

Hibbert, Christopher, *George IV, Vol. I* (London: Allen Lane, 1973)

Hinds, Allen (ed.), *Calendar of State Papers Relating to English Affairs in the Archives of Venice, Vol. 15, 1617–1619* (London: HMSO, 1909)

Holinshed, Raphael, *Holinshed's Chronicles* (1587)

Holmes, Elizabeth, *HRH: So Many Thoughts on Royal Style* (New York: Celadon Books, 2020)

Hooper, Wilfred, 'The Tudor Sumptuary Laws', *English Historical Review*, 30:119 (1915), pp. 433–49

Hopkirk, Mary, *Queen Adelaide* (London: John Murray, 1946)

Hughes, Clair, 'Uneasy Heads: Difficulties with Royal Hats', *Costume*, 47:2 (2013), pp. 234–47

Hume, Martin (ed.), *Chronicle of King Henry VIII of England* (London: G. Bell & Sons, 1889)

Ives, Eric, *Lady Jane Grey* (Oxford: Wiley-Blackwell, 2009)

Ives, Eric, *The Life and Death of Anne Boleyn* (Oxford: Blackwell, 2004)

Jesse, John Heneage, *Memoirs of the Court of England, Vol. III* (London: Richard Bentley, 1843)

Karim-Cooper, Farah, *Cosmetics in Shakespearean and Renaissance Drama* (Edinburgh: Edinburgh University Press, 2006)

Keay, Anna, *The Crown Jewels* (London: Thames & Hudson, 2011)

Kelly, Angela, *The Other Side of the Coin* (London: HarperCollins, 2022)

Knox, Kristin, *Alexander McQueen: Genius of a Generation* (London: A & C Black, 2010)

Langlade, Émile, *Rose Bertin: The Creator of Fashion at the Court of Marie Antoinette*, adapted from the French by Dr Angelo S. Rappoport (London: J. Long, 1913)

Lawson, Jane A., 'Rainbow for a Reign: The Colours of a Queen's Wardrobe', *Costume*, 41:1 (2007), pp. 26–44

Lee, Celia, *Jean, Lady Hamilton, 1861–1941* (Barnsley: Pen & Sword, 2020)

Lemon, Mark, *Up and Down the London Streets* (London: Chapman & Hall, 1867)

Leslie, Charles Robert, *Autobiographical Recollections, Vol. II* (London: John Murray, 1860)

Leslie, Shane, *Mrs Fitzherbert: A Life* (London: Burns, Oates, 1939)

Logan, T. and Smith, D. (eds.), The New Intellectuals (Lincoln, NE: University of Nebraska Press, 1977)

Longford, Elizabeth, *Victoria R.I.* (London: Weidenfeld & Nicolson, 1964)

Lynn, Eleri, *Tudor Fashion* (New Haven, CT: Yale University Press, 2017)

Maas, Jeremy, *The Prince of Wales's Wedding: The Story of a Picture* (London: David & Charles, 1977)

Madden, Frederick, *Privy Purse Expenses of the Princess Mary* (London: W. Pickering, 1831)

Magalotti, Lorenzo, *Lorenzo Magalotti at the Court of Charles II*, ed. & trans. W. E. K. Middleton (Waterloo, Canada: Wilfred Laurier University Press, 1980)

Malcolm-Davies, Jane, and Mikhaila, Ninya, *The Tudor Tailor* (London: Batsford, 2006)

Mansel, Philip, *Dressed to Rule* (New Haven, CT: Yale University Press, 2005)

Marley, D. de, *Fashion for Men: An Illustrated History* (London: Batsford, 1985)

Marschner, Joanna, 'Mary II: Her Clothes and Textiles', *Costume*, 34:1 (2000), pp. 44–50

Marschner, Joanna, 'Queen Caroline of Ansbach', *Costume*, 31:1 (1997), pp. 28–37

Matheson, Anne, *Princess Anne: A Girl of Our Time* (London, Muller, 1973)

Matthews, William (ed.), *The Diary of Dudley Ryder* (London: Methuen & Co., 1939)

Matthews David, Alison, *Fashion Victims* (London: Bloomsbury, 2015)

McClure, Norman, *The Letters of John Chamberlain* (Philadelphia, PA: American Philosophical Society, 1939)

Menkes, Suzy, *The Windsor Style* (London: Grafton, 1987)

Morra, Irene, *The New Elizabethan Age* (London, New York: I. B. Tauris, 2016)

Murphy, Deirdre, and Davies-Strodder, Cassie, *Modern Royal Fashion: Seven Royal Women and Their Style* (Surrey: Historic Royal Palaces, 2015)

Norton, Elizabeth, *Jane Seymour* (Stroud: Amberley Publishing, 2009)

Norton, Elizabeth, *The Temptation of Elizabeth Tudor* (London: Head of Zeus, 2015)

Nuckolls, Charles W., 'The Durbar Incident', *Modern Asian Studies*, 24:3 (1990), pp. 529–59

Papendiek, Charlotte, *Court and Private Life in the Time of Queen Charlotte, Vol. I* (London: Bentley & Son, 1887)

Parissien, Steven, *George IV: The Grand Entertainment* (London: John Murray, 2001)

Parker Bell, Barbara, *Inside the Wardrobe of Anne Boleyn* (Historical Fashion, 2014)

Pasternak, Anna, *The American Duchess: The Real Wallis Simpson* (Glasgow: William Collins, 2019)

Pepys, Samuel, *The Diary of Samuel Pepys*, ed. A. Spencer (1991)

Petican, Laura (ed.), *Fashion and Contemporaneity: Realms of the Visible* (Leiden, Netherlands: Brill, 2019)

Pimlott, Ben, *The Queen: Elizabeth II and the Monarchy* (London: Harper Collins, 2001)

Plumptre, George, *Edward VII* (London: Pavilion, 1995)

Pochna, Marie-France, *Christian Dior: The Man Who Made the World Look New* (New York: Arcade Publishing, 1996)

Pocock, Tom, *The Sailor King* (London: Sinclair-Stevenson, 1991)

Pope-Hennessy, James, *Queen Mary* (London: George Allen & Unwin Ltd, 1959)

Ribeiro, Aileen, *Dress and Morality* (Oxford, New York: Berg, 2003)

Richardson, Joanna, *The Disastrous Marriage* (London: Jonathan Cape, 1960)

Ridley, Jane, *Bertie: A Life of Edward VII* (London: Chatto & Windus, 2012)

Riehl, Anna, *The Face of Queenship* (Basingstoke: Palgrave Macmillan, 2010)

Russell, Gareth, *Young and Damned and Fair* (Glasgow: William Collins, 2017)

St Aubyn, Giles, *Edward VII: Prince and King* (London: Collins, 1979)

St Clair, Kassia, *The Secret Lives of Colour* (London: John Murray, 2016)

Sanders, Margaret, *Intimate Letters of England's Queens* (Stroud: Amberley Publishing, 2009)

Sandford, Francis, *The History of the Coronation of . . . James II . . . and . . . Queen Mary* (London: T. Newcomb, 1687)

Saussure, César de, *A Foreign View of England in the Reigns of George I & George II*, trans. & ed. Madame van Muyden (London: John Murray, 1902)

Schulte, Regina (ed.), *The Body of the Queen* (New York: Berghan Books, 2006)

Walter Scott, *Hints Addressed to the Inhabitants of Edinburgh, and Others, in Prospect of His Majesty's Visit. By an Old Citizen* (Edinburgh: Bell & Bradfute, 1822)

Shawcross, William, *The Queen Mother: The Official Biography* (London: Macmillan, 2009)

Sheppard, Edgar, *Memorials of St James's Palace* (London: Longmans & Co., 1894)

Sichel, Walter (ed.), *The Glenbervie Journals* (London: Constable & Co., 1910)

Smith, E. A., *George IV* (New Haven, CT: Yale University Press, 1999)

Smith, William James (ed.), *The Grenville Papers, Vol. III* (London: John Murray, 1853)

Somerset, Anne, *Queen Anne* (New York: Knopf, 2013)

Stanhope, Philip Dormer, *The Letters of P. D. Stanhope, Earl of Chesterfield, Vol. II*, ed. Lord Mahon (London: Richard Bentley, 1845

Staniland, Kay, *In Royal Fashion* (London: Museum of London, 1997)

Starkey, David, *Crown and Country: The Kings and Queens of England* (London: HarperPress, 2010)

Starkey, David, Ward, Philip, and Hawkyard, Alasdair, *The Inventory of Henry VIII: The Transcript* (London: Society of Antiquaries of London, 1998)

Stevenson, David, *The Beggar's Benison* (Edinburgh: Berlinn Ltd, 2013)

Stow, John, *Annals of England to 1603* (1603)

Strasdin, Kate, 'Fashioning Alexandra: A Royal Approach to Style 1863–1910', *Costume*, 47:2 (2013), pp. 180–97

Strasdin, Kate, *Inside the Royal Wardrobe* (London: Bloomsbury, 2017)

Strickland, Agnes, *Lives of the Queens of England, Vol. II* (London: Henry Colburn, 1843)

Strong, Roy, *Cecil Beaton: The Royal Portraits* (London: Thames & Hudson, 1988)

Strong, Roy, *Elizabeth R* (London: Secker & Warburg, 1971)

Strong, Roy, 'Three Royal Jewels: The Three Brothers, the Mirror of Great Britain and the Feather', *Burlington Magazine*, 108:760 (1966), pp. 350–53

Thomson, A. T. (ed.), *Memoirs of Sarah Duchess of Marlborough, Vol. II* (London: Henry Colburn, 1839)

Toynbee, Paget (ed.), *The Letters of Horace Walpole, Vol. V* (Oxford: Clarendon, 1904)

Trowbridge, William Rutherford Hayes, *Queen Alexandra: A Study of Royalty* (London: T. Fisher Unwin, 1923)

Tyler, Royall (ed.), *Calendar of State Papers, Spain, Vol. 13, 1554–1558* (London: HMSO, 1954)

Vanderbilt Balsan, Consuelo, *The Glitter and the Gold* (New York: Harper & Bros, 1952)

Vertot, R. A. de, *Ambassades de Messieurs de Noailles en Angleterre, Vol. II* (Paris: Dessaint and Saillant, 1763)

Vickers, Hugo, *Cecil Beaton: A Biography* (London: Weidenfeld & Nicolson, 1986)

Walpole, Horace, *Memoirs of the Reign of King George III, Vol. I* (London: Richard Bentley, 1845)

Weintraub, Stanley, *Victoria* (London: Allen & Unwin, 1987)

Weir, Alison, *The Lady in the Tower* (London: Vintage, 2009)

Weir, Alison, *The Six Wives of Henry VIII* (London: The Bodley Head, 1991)

Weiser, Brian, *Charles II and the Politics of Access* (Woodbridge: Boydell Press, 2003)

Wilkins, W. H., *Mrs Fitzherbert and George IV* (London: Longmans & Co., 1905)

Williams, Kate, *Young Elizabeth* (Cambridge: Pegasus, 2015)

Windsor, Edward, *A Family Album* (London: Cassell & Co., 1960)

Windsor, Edward, *A King's Story* (London: Cassell & Co., 1951)

Windsor, Wallis Warfield, *The Heart Has Its Reasons* (London: Michael Joseph, 1956)

Woodham-Smith, Cecil, *Queen Victoria* (London: Hamilton, 1972)

Worsley, Lucy, *Courtiers* (London: Faber & Faber, 2010)

Worsley, Lucy, *Queen Victoria* (London: Hodder & Stoughton, 2018)

Wriothesley, Charles, *Chronicle of England During the Reign of the Tudors*, ed. William Douglas Hamilton (London: Camden Society, 1875)

Yonge, Charlotte Mary, *The Victorian Half Century* (London: Macmillan, 1887)

Ziegler, Philip, *William IV* (London: Fontana, 1973)

Notes

INTRODUCTION

1 Christopher, Prince of Greece, *Memoirs of H.R.H. Prince Christopher of Greece* (London: Hurst & Blackett, 1938), pp. 89–90.
2 'We be men and nay aungel, wherefore we know nothinge but by outward signification.' H. H. S. Croft (ed.), *The Boke Named the Governour* (London: Kegan Paul, Trench & Co., 1883), p. 201.

PART ONE: THE TUDORS

1 Quoted in Eleri Lynn, *Tudor Fashion* (New Haven, CT: Yale University Press, 2017), p. 15.
2 Raphael Holinshed, *Holinshed's Chronicles* (1587), p. 762, and Saint John Fisher, *The English Works of John Fisher: Bishop of Rochester* (London: Early English Text Society, 1876), pp. 305–6.
3 Maria Hayward, *Fashion at the Court of Henry VIII* (2007), pp. 80–83.
4 *Warrants for the Keeper of the Great Wardrobe* (National Archive, E 101/412/15).
5 'Sleyvs of orange colour sarsenet', quoted in Kassia St Clair, *The Secret Lives of Colour* (London: John Murray, 2016), p. 93.
6 Hayward, *Fashion at the Court of Henry VIII*, p. 83.
7 Edward Hall, *Hall's Chronicle* (London: Richard Grafton, 1548), p. 493.
8 Isabella of Castile to Henry VII, quoted in Alison Weir, *The Six Wives of Henry VIII* (London: The Bodley Head, 1991), p. 24.
9 Hayward, *Fashion at the Court of Henry VIII*, p. 55.
10 Quoted in Margaret Sanders, *Intimate Letters of England's Queens* (Stroud: Amberley Publishing, 2009), p. 9.

11 Hayward, *Fashion at the Court of Henry VIII*, p. 53.
12 Venetian ambassador Sebastian Giustinian reported: '16 000 (ducats of his expenditure) for the wardrobe, for he is the best dressed sovereign in the world: his robes are the richest and most superb that can be imagined; and he puts on new clothes for every holiday'; quoted in *Four Years at the Court of Henry VIII, Vol. II* (London: Smith, Elder & Co., 1854), p. 313.
13 Henry VIII's 1510 Act of Parliament and other sumptuary legislation is detailed in Wilfred Hooper, 'The Tudor Sumptuary Laws', *English Historical Review*, 30:119 (1915), p. 433.
14 Kelly Hart, *The Mistresses of Henry VIII* (2014), p. 81.
15 Hayward, *Fashion at the Court of Henry VIII*, p. 179.
16 Eric Ives, *Life and Death of Anne Boleyn* (Oxford: Blackwell, 2004), p. 196.
17 Hayward, *Fashion at the Court of Henry VIII*, p. 47.
18 Quoted in Martin Hume (ed.), *Chronicle of King Henry VIII of England* (London: G. Bell & Sons, 1889), p. 14.
19 Barbara Parker Bell, *Inside the Wardrobe of Anne Boleyn* (Historical Fashion, 2014), p. 67.
20 Pendant analysis suggested by E. Ives (2003), p. 357, and Weir, *Six Wives*, p. 148.
21 Lynn, *Tudor Fashion*, p. 79.
22 Alison Weir, *The Lady in the Tower* (London: Vintage, 2009), p. 146.
23 Hume, *Chronicle*, p. 70, and S. Bentley, *Excerpta Historica* (London: S. Bentley, 1831), p. 264.
24 Jane Seymour's instructions to Anne Bassett were documented in a letter from John Husee to Lady Lisle in October 1537. See James Gairdner (ed.), *Letters and Papers, Foreign and Domestic, Henry VIII, Volume 12* (London: HMSO, 1891), p. 808.
25 Gairdner, *Letters and Papers*, p. 579.
26 Elizabeth Norton, *Jane Seymour* (Stroud: Amberley Publishing, 2009), p. 150.
27 Weir, *Six Wives*, p. 356.
28 Charles Wriothesley, *Chronicle of England During the Reign of the Tudors*, ed. William Douglas Hamilton (London: Camden Society, 1875), pp. 109–10.
29 *Ibid.*, p. 111.
30 Hayward, *Fashion at the Court of Henry VIII*, p. 184.
31 Gareth Russell, *Young and Damned and Fair* (Glasgow: William Collins, 2017), p. 391.
32 Hayward, *Fashion at the Court of Henry VIII*, p. 185.
33 Weir, *Six Wives*, p. 491.
34 Lynn, *Tudor Fashion*, p. 83.
35 *Ibid.*

36 Quoted in Alison Weir, *The Six Wives of Henry VIII*, p. 526.

37 Hayward, *Fashion at the Court of Henry VIII*, p. 210.

38 Jane Malcolm-Davies and Ninya Mikhaila, *The Tudor Tailor* (London: Batsford, 2006), p. 16.

39 Agnes Strickland, *Lives of the Queens of England, Vol. II* (London: Henry Colburn, 1843), p. 339.

40 John Aylmer (1559), quoted in Lucy Aikin, *Memoirs of the Court of Queen Elizabeth, Vol. II* (London: Longman, Hurst, Rees, Orme & Brown, 1819), p. 110.

41 Eric Ives, *Lady Jane Grey* (Oxford: Wiley-Blackwell, 2009), p. 163.

42 Hayward, *Fashion at the Court of Henry VIII*, p. 204.

43 *Ibid.*, p. 205

44 Mary Tudor to Thomas Cromwell on 1 July 1536, quoted in Frederic Madden, *Privy Purse Expenses of the Princess Mary* (London: W. Pickering, 1831), p. lxxiii.

45 R. A. de Vertot, *Ambassades de Messieurs de Noailles en Angleterre, Vol. II* (1763), p. 146.

46 A. J. Carter, 'Mary Tudor's Wardrobe', *Costume*, 18:1 (1984), p. 21.

47 Wriothesley, *Chronicle*, p. 93.

48 John Stow, *Annals of England to 1603* (1603), p. 1064.

49 Tracy Boreman, *Crown and Sceptre* (London: Hodder & Stoughton, 2021), p. 217.

50 Rawdon Brown (ed.), *Calendar of State Papers and Manuscripts Relating to English Affairs in the Archives of Venice, Vol. 5, 1534–1554* (London: HMSO, 1873), p. 533.

51 Carter, 'Mary Tudor's Wardrobe', p. 16.

52 David Starkey, Philip Ward and Alasdair Hawkyard, *The Inventory of Henry VIII: The Transcript* (London: Society of Antiquaries of London, 1998), p. 342.

53 Royall Tyler (ed.), *Calendar of State Papers, Spain, Vol. 13, 1554–1558* (London: HMSO, 1954), p. 37.

54 Maria Hayward, 'Dressed to Impress' in *Tudor Queenship: The Reigns of Mary and Elizabeth*, ed. Alice Hunt & Anna Whitelock (Basingtoke: Palgrave Macmillan, 2012), p. 88.

55 Hayward, *Dressed to Impress*, p. 82.

56 For Anne Boleyn's purchases, see Ives, *Life and Death of Anne Boleyn*, p. 358.

57 For Elizabeth's change in living standards, see Lynn, *Tudor Fashion*, p. 86.

58 Elizabeth Norton, *The Temptation of Elizabeth Tudor* (London: Head of Zeus, 2015), pp. 86, 92.

59 For Elizabeth's change in clothes, see Lynn, *Tudor Fashion*, p. 88.

60 Hayward, *Fashion at the Court of Henry VIII*, p. 85.

61 Roy Strong, *Elizabeth R* (London: Secker & Warburg, 1971), p. 85.

62 Sarah Bendall, *Shaping Femininity* (London: Bloomsbury, 2021), p. 180.

63 Aileen Ribeiro, *Dress and Morality* (New York: Berg, 2003), p. 65.

64 Janet Arnold, *Patterns of Fashion 3* (London: Macmillan, 1985), pp. 8–9.

65 Ribeiro, *Dress and Morality*, p. 68.

66 Jane A. Lawson, 'Rainbow for a Reign: The Colours of a Queen's Wardrobe', *Costume*, 41:1 (2007), p. 26.

67 Roy Strong, *The Elizabethan Image: An Introduction to English Portraiture 1558–1603* (New Haven, CT: Yale University Press, 2019), p. 192.

68 *Ibid.*, p. 28.

69 Anna Riehl, *The Face of Queenship* (Basingstoke: Palgrave Macmillan, 2010), pp. 50, 51.

70 Farah Karim-Cooper, *Cosmetics in Shakespearean and Renaissance Drama* (Edinburgh: Edinburgh University Press, 2006), p. 59.

PART TWO: THE STUARTS

1 Valerie Cumming, *Royal Dress* (London: Batsford, 1989), p. 18.

2 Roy Strong, 'Three Royal Jewels: The Three Brothers, the Mirror of Great Britain and the Feather', *Burlington Magazine*, 108:760 (1966), pp. 350–53.

3 For the Puritans and their opinion of the court, see Aileen Ribeiro, *Dress and Morality* (New York: Berg, 2003), p. 85. And see p. 67 for shift in blame regarding the moral behaviour of a monarch's court.

4 For James's bathing habits, see Ribeiro, *Dress and Morality*, p. 74. For the bathroom at Whitehall Palace, see Lynn, *Tudor Fashion*, p. 124.

5 Ribeiro, *Dress and Morality*, p. 74.

6 Quoted in D. de Marley, *Fashion for Men: An Illustrated History* (London: Batsford, 1985).

7 Cumming, *Royal Dress*, p. 20.

8 T. Logan, and D. Smith, (eds.), *The New Intellectuals* (Lincoln, NE: University of Nebraska Press, 1977).

9 Quoted in Ribeiro, *Dress and Morality*, p. 80.

10 H. Busino (1617), quoted in Allen Hinds (ed.), *Calendar of State Papers Relating to English Affairs in the Archives of Venice, Vol. 15, 1617–1619* (London: HMSO, 1909), p. 80.

11 Sarah Bendall, *Shaping Femininity* (London: Bloomsbury, 2021), p. 180.

12 Quoted in Ribeiro, *Dress and Morality*, p. 80.

13 *Ibid.*, p. 75. For further detail on the Anne Turner case and the negative associations of the yellow ruff, see also A. Bellany 'Mistress Turner's Deadly Sins: Sartorial Transgression, Court Scandal, and Politics in Early

Stuart England', *Huntington Library Quarterly*, 58:2 (1995), pp. 189–94. Note however that Ribeiro mistakenly writes that Anne Turner assisted in the killing of Frances Howard's first husband as opposed to Sir Thomas Overbury, the actual victim.

14 Quoted in J. M. Rodney, *Henry Frederick, Prince of Wales, and His Circle* (PhD dissertation, Cornell University, 1965), p. 35.

15 Cumming, *Royal Dress*, pp. 18–20.

16 Charles Carlton, *Charles I: The Personal Monarch* (London: Routledge, 1995), p. 10.

17 Carolyn Harris, *Queenship and Revolution in Early Modern Europe* (Basingstoke: Palgrave Macmillan, 2016), p. 84.

18 New clothing rules at court are documented in a letter from John Chamberlain to Sir Dudley Carleton on 4 January 1623, quoted in Norman McClure, *The Letters of John Chamberlain* (Philadelphia, PA: American Philosophical Society, 1939), p. 70.

19 David Cressy, *Charles I and the People of England* (Oxford & New York: Oxford University Press, 2015), p. 25.

20 Henrietta Maria records the experience of raising funds in the Netherlands in a letter to Charles I in May 1642, edited by Mary Anne Everett Green in *Letters of Queen Henrietta Maria* (London: Richard Bentley, 1857), p. 63.

21 Peter Heylyn, *Aerius Redivivus: Or, The History of the Presbyterians* (London: Jo. Crosley, 1670), p. 461.

22 Thomas Herbert, *Memoirs of the Last Two Years of the Reign of King Charles I* (London: G. & W. Nicol, W. Bulmer & Co., 1815), p. 178.

23 Antonia Fraser, *King Charles II* (London: Weidenfeld & Nicolson, 1979), p. 184.

24 Philip Mansel, *Dressed to Rule* (New Haven, CT: Yale University Press, 2005), pp. 2–3.

25 Brian Weiser, *Charles II and the Politics of Access* (Woodbridge: Boydell Press, 2003), p. 35.

26 Anna Keay, *The Crown Jewels* (London: Thames & Hudson, 2011), pp. 39–40.

27 Cumming, *Royal Dress*, p. 28.

28 Ribeiro, *Dress and Morality*, p. 87.

29 Charles's decision to adopt the vest was documented by Samuel Pepys; see Samuel Pepys, *The Diary of Samuel Pepys*, ed. A. Spencer (1991), p. 207.

30 Lorenzo Magalotti, *Lorenzo Magalotti at the Court of Charles II*, ed. & trans. W. E. K. Middleton (Waterloo, Canada: Wilfred Laurier University Press, 1980), pp. 29–30.

31 Lillias Campbell Davidson, *Catherine of Braganza* (London: John Murray, 1908), p. 125.

32 Pepys, *Diary*, p. 120.

33 In November 1663, Pepys observed in his *Diary*, 'I never till this day observed that the King is mighty grey', p. 128.

34 David Stevenson, *The Beggar's Benison* (Edinburgh: Berlinn Ltd, 2013), p. 326.

35 Francis Sandford, *The History of the Coronation of . . . James II . . . and . . . Queen Mary* (London: T. Newcomb, 1687), pp. 43–4.

36 Tracy Boreman, *Crown and Sceptre* (London: Hodder & Stoughton, 2021), p. 302.

37 Pepys, *Diary*, pp. 128 and 207–8.

38 *Ibid.*, p. 194.

39 R. Doebner (ed.), *The Memoirs of Mary, Queen of England, 1689–1693* (London: David Nutt, 1886), p. 3.

40 *Ibid.*

41 Edward Gregg, *Queen Anne* (London: Routledge & Kegan Paul, 1980), p. 68.

42 Cumming, *Royal Dress*, p. 37.

43 Keay, *Crown Jewels*, p. 113.

44 Joanna Marschner, 'Mary II: Her Clothes and Textiles', *Costume*, 34:1 (2000), pp. 48–9.

45 Francis Lawrence Bickley, *The Life of Matthew Prior* (New York: Sir Isaac Pitman & Sons, 1914), p. 36.

46 Cumming, *Royal Dress*, pp. 41–2.

47 *Ibid.*

48 Mansel, *Dressed to Rule*, p. 12.

49 Winston Churchill, *Marlborough, Vol. I* (London: George G. Harrap & Co., 1947), p. 499.

50 *Ibid.*

51 Gregg, *Queen Anne*, p. 79.

52 Quoted in Edgar Sheppard, *Memorials of St James's Palace* (London: Longmans & Co., 1894), p. 81.

53 Nigel Arch and Joanna Marschner, *Splendour at Court* (London: Unwin Hyman, 1987), p. 18.

54 Cannadine, David (ed.), *Tudors to Windsors: British Royal Portraits* (London: National Portrait Gallery, 2018), p. 107.

55 Cumming, *Royal Dress*, p. 46.

56 Gregg, *Queen Anne*, p. 384.

57 Quoted in Robert Bucholz, *The Augustan Court: Queen Anne and the Decline of Court Culture* (Stanford, CA: Stanford University Press, 1993), p. 239.

58 *Ibid.*

59 Gregg, *Royal Dress*, p. 231.

60 Bucholz, *The Augustan Court*, p. 240.

61 Gregg, *Royal Dress*, p. 392.

62 Anne Somerset, *Queen Anne* (New York: Knopf, 2013), p. 201.
63 A. T. Thomson (ed.), *Memoirs of Sarah Duchess of Marlborough, Vol. II* (London: Henry Colburn, 1839), p. 165.

PART THREE: THE FOUR GEORGES

1 Gilbert Burnet, *Bishop Burnet's History of His Own Time* (London: Henry G. Bohn, 1857), p. 784.
2 Philip Dormer Stanhope, *The Letters of P. D. Stanhope, Earl of Chesterfield, Vol. II*, ed. Lord Mahon (London: Richard Bentley, 1845), p. 440.
3 Quoted in Edgar Sheppard, *Memorials of St James's Palace* (London: Longmans & Co., 1894), p. 88.
4 Norman Hartnell, *Royal Courts of Fashion* (London: Cassell, 1971), p. 84.
5 Quoted in John Beattie, *The English Court in the Reign of George I* (Cambridge: Cambridge University Press, 1967), p. 56.
6 *Ibid.*, p. 260.
7 César de Saussure, *A Foreign View of England in the Reigns of George I & George II*, trans. & ed. Madame van Muyden (London: John Murray, 1902), p. 140.
8 William Matthews (ed.), *The Diary of Dudley Ryder* (London: Methuen & Co., 1939).
9 Ragnhild Hatton, *George I* (London: Thames & Hudson, 1978), pp. 77–8.
10 Hartnell, *Royal Courts*, p. 86.
11 George Edward Cokagne, *The Complete Peerage of England, Scotland, Ireland, Great Britain and the United Kingdom Vol. VII* (London: St Catherine's Press, 1910), p. 111.
12 Claudia Gold, *The King's Mistress* (London: Quercus, 2012), p. 155.
13 Valerie Cumming, *Royal Dress* (London: Batsford, 1989), p. 52.
14 Mary Cowper, *Diary of Mary, Countess Cowper* (London: John Murray, 1864), p. 25.
15 Lucy Worsley, *Courtiers* (London: Faber & Faber, 2010), p. 27.
16 Augusta Hall (ed.), *The Autobiography and Correspondence of Mrs Delany* (London: Richard Bentley, 1861), p. 76.
17 Tracy Boreman, *Crown and Sceptre* (London: Hodder & Stoughton, 2021), p. 338.
18 *Ibid.*, p. 339.
19 Sheppard, *Memorials of St James's Palace*, p. 92.
20 Cumming, *Royal Dress*, pp. 52–3.
21 John Hervey, *Memoirs of the Reign of George the Second, Vol. I* (London: John Murray, 1855), p. 93.

22 *Ibid.*

23 Sheppard, *Memorials of St James's Palace*, p. 95.

24 Joanna Marschner, 'Queen Caroline of Ansbach', *Costume*, 31:1 (1997), pp. 30–31.

25 Cumming, *Royal Dress*, p. 53.

26 John Heneage Jesse, *Memoirs of the Court of England, Vol. III* (London: Richard Bentley, 1843), p. 204.

27 Worsley, *Courtiers*, p. 121.

28 *Ibid.*, p. 120.

29 BL Add MS 22629 ff. 117–18.

30 Quoted in David Starkey, *Crown and Country: The Kings and Queens of England* (London: HarperPress, 2010), p. 421.

31 John Hervey, *Some Materials Towards Memoirs of the Reign of George II, Vol. II* (London: Eyre & Spottiswoode, 1931), p. 874.

32 *Gentleman's Magazine, Vol. VI* (1736), p. 230.

33 Mark Lemon, *Up and Down the London Streets* (London: Chapman & Hall, 1867), p. 328.

34 Peter Cunningham (ed.), *The Letters of Horace Walpole, Vol. II* (London: Richard Bentley, 1857), p. 152.

35 Cumming, *Royal Dress*, p. 57.

36 *Ibid.*

37 Cunningham, *Letters of Horace Walpole*, p. 107.

38 Quoted in Catherine Curzon, *Queens of Georgian Britain* (Barnsley: Pen & Sword, 2017), p. 97.

39 Cunningham, *Letters of Horace Walpole*, p. 243.

40 James Greig (ed.), *The Diaries of a Duchess: Extracts from the Diaries of the First Duchess of Northumberland* (London: Hodder & Stoughton, 1926), p. 35.

41 Cumming, *Royal Dress*, p. 75.

42 Paget Toynbee (ed.), *The Letters of Horace Walpole, Vol. V* (Oxford: Clarendon, 1904), p. 107.

43 Greig, *Diaries of a Duchess*, p. 34.

44 Horace Walpole, *Memoirs of the Reign of King George III, Vol. I* (London: Richard Bentley, 1845), p. 72.

45 Toynbee, *Letters of Horace Walpole*, p. 185.

46 Quoted in Nigel Arch and Joanna Marschner, *Splendour at Court* (London: Unwin Hyman, 1987), p. 35.

47 Quoted in Cumming, *Royal Dress*, p. 68.

48 Sheppard, *Memorials of St James's Palace*, p. 256.

49 Quoted in Philip Mansel, *Dressed to Rule* (New Haven, CT: Yale University Press, 2005), p. 60.

50 *Ibid.*, p. 58.

51 Quoted in Arch and Marschner, *Splendour at Court*, p. 40.

52 Cumming, *Royal Dress*, p. 81

53 Fanny Burney, *Diary and Letters of Madame D'Arblay, Vol. I* (London: Henry Colburn, 1842), p. 246.

54 *Ibid.*, p. 422.

55 *Ibid.*

56 Quoted in John Brooke, *George III* (London: Constable, 1972), p. 216.

57 Burney, *Diary*, p. 430.

58 William James Smith (ed.), *The Grenville Papers, Vol. III* (London: John Murray, 1853), p. 122.

59 Boreman, *Crown and Sceptre*, p. 355.

60 Mansel, *Dressed to Rule*, p. 60.

61 *Ibid.*, p. 59.

62 John Hall (ed.), *250 Royal Speeches* (Charleston, SC: Nabu Press, 2011), p. 12.

63 'July 19-1821', from Rev. W. Monsell to Rev. J. Drake, Royal Ceremonial Dress Collection, object no. 350130.

64 Quoted in Shane Leslie, *Mrs Fitzherbert: A Life* (London: Burns, Oates, 1939), p. 370.

65 Boreman, *Crown and Sceptre*, p. 353.

66 Charlotte Papendiek, *Court and Private Life in the Time of Queen Charlotte, Vol. I* (London: Bentley & Son, 1887), p. 132.

67 Quoted in E. A. Smith, *George IV* (New Haven, CT: Yale University Press, 1999), p. 44.

68 Kay Staniland, *In Royal Fashion* (London: Museum of London, 1997), p. 32.

69 Mansel, *Dressed to Rule*, p. 29.

70 Quoted in Christopher Hibbert, *George IV, Vol. I* (1974), p. 43.

71 Staniland, *In Royal Fashion*, p. 32, and Cumming, *Royal Dress*, p. 89.

72 W. H. Wilkins, *Mrs Fitzherbert and George IV* (London: Longmans & Co., 1905), p. 111.

73 Mansel, *Dressed to Rule*, p. 58.

74 Wilkins, *Mrs Fitzherbert and George IV*, p. 400.

75 J. H. Harris (ed.), *Diaries and Correspondence of James Harris, First Earl of Malmesbury, Vol. III* (London: Richard Bentley, 1844), p. 182.

76 *Ibid.*, p. 211.

77 *Ibid.*, p. 211, and Joanna Richardson, *The Disastrous Marriage* (London: Jonathan Cape, 1960), pp. 31–2.

78 Harris, *Diaries*, p. 218.

79 Charlotte Bury (ed.), *Memoirs of a Peeress, Vol. I* (London: Henry Colburn, 1837), pp. 139–40.

80 Staniland, *In Royal Fashion*, pp. 45–6.

81 Hibbert, *George IV*, p. 48.

82 Walter Sichel (ed.), *The Glenbervie Journals* (London: Constable & Co., 1910), pp. 152–3.

83 The jewellery is currently part of the Victoria & Albert Museum collection: M.13.1 to 9-2013.

84 Staniland, *In Royal Fashion*, p. 57.

85 Smith, *George IV*, pp. 232–3.

86 Steven Parissien, *George IV: The Grand Entertainment* (London: John Murray, 2001), p. 171.

87 *The Shilling Magazine* in *Weekly Dispatch* (18 March 1866), p. 38.

88 Walter Scott, *Hints Addressed to the Inhabitants of Edinburgh, and Others, in Prospect of His Majesty's Visit. By an Old Citizen* (Edinburgh: Bell & Bradfute, 1822).

89 Quoted in Smith, *George IV*, p. 266.

90 Hibbert, *George IV*, p. 218.

91 Leslie, *Mrs Fitzherbert*, pp. 277–82.

PART FOUR: THE VICTORIA EFFECT

1 Quoted in Lucy Worsley, *Queen Victoria* (London: Hodder & Stoughton, 2018), p. 17.

2 Émile Langlade, *Rose Bertin: The Creator of Fashion at the Court of Marie Antoinette*, adapted from the French by Dr Angelo S. Rappoport (London: J. Long, 1913), p. 79.

3 A. Aspinall (ed.), *The Later Correspondence of George III, Vol. I* (Cambridge: Cambridge University Press, 1966), pp. 273–4.

4 Quoted in Tom Pocock, *The Sailor King* (London: Sinclair-Stevenson, 1991), p. 23.

5 *Ibid.*, pp. 174–5.

6 A. Aspinall (ed.), *Mrs Jordan and Her Family* (London: Arthur Barker Ltd, 1951), p. 7.

7 James Boaden, *The Life of Mrs Jordan* (London: E. Bull, 1831), pp. 248–9.

8 Quoted in Mary Hopkirk, *Queen Adelaide* (London: John Murray, 1946), p. 107.

9 Quoted in Valerie Cumming, *Royal Dress* (London: Batsford, 1989), p. 103.

10 Tracy Boreman, *Crown and Sceptre* (London: Hodder & Stoughton, 2021), p. 369.

11 Quoted in Edgar Sheppard, *Memorials of St James's Palace* (London: Longmans & Co., 1894), p. 104.

12 Quoted in Norman Hartnell, *Royal Courts of Fashion* (London: Cassell, 1971), p. 147.

13 Hopkirk, *Queen Adelaide*, p. 102.

14 *Ibid.*, p. 153.

15 Quoted in Philip Ziegler, *William IV* (London: Fontana, 1973), p. 312.

16 RA VIC/MAIN/QVJ (W) 20 June 1837 (Lord Esher's Typescripts).

17 Kay Staniland, *In Royal Fashion* (London: Museum of London, 1997), p. 88.

18 RA VIC/MAIN/QVJ (W) 17 September 1836.

19 Madeleine Ginsburg, 'The Young Queen and Her Clothes', *Costume*, 54:1, p. 41.

20 RA VIC/MAIN/QVJ (W) 9 January 1838, and Worsley, *Queen Victoria*, pp. 87–8.

21 RA VIC/MAIN/QVJ (W) 20 June 1837.

22 Quoted in Staniland, *In Royal Fashion*, p. 102.

23 Quoted in Charlotte Mary Yonge, *The Victorian Half Century* (London: Macmillan, 1887), p. 9, and Charles Robert Leslie, *Autobiographical Recollections, Vol. II* (London: John Murray, 1860), p. 239.

24 John Campbell, *V.R.I.: Queen Victoria, Her Life and Empire* (London: Harmsworth Bros, 1901), p. 82.

25 RA VIC/MAIN/QVJ (W) 28 June 1838.

26 RA VIC/MAIN/QVJ (W) 28 September 1837.

27 Cumming, *Royal Dress*, p. 108.

28 RA VIC/MAIN/QVJ (W) 18 April 1839.

29 'Letter to the Editor', *The Times*, 8 February 1840.

30 RA VIC/MAIN/QVJ (W) 19 December 1893.

31 *Ibid.*

32 *Ibid.*, 10 February 1840.

33 RCIN 65293, Royal Collection.

34 Frances Dimond, 'Queen Victoria and Fashions for the Young', *Costume*, 22:1 (1988), p. 7.

35 Roger Fulford (ed.), *Dearest Child: Private Correspondence of Queen Victoria and the Princess Royal 1858–1861* (London: Evans Bros, 1977), p. 35.

36 Cumming, *Royal Dress*, p. 112.

37 Ginsburg, 'The Young Queen', p. 43.

38 Laura Forsberg, *Worlds Beyond: Miniatures and Victorian Fiction* (New Haven, CT: Yale University Press, 2021), p. 46.

39 RA VIC/MAIN/QVJ (W) 14 October 1838.

40 RA VIC/MAIN/QVJ (W) 17 January 1852 and RCIN 2932491, Royal Collection.

41 Worsley, *Queen Victoria*, p. 397.

42 Report on the House of Commons, Tuesday, 19 March, in *The Times*, 20 March 1861.

43 Sarah Carter and Maria Nugent (eds.), *Mistress of Everything: Queen Victoria in Indigenous Worlds* (Manchester: Manchester University Press, 2016), p. 132.

44 Cecil Woodham-Smith, *Queen Victoria* (London: Hamilton, 1972), p. 345.

45 Regina Schulte (ed.), *The Body of the Queen* (New York: Berghan Books, 2006), p. 179.

46 Matthew Dennison, *The Last Princess: The Devoted Life of Queen Victoria's Youngest Daughter* (London: Hachette, 2010), p. 41.

47 Woodham-Smith, *Queen Victoria*, p. 429.

48 Florence Hartley, *The Ladies' Book of Etiquette and Manual of Politeness* (Boston, MA: G. W. Cottrell, 1860), pp. 82–3.

49 'Court Circular' in *The Times*, 6 April 1864.

50 'The Opening of Parliament by the Queen in Person', *The Times*, 7 February 1866.

51 Elizabeth Longford, *Victoria R.I.* (London: Weidenfeld & Nicolson, 1964), p. 563.

52 Stanley Weintraub, *Victoria* (London: Allen & Unwin, 1987), p. 638.

53 Quoted in Jane Ridley, *Bertie: A Life of Edward VII* (London: Chatto & Windus, 2012), p. 39.

54 Virginia Cowles, *Gay Monarch: The Life and Pleasures of Edward VII* (New York: Harper, 1956), p. 36.

55 Giles St Aubyn, *Edward VII: Prince and King* (London: Collins, 1979), p. 33.

56 George Plumptre, *Edward VII* (London: Pavilion, 1995), p. 48.

57 Georgina Battiscombe, *Queen Alexandra* (London: Constable, 1984), p. 19.

58 *Ibid.*, p. 17.

59 *Ibid.*, pp. 24–5, and David Duff, *Alexandra, Princess and Queen* (London: Collins, 1980), p. 37.

60 Deirdre Murphy and Cassie Davies-Strodder, *Modern Royal Fashion: Seven Royal Women and Their Style* (Surrey: Historic Royal Palaces, 2015), p. 28.

61 Duff, *Alexandra*, p. 41.

62 *Ibid.*, p. 33.

63 Jane Welsh Carlyle to Grace Welsh in Thomas Carlyle (ed.), *Letters and Memorials of Jane Welsh Carlyle, Vol. I* (London: Longmans & Co., 1883), pp. 197–8.

64 Kate Strasdin, 'Fashioning Alexandra: A Royal Approach to Style 1863–1910', *Costume*, 47:2 (2013), pp. 180–97.

65 Cumming, *Royal Dress*, p. 131.

66 Battiscombe, *Queen Alexandra*, p. 49.

67 Jeremy Maas, *The Prince of Wales's Wedding: The Story of a Picture* (London: David & Charles, 1977), p. 64.

68 Cowles, *Gay Monarch*, p. 128.

69 Plumptre, *Edward VII*, p. 216, and Cowles, *Gay Monarch*, p. 130.

70 Plumptre, *Edward VII*, p. 83.

71 Murphy and Davies-Strodder, *Modern Royal Fashion*, p. 9.

72 Celia Lee, *Jean, Lady Hamilton, 1861–1941* (Barnsley: Pen & Sword, 2020), pp. 45–6.

73 Alison Matthews David, *Fashion Victims* (London: Bloomsbury, 2015), p. 163.

74 Hartnell, *Royal Courts*, pp. 164–8, 175–6.

75 Strasdin, 'Fashioning Alexandra', pp. 180–97.

76 W. R. H. Trowbridge, *Queen Alexandra, A Study of Royalty* (London: T. Fisher Unwin, 1923), pp. 200–201.

77 Strasdin, 'Fashioning Alexandra', pp. 180–97.

78 *London Gazette*, 23 January 1901.

79 Maurice V. Brett (ed.), *Journals and Letters of Reginald Viscount Esher, Vol. I* (London: Nicholson & Watson, 1934), p. 318.

80 Anna Keay, *The Crown Jewels* (London: Thames & Hudson, 2011), p. 147.

81 Kate Strasdin, *Inside the Royal Wardrobe* (London: Bloomsbury, 2017), p. 133.

82 Consuelo Vanderbilt Balsan, *The Glitter and the Gold* (New York: Harper & Bros, 1952), p. 142.

83 Brett, *Journals and Letters*, p. 309.

84 Cecil Beaton, *The Glass of Fashion* (London: Weidenfeld & Nicolson, 1954), pp. 274–6.

85 Plumptre, *Edward VII*, p. 255.

PART FIVE: THE WINDSORS

1 James Pope-Hennessy, *Queen Mary* (London: George Allen & Unwin Ltd, 1959), p. 164.

2 *Ibid.*

3 *Ibid.*, p. 217.

4 Maurice V. Brett (ed.), *Journals and Letters of Reginald Viscount Esher, Vol. III* (London: Nicholson & Watson, 1934), p. 49.

5 Charles W. Nuckolls, 'The Durbar Incident', *Modern Asian Studies*, 24:3 (1990), pp. 554–5.

6 Pope-Hennessy, *Queen Mary*, p. 430.

7 Norman Hartnell, *Silver and Gold* (London: V&A, 2019), pp. 90–91.

8 Valerie Cumming, *Royal Dress* (London: Batsford, 1989), pp. 156–7.

9 Anne Edwards, *Matriarch: Queen Mary and the House of Windsor* (New York: William Morrow & Co., 1984), p. 376.

10 Jennifer Ellis (ed.), *Thatched with Gold: The Memoirs of Mabell, Countess of Airlie* (London: Hutchinson, 1962), p. 128.

11 *Ibid.*

12 Edward Windsor, *A Family Album* (London: Cassell & Co., 1960), pp. 12–13.

13 Ellis, *Thatched with Gold*, p. 216.

14 Clair Hughes, 'Uneasy Heads: Difficulties with Royal Hats', *Costume*, 47:2 (2013), pp. 234–47.

15 Joe Dolce, 'Cullinan', *Quadrant*, 64:4 (2017).

16 Edward Windsor, *A King's Story* (London: Cassell & Co., 1951), p. 8.

17 Windsor, *Family Album*, p. 24.

18 *Ibid.*, p. 45.

19 Windsor, *A King's Story*, p. 83.

20 Windsor, *Family Album*, p. 25.

21 Windsor, *A King's Story*, p. 115.

22 Elizabeth Dawson, '"Comfort and Freedom": The Duke of Windsor's Wardrobe', *Costume*, 47:2 (2013), pp. 198–215.

23 Windsor, *A King's Story*, p. 116.

24 'H.R.H Started It', *Vogue*, 15 January 1934.

25 Wallis Warfield Windsor, *The Heart Has Its Reasons* (London: Michael Joseph, 1956), p. 130.

26 *Ibid.*, p. 163.

27 *Ibid.*

28 *Ibid.*, p. 164.

29 'Mrs. Simpson', *Vogue*, 1 February 1937.

30 Windsor, *A King's Story*, p. 296, and G. P. Dyer, *The Proposed Coinage of King Edward VIII* (London: HMSO, 1973), p. 3.

31 Windsor, *A King's Story*, p. 355.

32 Anna Pasternak, *The American Duchess: The Real Wallis Simpson* (Glasgow: William Collins, 2019), p. 189.

33 Suzy Menkes, *The Windsor Style* (London: Grafton, 1987), p. 120.

34 *Ibid.*, p. 104, and 'The Future Duchess of Windsor', *Vogue*, 1 June 1937.

35 Laura Petican (ed.), *Fashion and Contemporaneity: Realms of the Visible* (Leiden, Netherlands: 2019), p. 74.

36 Menkes, *The Windsor Style*, p.113.

37 Windsor, *A King's Story*, p. 277, and Piers Brendan, *Edward VIII: Uncrowned King* (London: Penguin, 2018), pp. 38–9.

38 Hartnell, *Silver and Gold*, p. 87.

39 *Ibid.*, p. 88.

40 *Ibid.*, pp. 88–9.

41 *Ibid.*, p. 89.

42 'The Wedding Gown of H.R.H. The Duchess of York', *Vogue*, 15 June 1923.

43 William Shawcross, *The Queen Mother: The Official Biography* (London: Macmillan, 2009), p. 177.

44 Hugo Vickers, *Cecil Beaton: A Biography* (London: Weidenfeld & Nicolson, 1986), p. 268.

45 An extensive collection of Madame Handley-Seymour's fashion designs was donated to the Victoria & Albert Museum after her death and can be viewed on their collections website.

46 Advertisement for Handley-Seymour, *The Times*, 4 September 1914.

47 'Lady E. Bowes-Lyon's Trousseau', *The Times*, 23 April 1923.

48 Cumming, *Royal Dress*, p. 174.

49 Hartnell, *Silver and Gold*, p. 94.

50 *Ibid.*, p. 95.

51 *Ibid.*, p. 96.

52 *Ibid.*, p. 97.

53 *Ibid.*, p. 92.

54 *Ibid.*, p. 100.

55 Shawcross, *The Queen Mother*, p. 526.

56 Hartnell, *Silver and Gold*, p. 101.

57 Shawcross, *The Queen Mother*, p. 527.

58 Deirdre Murphy and Cassie Davies-Strodder, *Modern Royal Fashion: Seven Royal Women and Their Style* (Surrey: Historic Royal Palaces, 2015), p. 51.

59 Ben Pimlott, *The Queen: Elizabeth II and the Monarchy* (London: Harper Collins, 2001), p. 5.

60 *Ibid.*

61 Marion Crawford, *The Little Princesses* (London: Cassell & Co., 1950), p. 34.

62 *Ibid.*, pp. 77 and 170.

63 *Ibid.*, p. 34.

64 Marion Crawford, *The Little Princesses*, p. 72.

65 *Ibid.*, p. 72.

66 *Ibid.*, p. 91.

67 *Ibid.*, p. 89.

68 Kate Williams, *Young Elizabeth* (Cambridge: Pegasus, 2015), p. 125.

69 Jane Eastoe, *Elizabeth II: Reigning in Style* (London: HarperCollins, 2012), p. 23.

70 Crawford, *The Little Princesses*, p. 165, and Roy Strong, *Cecil Beaton: The Royal Portraits* (London: Thames & Hudson, 1988), p. 91.

71 Crawford, *The Little Princesses*, p. 170.

72 Williams, *Young Elizabeth*, p. 145.

73 Crawford, *The Little Princesses*, p. 198.

74 *Ibid.*, p. 169.

75 For Hartnell's Renaissance inspiration, see Hartnell, *Silver and Gold*, p. 111.

76 *Ibid.*, p. 112.

77 Helen Cathcart, *The Queen Mother Herself* (London: W. H. Allen, 1979), p. 165, and Robert Hardman, *Queen of Our Times* (London: Pan Macmillan, 2022), p. 96.

78 Pimlott, *The Queen*, p. 179.

79 Hartnell, *Silver and Gold*, p. 123.

80 *Ibid.*, p. 117.

81 Eastoe, *Elizabeth II*, p. 46.

82 *Ibid.*, p. 62.

83 *Ibid.*, p. 96.

84 'He Borrowed the Queen's Coronet', in the *Australasian Post*, 2 June 1955, p. 10.

85 Kate Strasdin, *Inside the Royal Wardrobe* (London: Bloomsbury, 2017), p. 70.

86 Theo Aronson, *Princess Margaret* (London: Michael O'Mara, 2001), p. 98.

87 Christian Dior, *Dior by Dior*, trans. Antonia Fraser (London: V&A, 2018), p. 171.

88 Marie-France Pochna, *Christian Dior: The Man Who Made the World Look New* (New York: Arcade Publishing, 1996), p. 162.

89 Strong, *Cecil Beaton*, p. 148.

90 'Fashion and Princess Margaret', *Picture Post*, 27 June 1953.

91 Angela Kelly, *The Other Side of the Coin* (London: HarperCollins, 2022), p. 109.

92 *Ibid.*, p. 80.

93 *Ibid.*, p. 81.

94 Irene Morra, *The New Elizabethan Age* (London, New York: I. B. Tauris, 2016), p. 67.

95 Anne Matheson, *Princess Anne: A Girl of Our Time* (London, Muller, 1973).

96 Joanne Entwistle, *The Fashioned Body* (Cambridge: Polity Press, 2015), p. 49.

97 'Edward Enninful Interviews Prince Charles', *British Vogue*, December 2020.

98 Rosalind Coward, *Diana: The Portrait* (London: HarperCollins, 2004), p. 74.

99 *Ibid.*

100 'The Fabulously Frou-Frou Dress That Changed Princess Diana's Style', *British Vogue*, 13 December 2020.

101 David Emanuel and Elizabeth Emanuel, *A Dress for Diana* (London: Pavilion, 2006), p. 87.

102 David Emanuel, quoted in 'Princess Diana Had a Second Wedding Dress – But She Didn't Know It', *Town & Country*, September 2020.

Notes

103 'Vogue's Anna Harvey on Dressing Princess Diana', Vogue, October 1997.

104 Elizabeth Holmes, HRH: So Many Thoughts on Royal Style (New York: Celadon Books, 2020), p. 140.

105 'Edward Enninful Interviews Prince Charles', British Vogue, December 2020.

106 'HRH The Duchess of Cornwall Makes Her Debut in British Vogue', British Vogue, July 2022.

107 Kristin Knox, Alexander McQueen: Genius of a Generation (London: A & C Black, 2010), p. 8.

PART SIX: THE NEXT GENERATION

1 Cecil Beaton, The Glass of Fashion (London: Weidenfeld & Nicolson, 1954), p. 274.

2 Mary Fellowes, quoted in 'Princesses Beatrice and Eugenie's stylist reveals the story behind their fashion makeover', Telegraph, 9 August 2021.

3 Mary Fellowes (@mary_fellowes), 8 August 2021.

4 Princess Eugenie, interviewed before her wedding by Ruth Langsford and Eammon Holmes, This Morning, 12 October 2018.

5 Quoted in 'The Duchesses Inventory', Marie Claire, 17 January 2022.

6 Portrait of the Duke and Duchess of Cambridge by Jamie Coreth (2022), Fitzwilliam Museum, Cambridge.

7 Marion Crawford, The Little Princesses (London: Cassell & Co., 1950), p. 33.

8 The Royal Family: A Centenary Portrait by John Wonnacott (2000), NPG 6479, and William, Prince of Wales; Prince Harry, Duke of Sussex by Nicky Philipps (2009), NPG 6876.

9 Norman Hartnell, Silver and Gold (London: V&A, 2019), p. 98.

Index

INDEX

Index

INDEX

Index

INDEX